Splatoon
SQUID KIDS COMEDY SHOW

5

STORY AND ART BY
HIDEKI GOTO

Volume 5
VIZ Media Edition

Story and Art by
Hideki Goto

Translation **Tetsuichiro Miyaki**
English Adaptation **Bryant Turnage**
Lettering **John Hunt**
Design **Kam Li**
Editor **Joel Enos**

TM & © 2021 Nintendo. All rights reserved.

SPLATOON IKASU KIDS 4KOMA FES Vol. 5 by Hideki GOTO
© 2018 Hideki GOTO
All rights reserved.
Original Japanese edition published by SHOGAKUKAN.
English translation rights in the United States of America, Canada, the United Kingdom, Ireland, Australia and New Zealand arranged with SHOGAKUKAN.

Original Design vol.ONE

Printed in the U.S.A.

Published by VIZ Media, LLC
P.O. Box 77010
San Francisco, CA 94107

10 9 8 7 6 5 4 3 2 1
First Printing, November 2021

PARENTAL ADVISORY
SPLATOON: SQUID KIDS
COMEDY SHOW is rated A and
is suitable for readers of all ages.

Maika
A city girl who uses Dualies.

Characters

Kou
An elite boy with three big advantages going for him—he's tall, rich and smart.

Hit
A boy from the countryside who came to the city to be a cool squid kid!

Contents

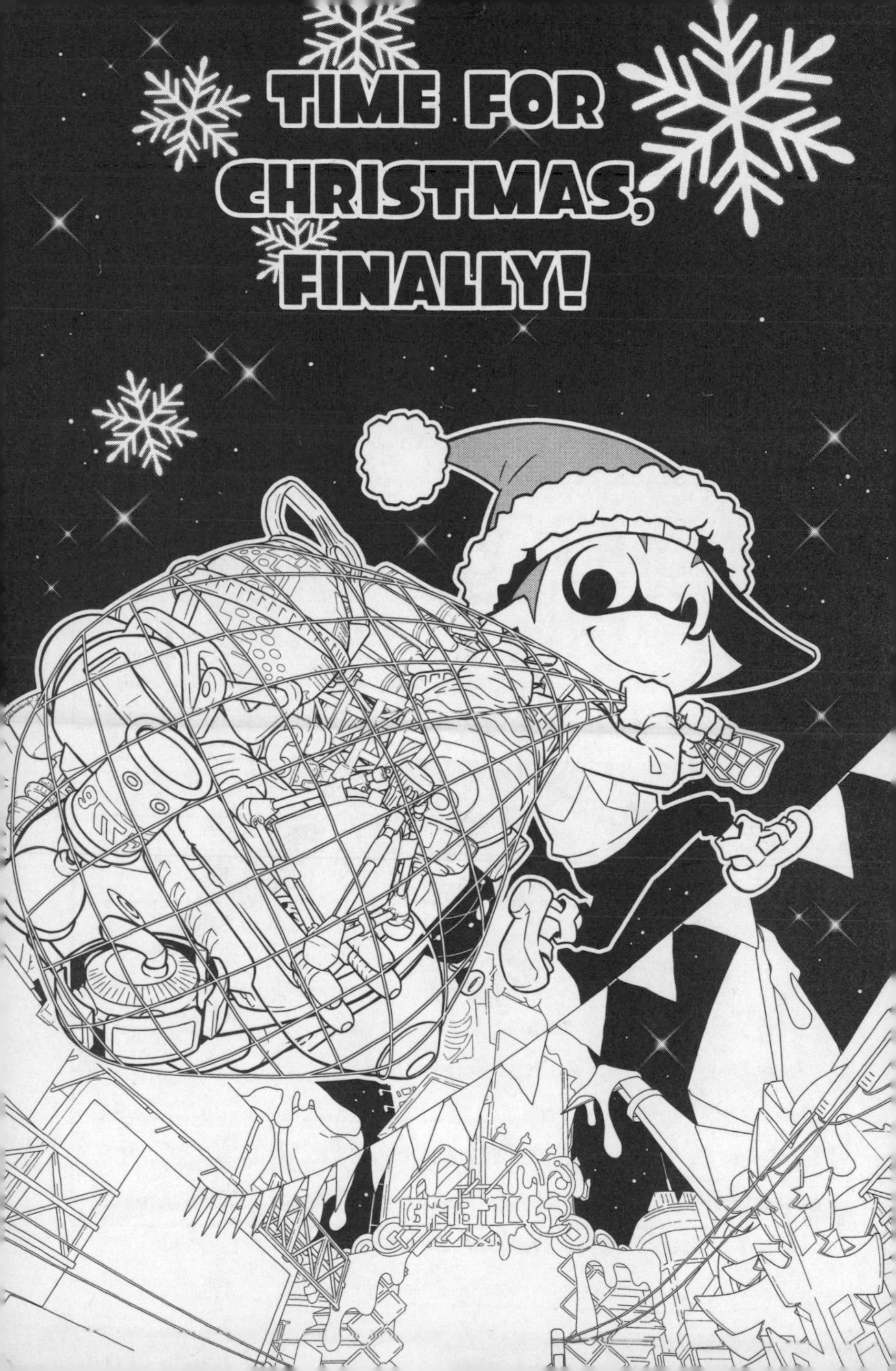
TIME FOR CHRISTMAS, FINALLY!

HOLOGRAM HOLIDAY

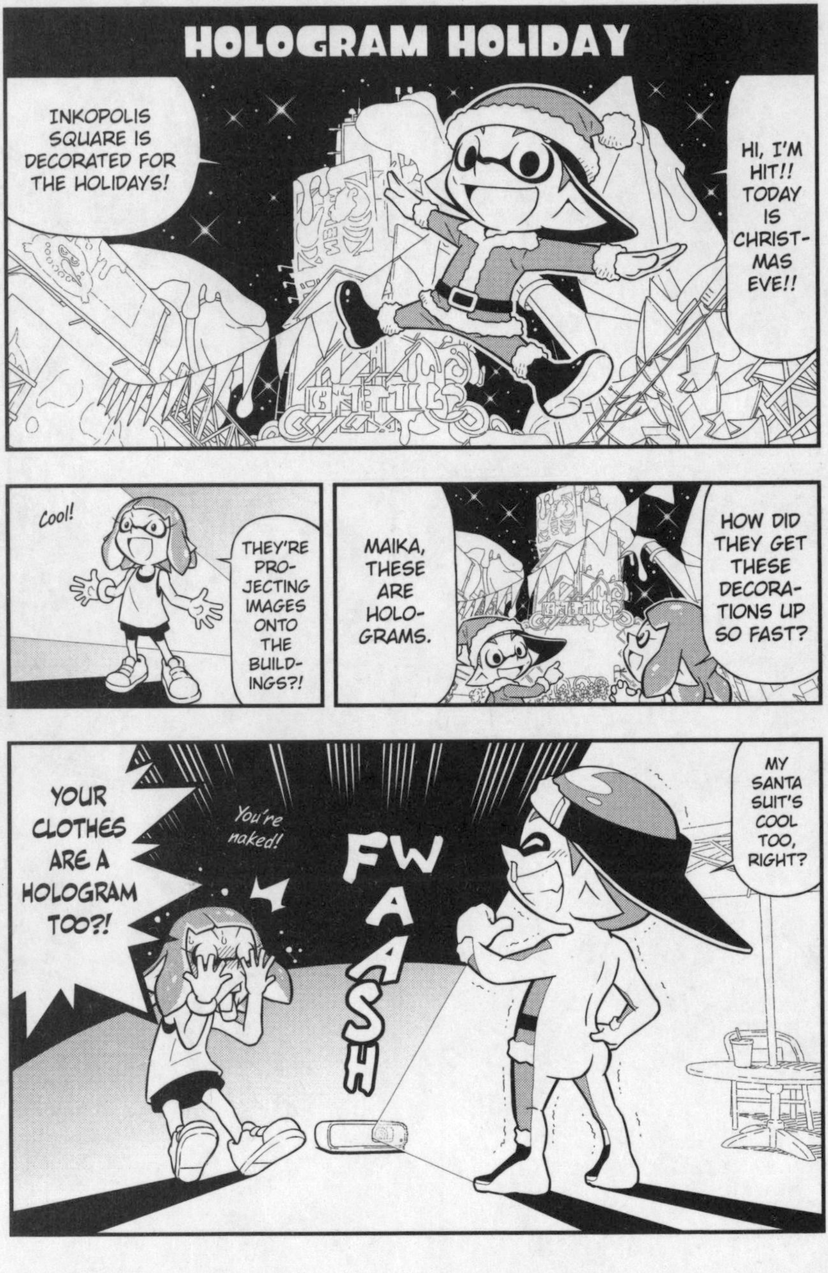

HI, I'M HIT!! TODAY IS CHRIST-MAS EVE!!
INKOPOLIS SQUARE IS DECORATED FOR THE HOLIDAYS!
HOW DID THEY GET THESE DECORA-TIONS UP SO FAST?
MAIKA, THESE ARE HOLO-GRAMS.
THEY'RE PRO-JECTING IMAGES ONTO THE BUILD-INGS?!
Cool!
MY SANTA SUIT'S COOL TOO, RIGHT?
FWAASH
YOUR CLOTHES ARE A HOLOGRAM TOO?!
You're naked!

SPECIAL DECORATIONS

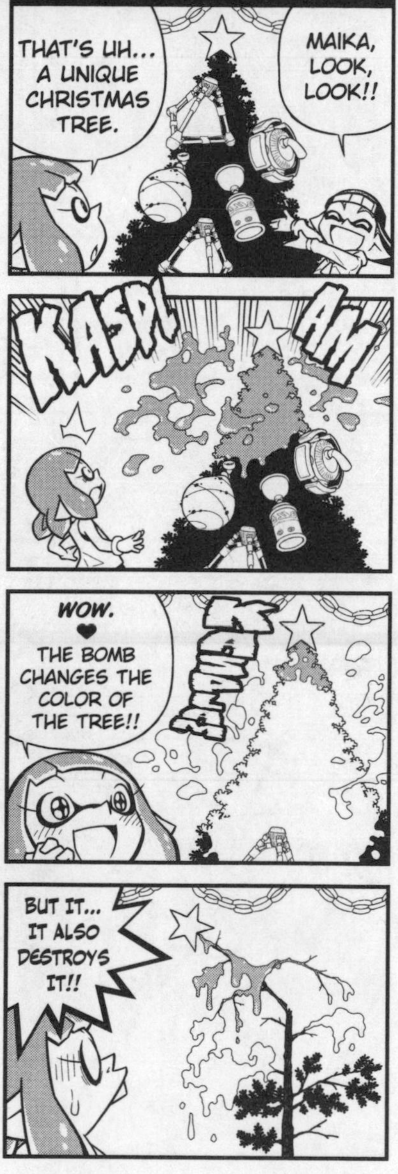
MAIKA, LOOK, LOOK!!
THAT'S UH... A UNIQUE CHRISTMAS TREE.
KASPLAM
WOW. ♥ THE BOMB CHANGES THE COLOR OF THE TREE!!
BUT IT... IT ALSO DESTROYS IT!!

HO HO HO

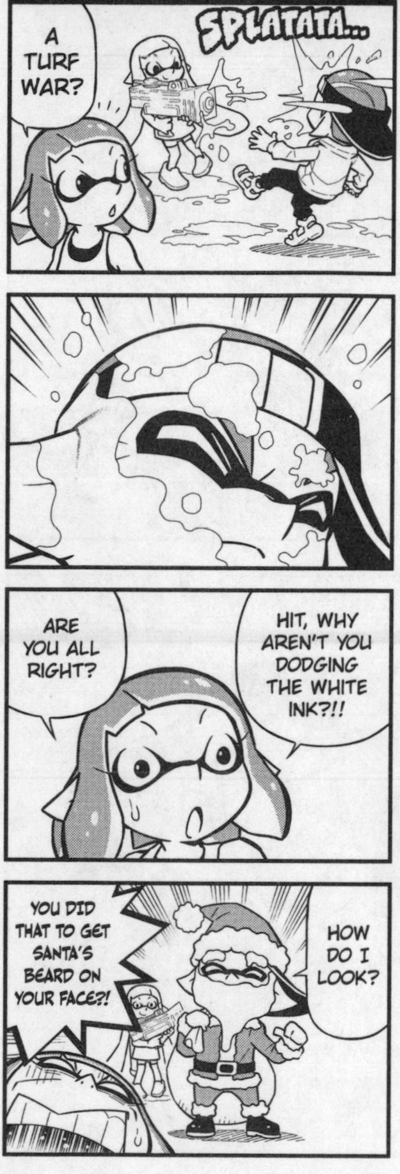
SPLATATA...
A TURF WAR?
HIT, WHY AREN'T YOU DODGING THE WHITE INK?!!
ARE YOU ALL RIGHT?
HOW DO I LOOK?
YOU DID THAT TO GET SANTA'S BEARD ON YOUR FACE?!

CHRISTMAS INKING BATTLE

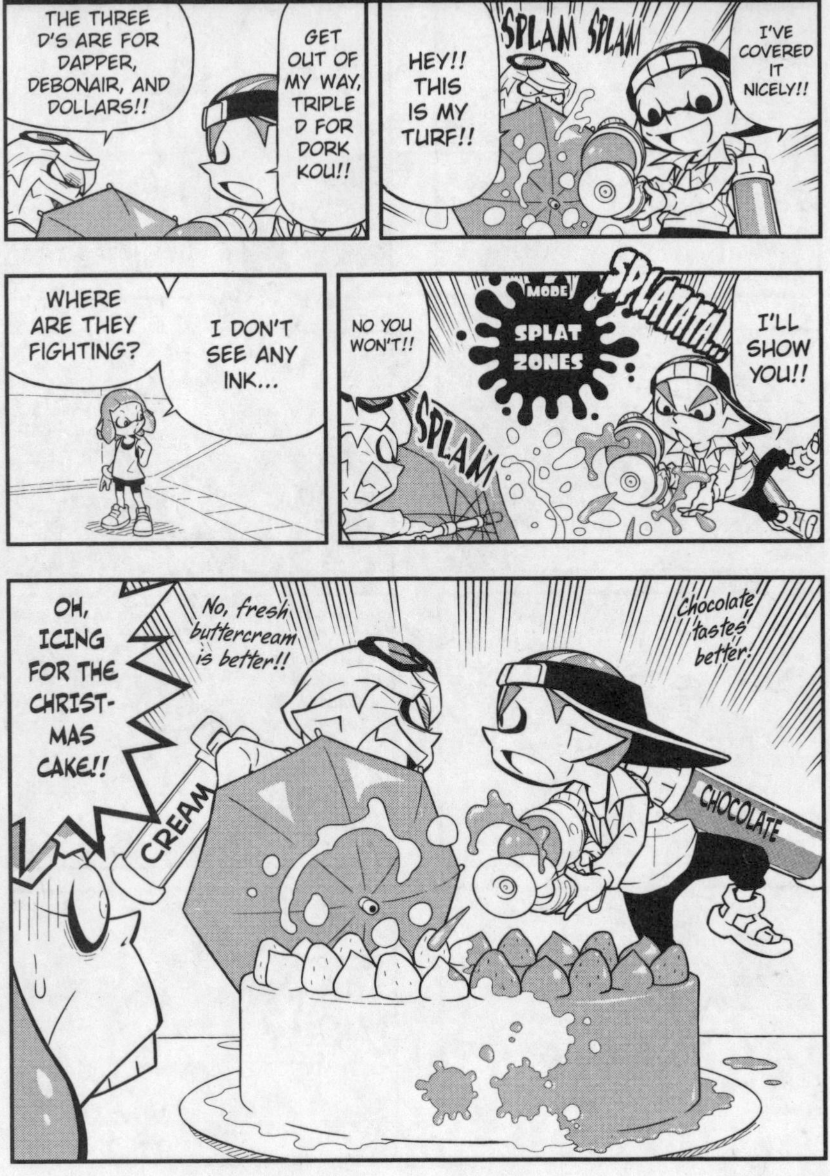
I'VE COVERED IT NICELY!!
SPLAM SPLAM
HEY!! THIS IS MY TURF!!
GET OUT OF MY WAY, TRIPLE D FOR DORK KOU!!
THE THREE D'S ARE FOR DAPPER, DEBONAIR, AND DOLLARS!!
SPLATATA...
I'LL SHOW YOU!!
MODE
SPLAT ZONES
NO YOU WON'T!!
SPLAM
I DON'T SEE ANY INK...
WHERE ARE THEY FIGHTING?
Chocolate tastes better.
No, fresh buttercream is better!!
OH, ICING FOR THE CHRIST-MAS CAKE!!
CHOCOLATE
CREAM

CHEERS

THE CHRISTMAS SWEETS ARE READY!!
WOW!! THEY LOOK GOOOOD. ♪
KLINK
THE GROWN-UPS WILL MAKE A TOAST WITH CHAMPAGNE !!
KLANK
AND THE KIDS WILL MAKE A TOAST WITH SODA POP!!
KA-SPLAM-SPLAM-SPLAM
SPLAM
SPLAM
THAT WAS A FIZZY BOMB!!
SPLAM

RING

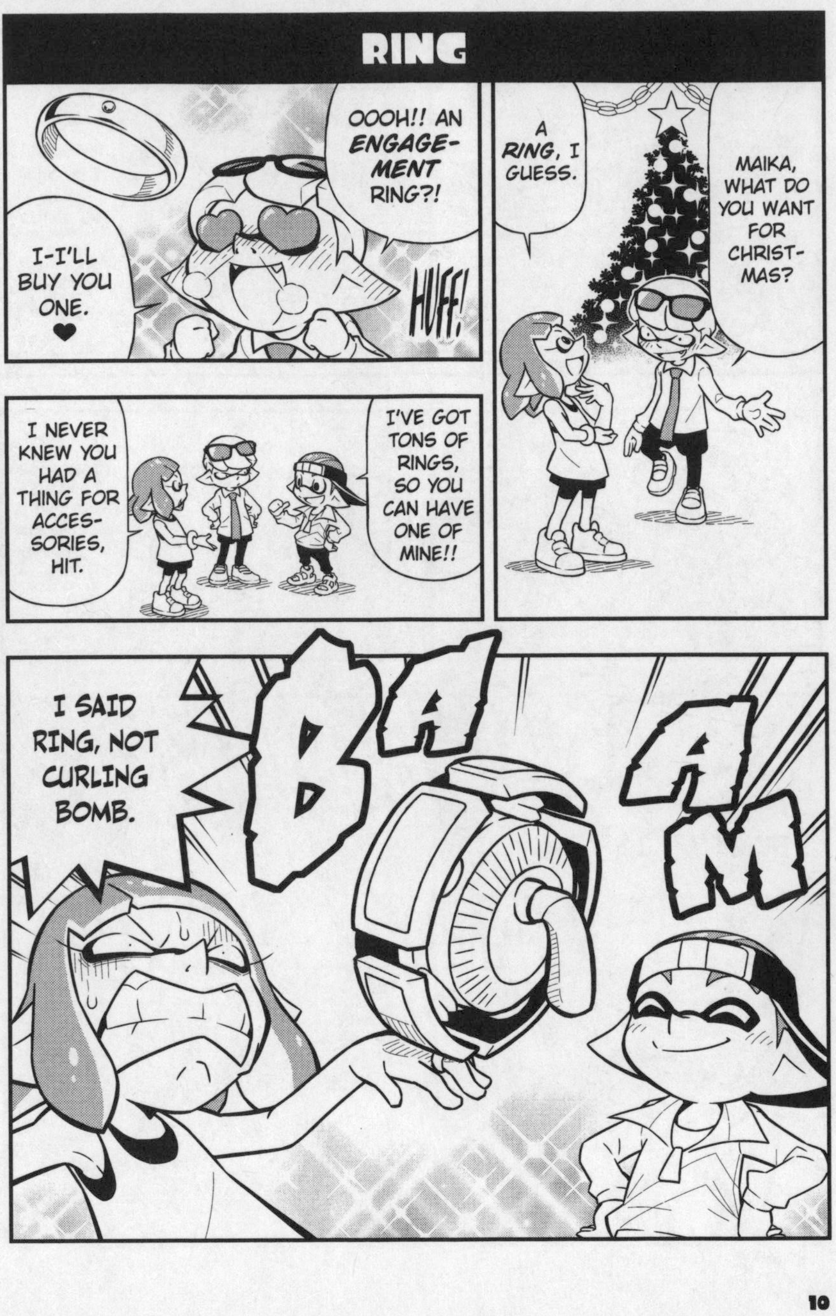
MAIKA, WHAT DO YOU WANT FOR CHRIST-MAS?
A *RING*, I GUESS.
OOOH!! AN *ENGAGE-MENT* RING?!
HUFF!
I-I'LL BUY YOU ONE. ❤
I'VE GOT TONS OF RINGS, SO YOU CAN HAVE ONE OF MINE!!
I NEVER KNEW YOU HAD A THING FOR ACCES-SORIES, HIT.
BAAM
I SAID RING, NOT CURLING BOMB.

A NEW WEAPON

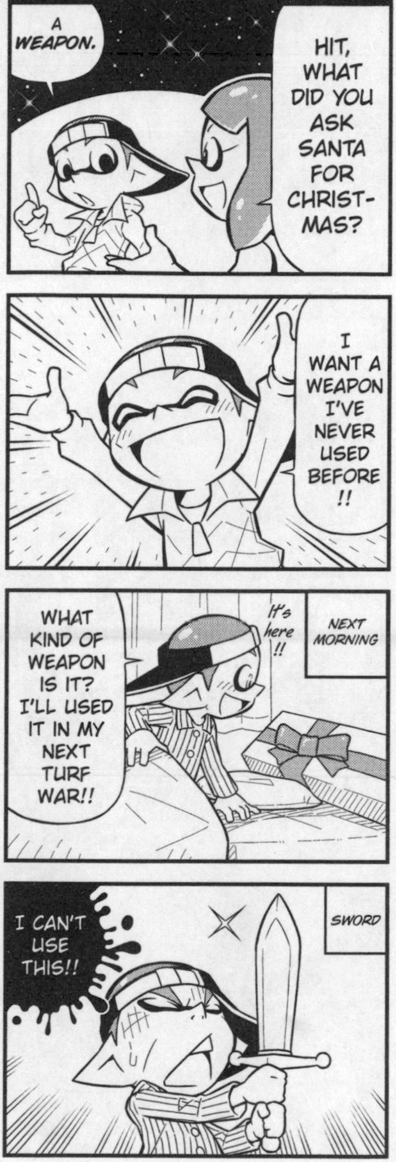
HIT, WHAT DID YOU ASK SANTA FOR CHRIST-MAS?
A WEAPON.
I WANT A WEAPON I'VE NEVER USED BEFORE!!
NEXT MORNING
It's here!!
WHAT KIND OF WEAPON IS IT? I'LL USED IT IN MY NEXT TURF WAR!!
SWORD
I CAN'T USE THIS!!

A BOOYAH PRESENT

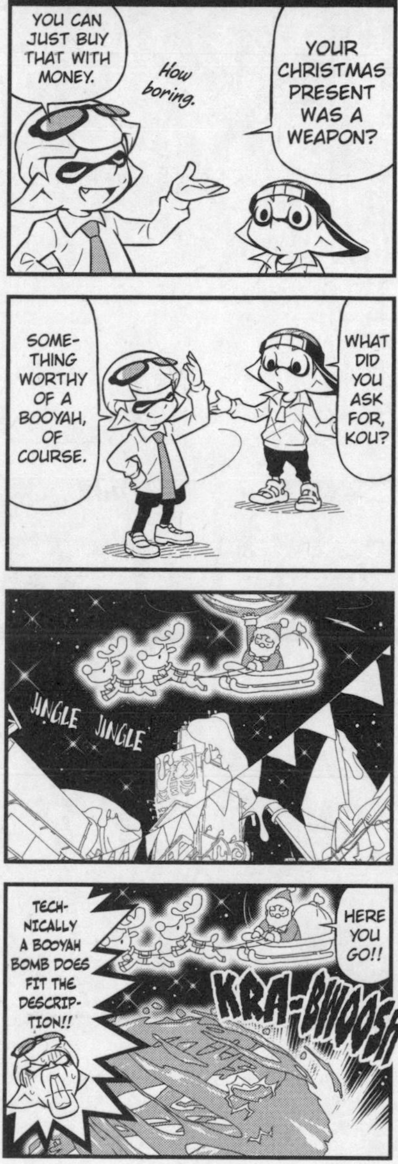
YOUR CHRISTMAS PRESENT WAS A WEAPON?
YOU CAN JUST BUY THAT WITH MONEY.
How boring.
WHAT DID YOU ASK FOR, KOU?
SOME-THING WORTHY OF A BOOYAH, OF COURSE.
JINGLE JINGLE
HERE YOU GO!!
KRA-BWOOSH
TECH-NICALLY A BOOYAH BOMB DOES FIT THE DESCRIP-TION!!

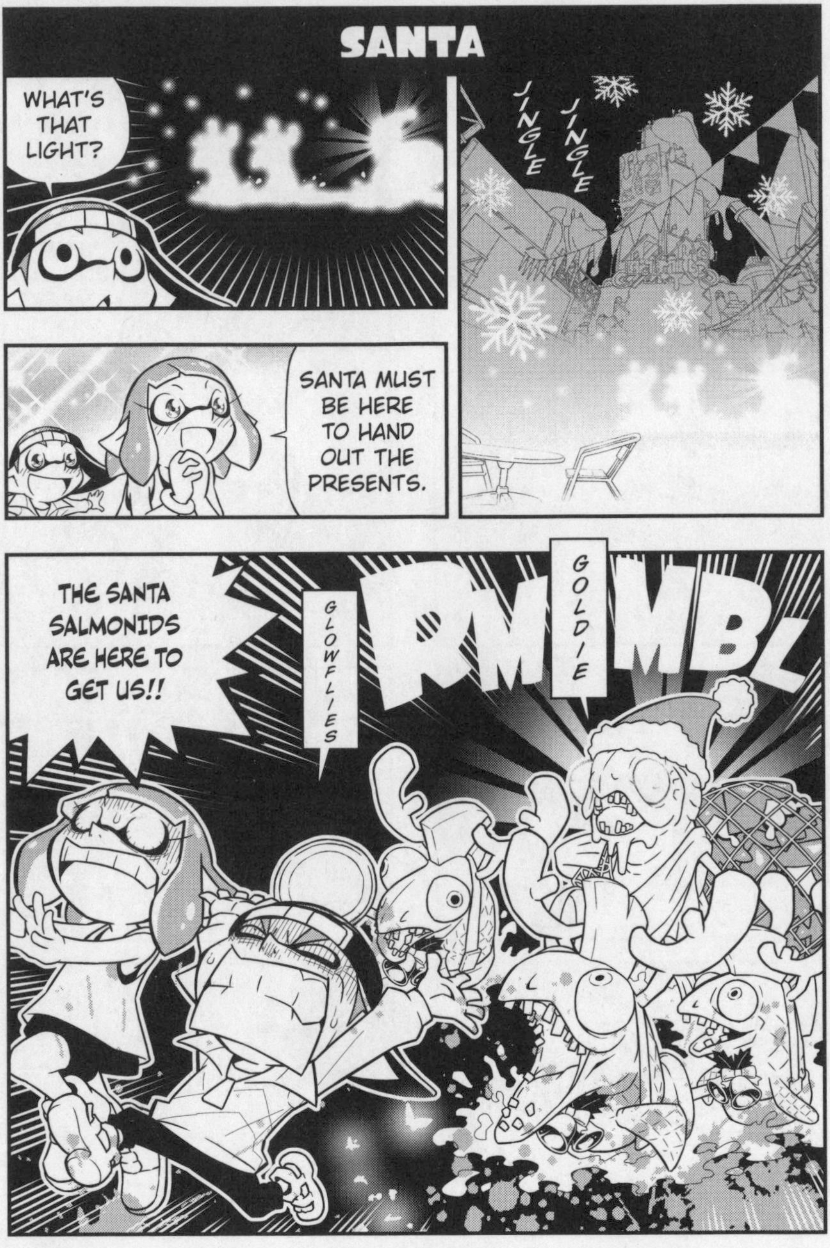
SANTA
JINGLE JINGLE
WHAT'S THAT LIGHT?
SANTA MUST BE HERE TO HAND OUT THE PRESENTS.
RMMBL
GOLDIE
GLOWFLIES
THE SANTA SALMONIDS ARE HERE TO GET US!!

Splatoon
SQUID KIDS
COMEDY SHOW

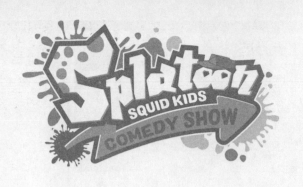

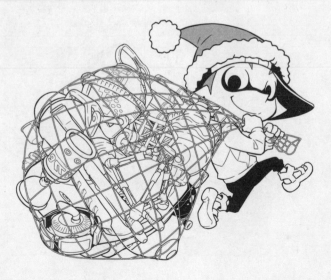

Splatoon SQUID KIDS COMEDY SHOW

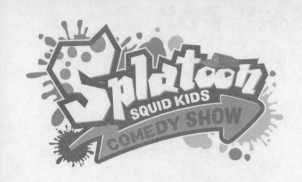

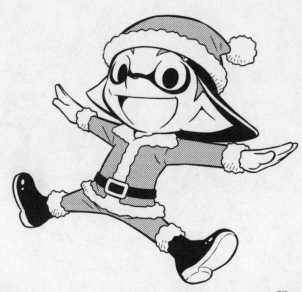

TIME FOR A CHERRY-BLOSSOM TURF WAR!

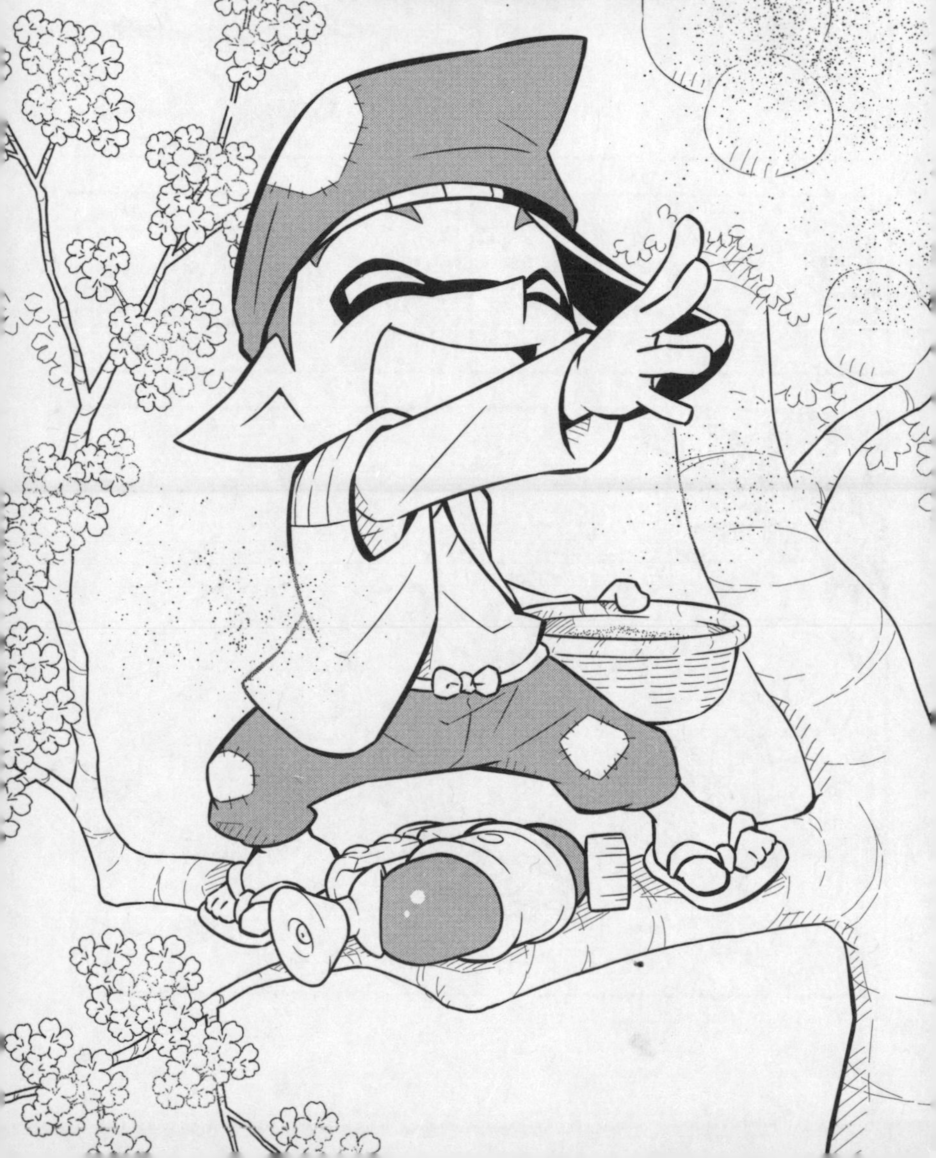

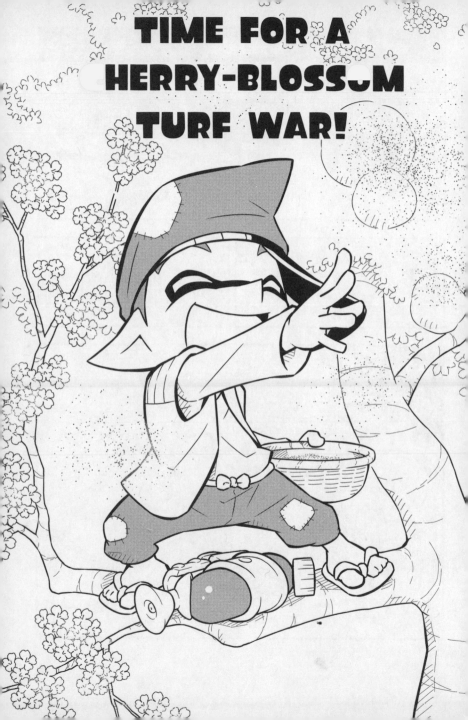

PICNIC

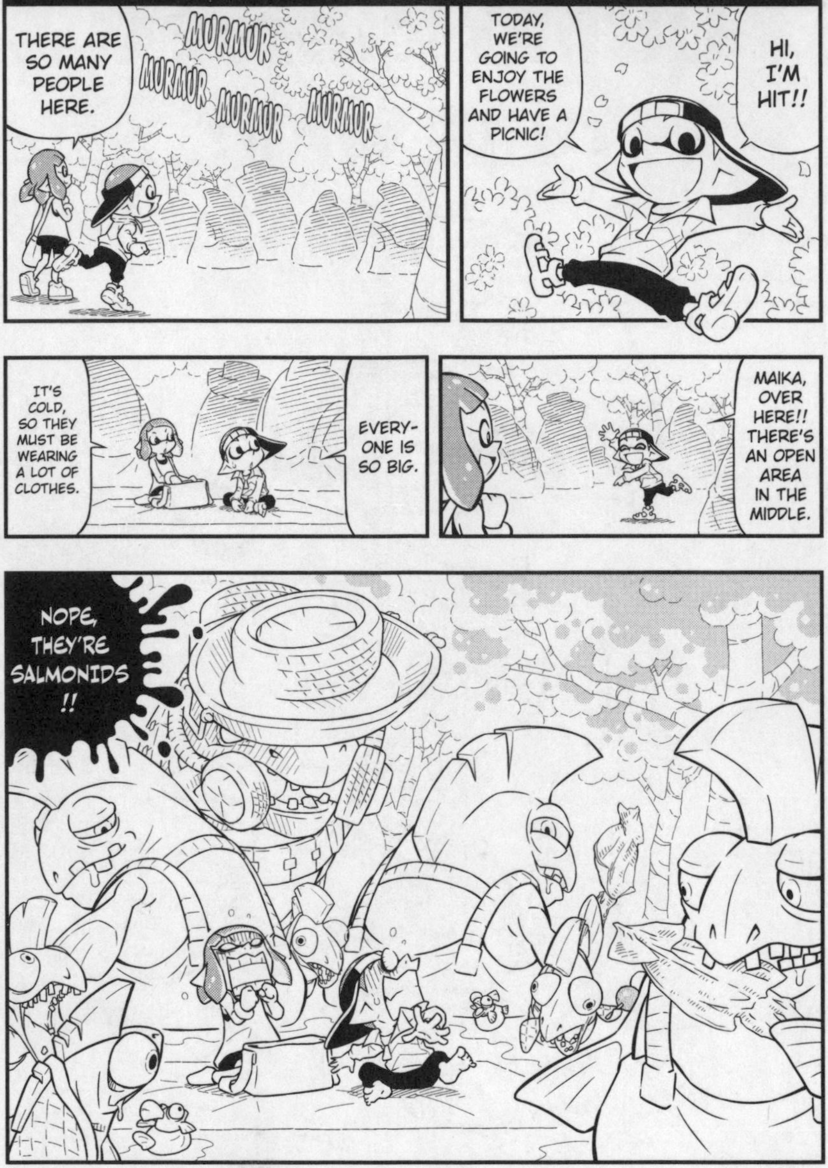
HI, I'M HIT!!
TODAY, WE'RE GOING TO ENJOY THE FLOWERS AND HAVE A PICNIC!
THERE ARE SO MANY PEOPLE HERE.
MURMUR
MURMUR
MURMUR
MURMUR
MAIKA, OVER HERE!! THERE'S AN OPEN AREA IN THE MIDDLE.
EVERY-ONE IS SO BIG.
IT'S COLD, SO THEY MUST BE WEARING A LOT OF CLOTHES.
NOPE, THEY'RE SALMONIDS!!

HAPPINESS IS WARM INK

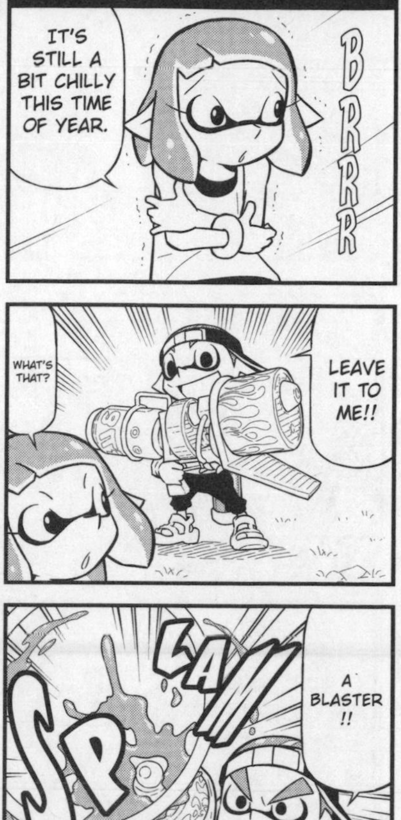
IT'S STILL A BIT CHILLY THIS TIME OF YEAR.
BRRR
LEAVE IT TO ME!!
WHAT'S THAT?
A BLASTER !!
SPLAM
DID I BLAST THE CHILL AWAY?
SPLUUB...
NOW I'M COLD AND INKED.

FULL BLOOM

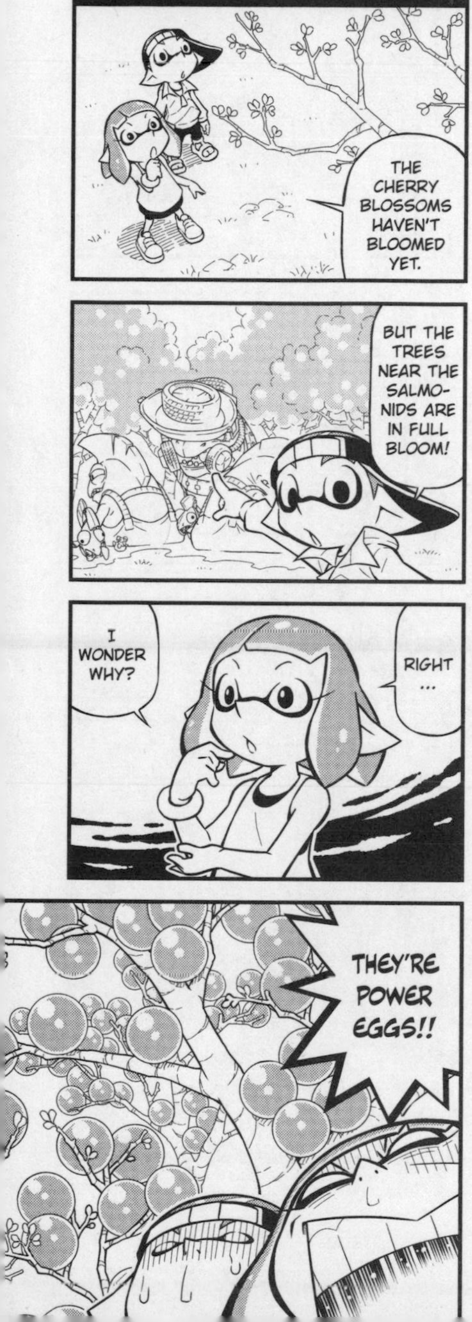
THE CHERRY BLOSSOMS HAVEN'T BLOOMED YET.
BUT THE TREES NEAR THE SALMONIDS ARE IN FULL BLOOM!
RIGHT ...
I WONDER WHY?
THEY'RE POWER EGGS!!

FLOWER BLOOMER HIT

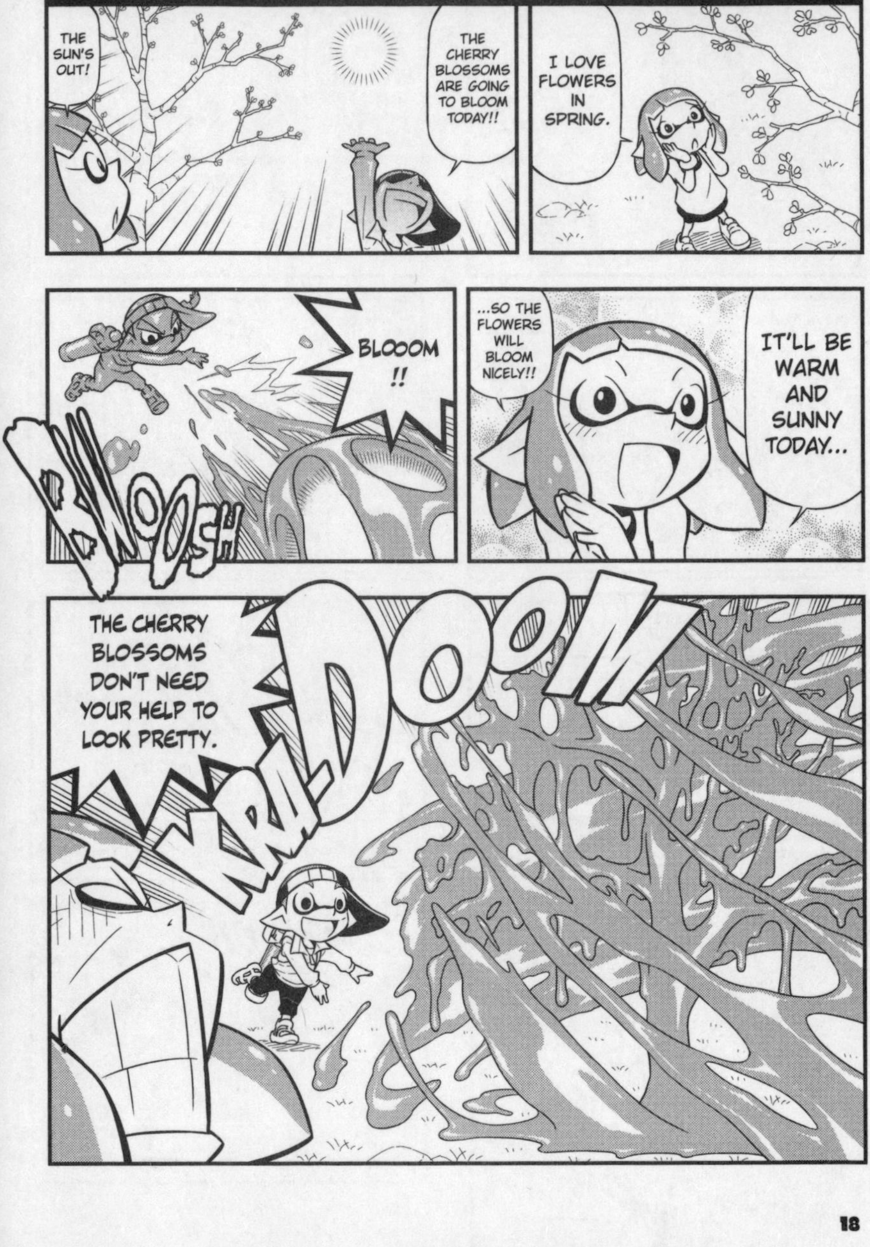
I LOVE FLOWERS IN SPRING.
THE CHERRY BLOSSOMS ARE GOING TO BLOOM TODAY!!
THE SUN'S OUT!
IT'LL BE WARM AND SUNNY TODAY...
...SO THE FLOWERS WILL BLOOM NICELY!!
BLOOOM !!
BWOOSH
KRA-DOOOM
THE CHERRY BLOSSOMS DON'T NEED YOUR HELP TO LOOK PRETTY.

BENTO BOX

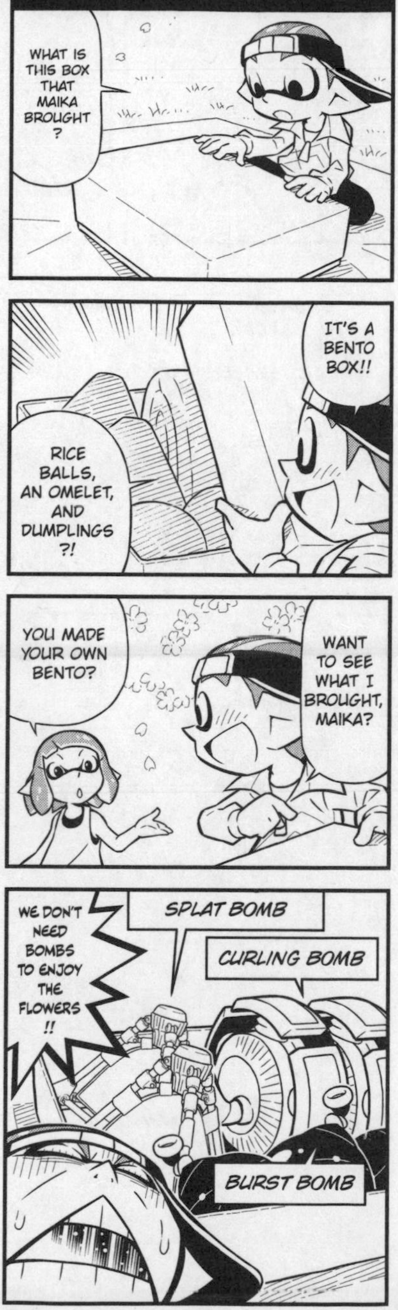
WHAT IS THIS BOX THAT MAIKA BROUGHT?
IT'S A BENTO BOX!!
RICE BALLS, AN OMELET, AND DUMPLINGS?!
WANT TO SEE WHAT I BROUGHT, MAIKA?
YOU MADE YOUR OWN BENTO?
SPLAT BOMB
CURLING BOMB
BURST BOMB
WE DON'T NEED BOMBS TO ENJOY THE FLOWERS!!

TRASH CAN

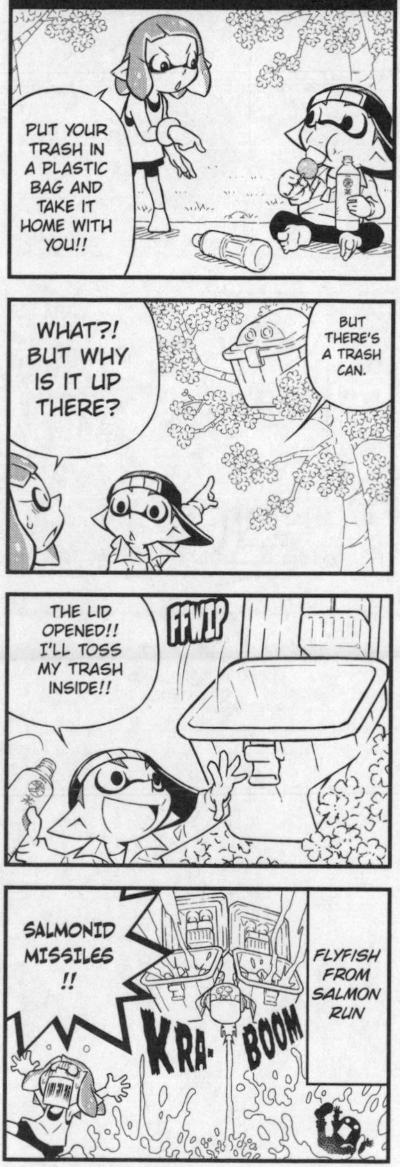
PUT YOUR TRASH IN A PLASTIC BAG AND TAKE IT HOME WITH YOU!!
BUT THERE'S A TRASH CAN.
WHAT?! BUT WHY IS IT UP THERE?
FFWIP
THE LID OPENED!! I'LL TOSS MY TRASH INSIDE!!
FLYFISH FROM SALMON RUN
SALMONID MISSILES!!
KRA-BOOM

A SPRING WALL

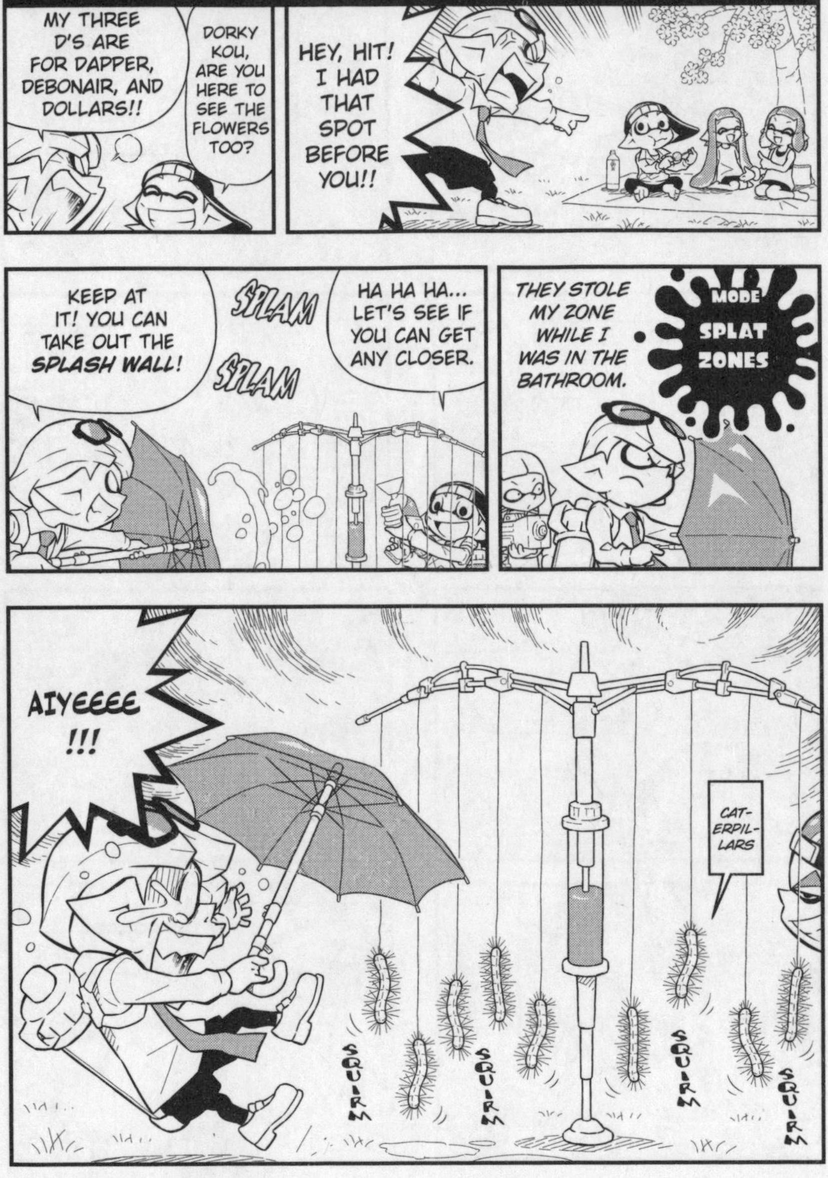
HEY, HIT! I HAD THAT SPOT BEFORE YOU!!
DORKY KOU, ARE YOU HERE TO SEE THE FLOWERS TOO?
MY THREE D'S ARE FOR DAPPER, DEBONAIR, AND DOLLARS!!
MODE
SPLAT ZONES
THEY STOLE MY ZONE WHILE I WAS IN THE BATHROOM.
HA HA HA... LET'S SEE IF YOU CAN GET ANY CLOSER.
SPLAM
SPLAM
KEEP AT IT! YOU CAN TAKE OUT THE SPLASH WALL!
CAT-ERPIL-LARS
AIYEEEE !!!
SQUIRM
SQUIRM
SQUIRM
SQUIRM
SQUIRM

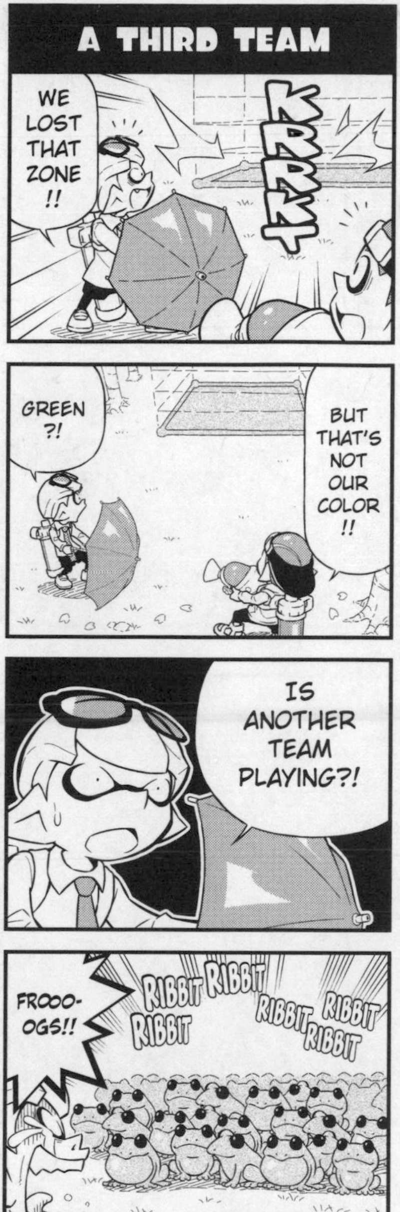
A THIRD TEAM
WE LOST THAT ZONE!!
KRRKT
GREEN?!
BUT THAT'S NOT OUR COLOR!!
IS ANOTHER TEAM PLAYING?!
FROOO-OGS!!
RIBBIT RIBBIT
RIBBIT
RIBBIT RIBBIT
RIBBIT
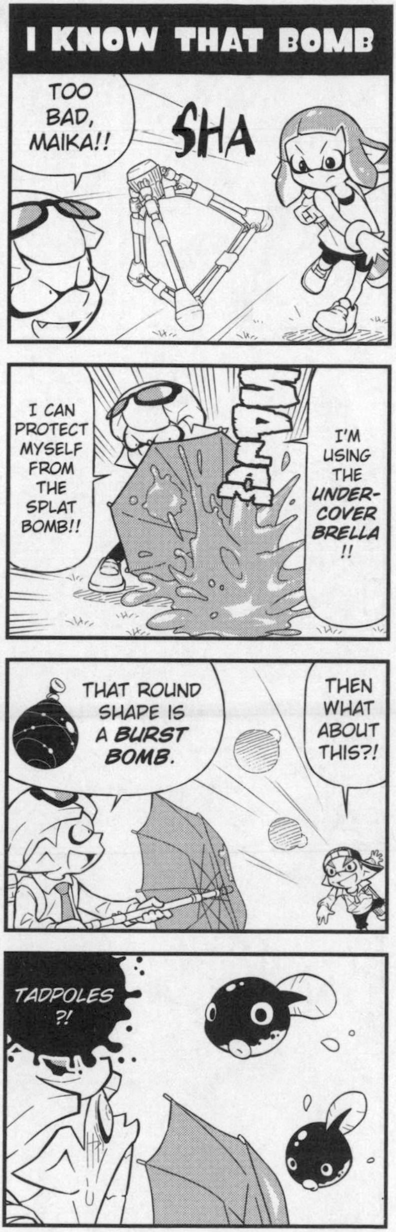
I KNOW THAT BOMB
TOO BAD, MAIKA!!
SHA
I CAN PROTECT MYSELF FROM THE SPLAT BOMB!!
SPLAT
I'M USING THE UNDERCOVER BRELLA!!
THAT ROUND SHAPE IS A BURST BOMB.
THEN WHAT ABOUT THIS?!
TADPOLES?!

SPRING BREAK

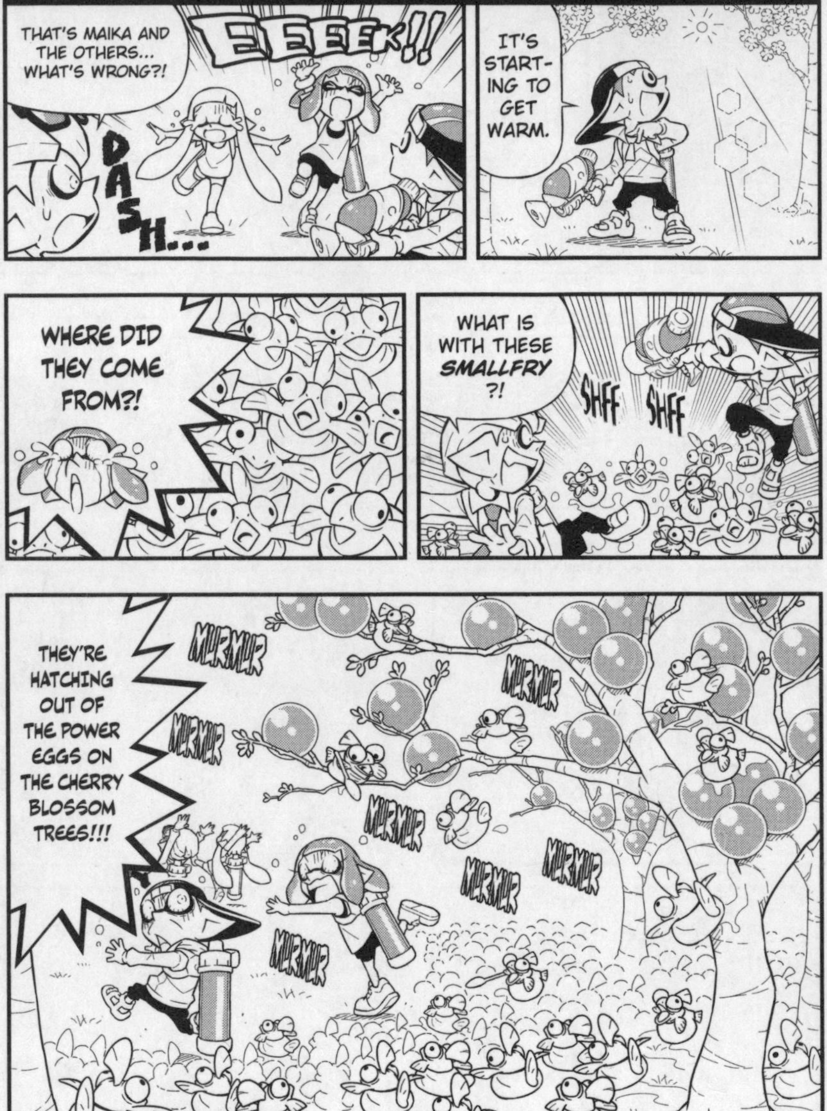
IT'S START-ING TO GET WARM.
EEEEK!!
THAT'S MAIKA AND THE OTHERS... WHAT'S WRONG?!
DASH...
WHAT IS WITH THESE *SMALLFRY* ?!
SHFF
SHFF
WHERE DID THEY COME FROM?!
MURMUR
MURMUR
THEY'RE HATCHING OUT OF THE POWER EGGS ON THE CHERRY BLOSSOM TREES!!!
MURMUR
MURMUR
MURMUR
MURMUR
MURMUR

THE FATAL INK STORM

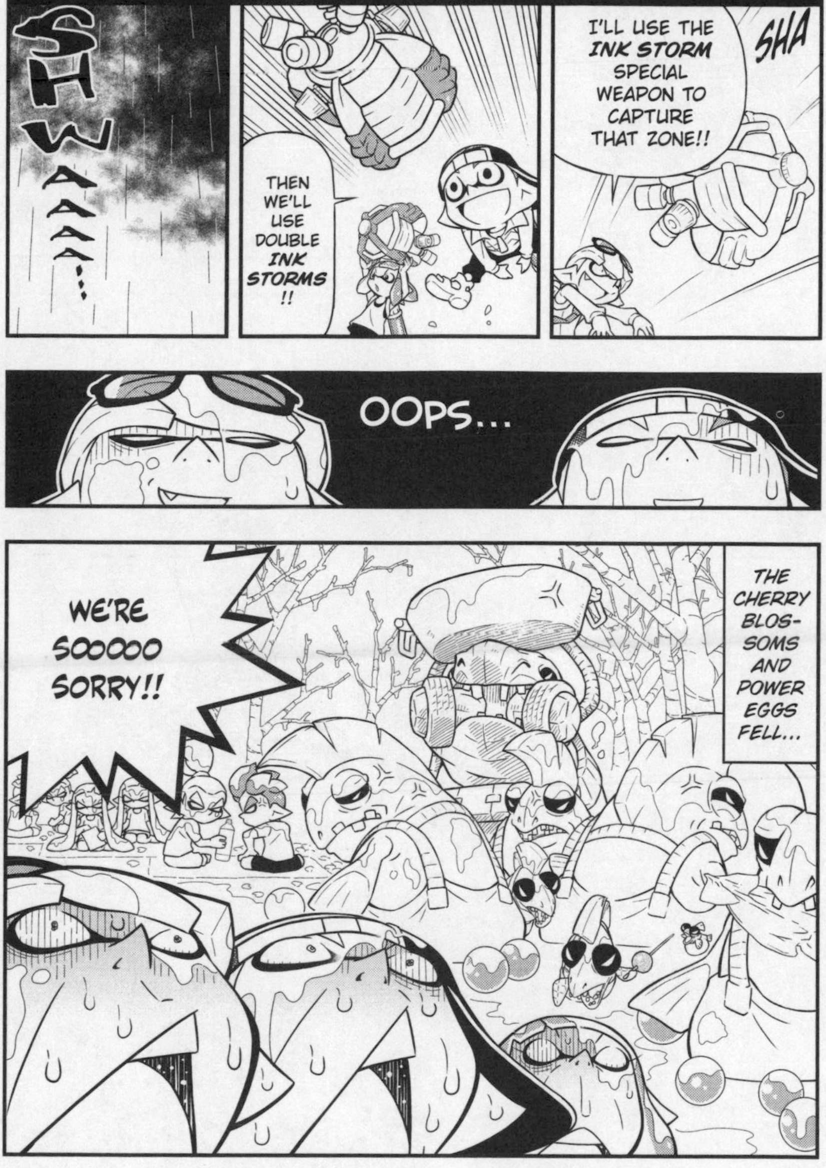

SHA
I'LL USE THE INK STORM SPECIAL WEAPON TO CAPTURE THAT ZONE!!
THEN WE'LL USE DOUBLE INK STORMS!!
SHWAAAA...
OOPS...
THE CHERRY BLOSSOMS AND POWER EGGS FELL...
WE'RE SOOOOO SORRY!!

Splatoon
SQUID KIDS COMEDY SHOW

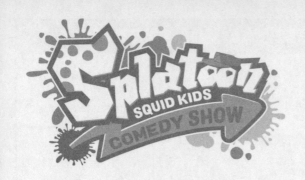

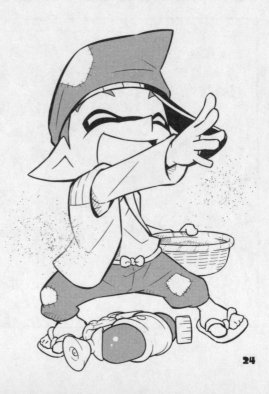

TIME TO ENJOY SOME EXERCISE!

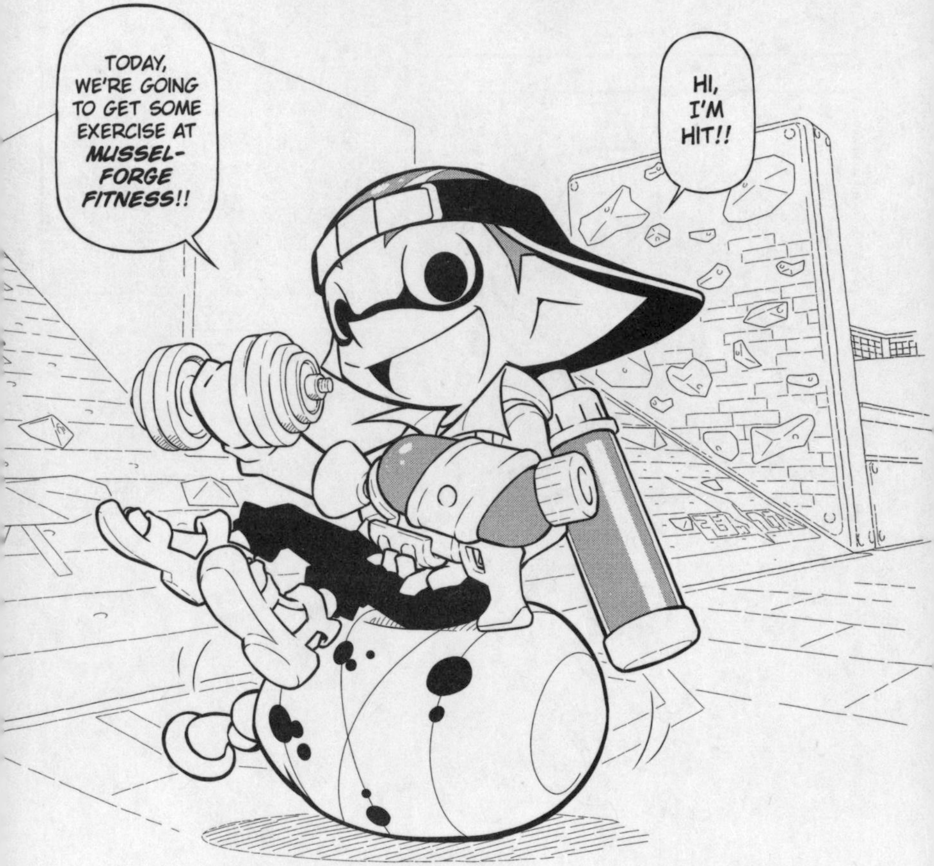
HI, I'M HIT!!
TODAY, WE'RE GOING TO GET SOME EXERCISE AT MUSSEL-FORGE FITNESS!!

MUSSELFORGE FITNESS DURING THE RAINY SEASON

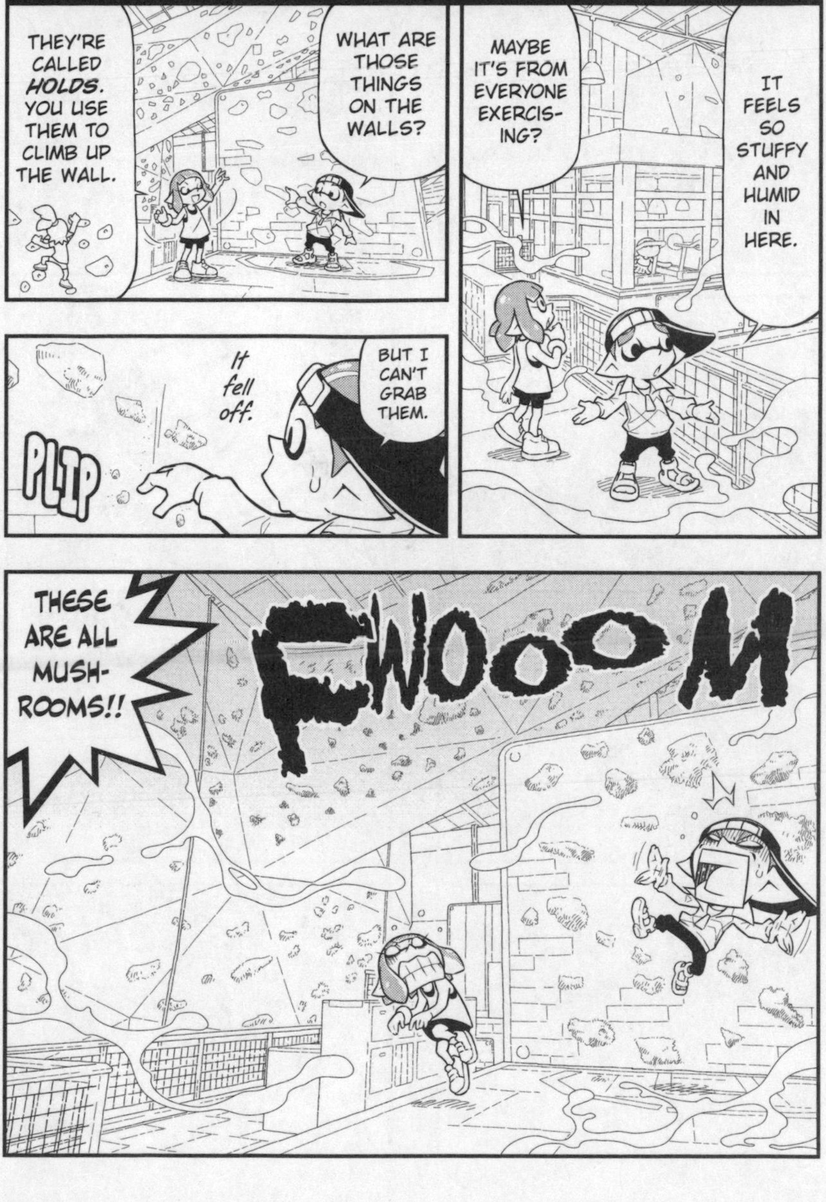
IT FEELS SO STUFFY AND HUMID IN HERE.
MAYBE IT'S FROM EVERYONE EXERCIS-ING?
WHAT ARE THOSE THINGS ON THE WALLS?
THEY'RE CALLED *HOLDS*. YOU USE THEM TO CLIMB UP THE WALL.
BUT I CAN'T GRAB THEM.
It fell off.
PLIP
FWOOOM
THESE ARE ALL MUSH-ROOMS!!

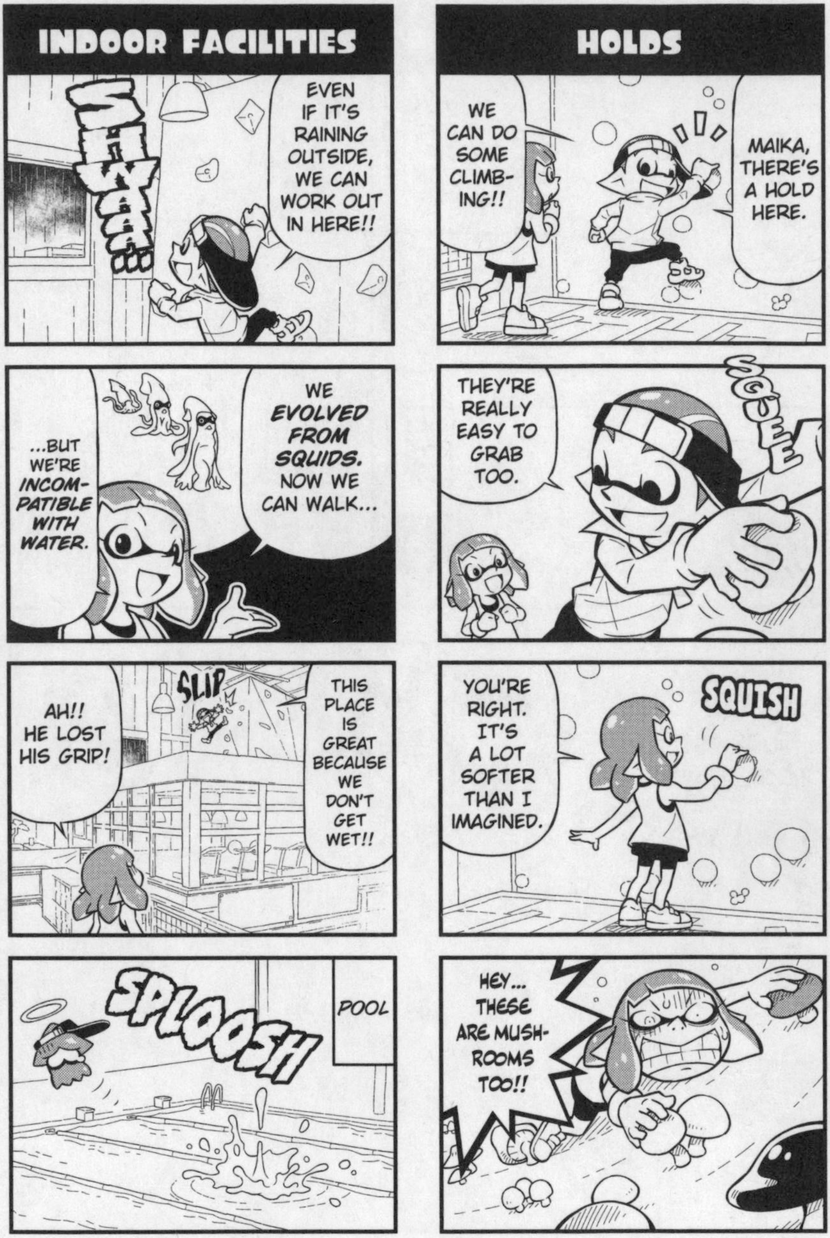
HOLDS
MAIKA, THERE'S A HOLD HERE.
WE CAN DO SOME CLIMBING!!
SQUEE
THEY'RE REALLY EASY TO GRAB TOO.
SQUISH
YOU'RE RIGHT. IT'S A LOT SOFTER THAN I IMAGINED.
HEY... THESE ARE MUSHROOMS TOO!!
INDOOR FACILITIES
EVEN IF IT'S RAINING OUTSIDE, WE CAN WORK OUT IN HERE!!
WE EVOLVED FROM SQUIDS. NOW WE CAN WALK...
...BUT WE'RE INCOMPATIBLE WITH WATER.
THIS PLACE IS GREAT BECAUSE WE DON'T GET WET!!
SLIP
AH!! HE LOST HIS GRIP!
POOL
SPLOOSH

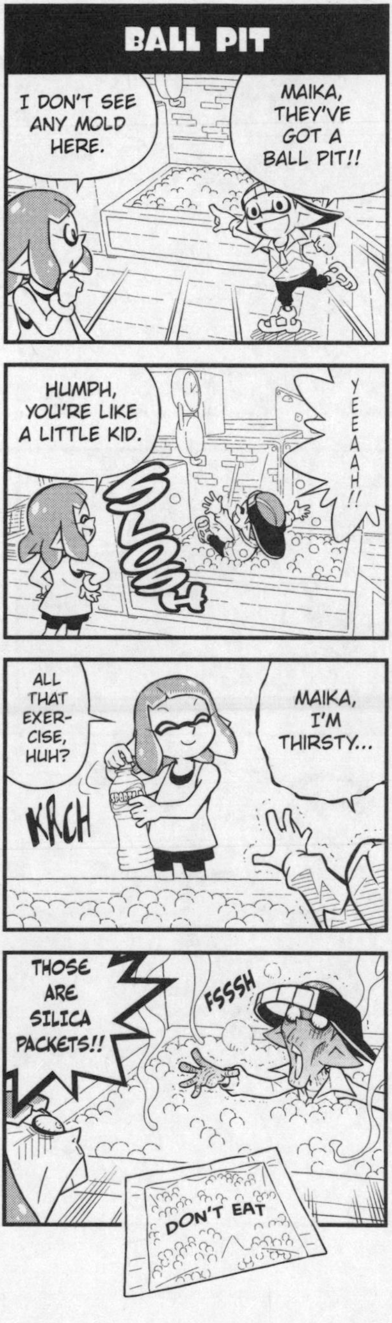
BALL PIT
MAIKA, THEY'VE GOT A BALL PIT!!
I DON'T SEE ANY MOLD HERE.
YEEAAH!!
HUMPH, YOU'RE LIKE A LITTLE KID.
SLOOSH
MAIKA, I'M THIRSTY...
ALL THAT EXERCISE, HUH?
KRCH
FSSSH
THOSE ARE SILICA PACKETS!!
DON'T EAT
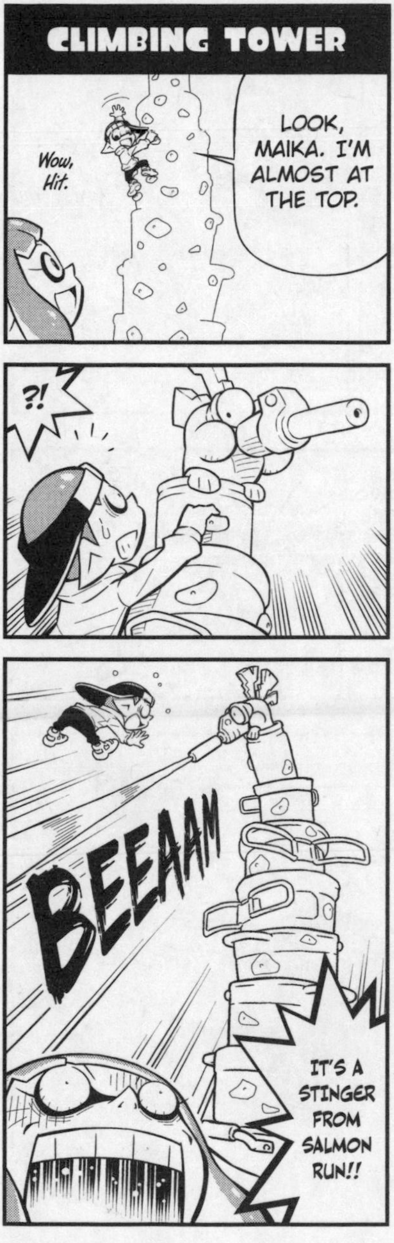
CLIMBING TOWER
LOOK, MAIKA. I'M ALMOST AT THE TOP.
Wow, Hit.
?!
BEEAAM
IT'S A STINGER FROM SALMON RUN!!

MATCHING FASHION

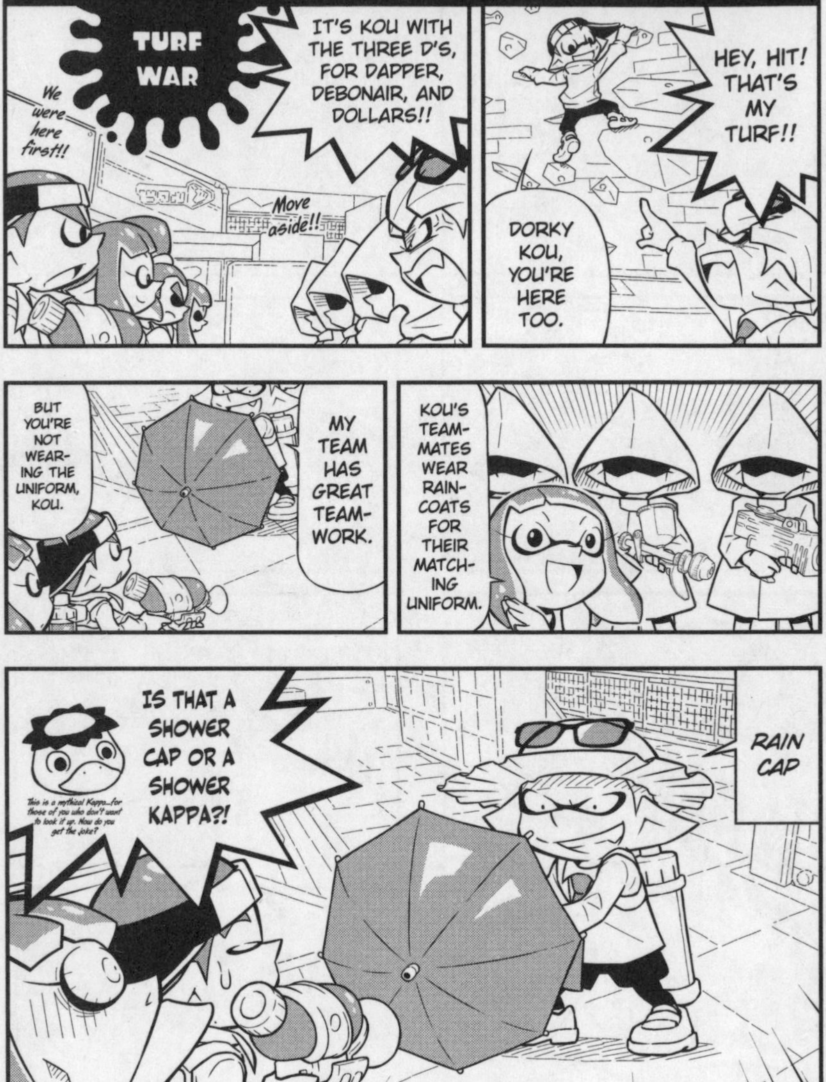
HEY, HIT! THAT'S MY TURF!!
DORKY KOU, YOU'RE HERE TOO.
IT'S KOU WITH THE THREE D'S, FOR DAPPER, DEBONAIR, AND DOLLARS!!
TURF WAR
We were here first!!
Move aside!!
KOU'S TEAM-MATES WEAR RAIN-COATS FOR THEIR MATCH-ING UNIFORM.
MY TEAM HAS GREAT TEAM-WORK.
BUT YOU'RE NOT WEAR-ING THE UNIFORM, KOU.
RAIN CAP
IS THAT A SHOWER CAP OR A SHOWER KAPPA?!
This is a mythical Kappa...for those of you who don't want to look it up. Now do you get the joke?

STUCK

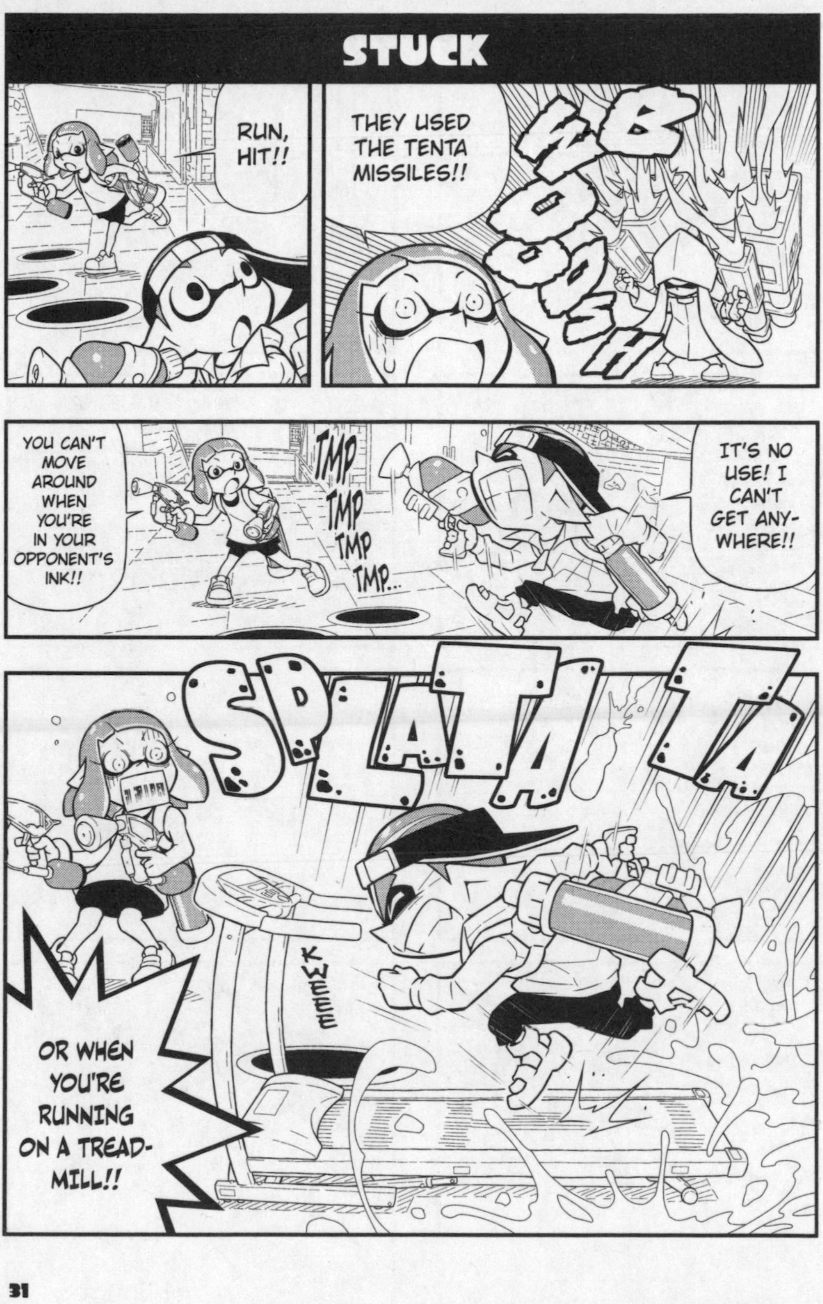
THEY USED THE TENTA MISSILES!!
BWOOOSH
RUN, HIT!!
IT'S NO USE! I CAN'T GET ANY-WHERE!!
TMP TMP TMP TMP...
YOU CAN'T MOVE AROUND WHEN YOU'RE IN YOUR OPPONENT'S INK!!
SPLATTA
KWEEE
OR WHEN YOU'RE RUNNING ON A TREAD-MILL!!

CURLING BOMB LAUNCHER

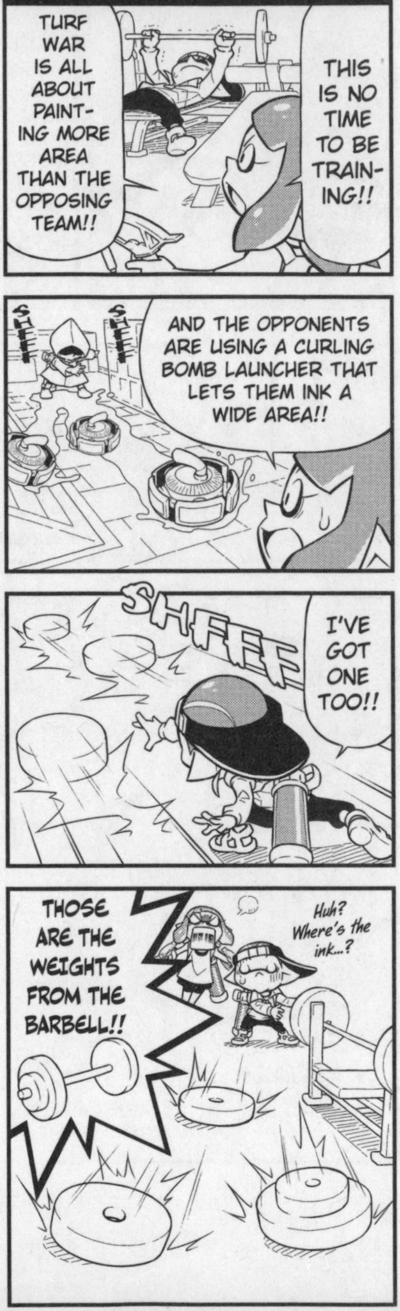
THIS IS NO TIME TO BE TRAIN-ING!!
TURF WAR IS ALL ABOUT PAINT-ING MORE AREA THAN THE OPPOSING TEAM!!
SHFF
SHFF
AND THE OPPONENTS ARE USING A CURLING BOMB LAUNCHER THAT LETS THEM INK A WIDE AREA!!
I'VE GOT ONE TOO!!
SHFFF
Huh? Where's the ink...?
THOSE ARE THE WEIGHTS FROM THE BARBELL!!

INVISIBLE INK

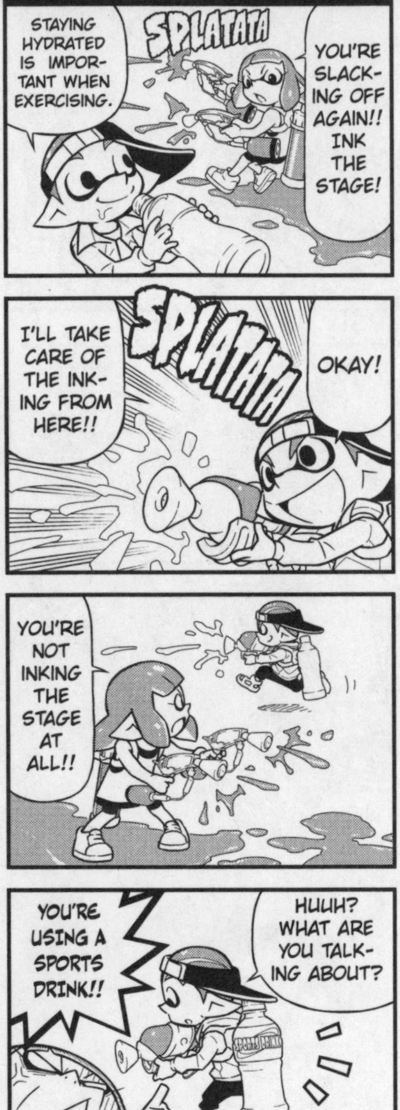
YOU'RE SLACK-ING OFF AGAIN!! INK THE STAGE!
SPLATATA
STAYING HYDRATED IS IMPOR-TANT WHEN EXERCISING.
OKAY!
SPLATATA
I'LL TAKE CARE OF THE INK-ING FROM HERE!!
YOU'RE NOT INKING THE STAGE AT ALL!!
HUUH? WHAT ARE YOU TALK-ING ABOUT?
YOU'RE USING A SPORTS DRINK!!
SPORTS DRINK

COLOR-CHANGING INK

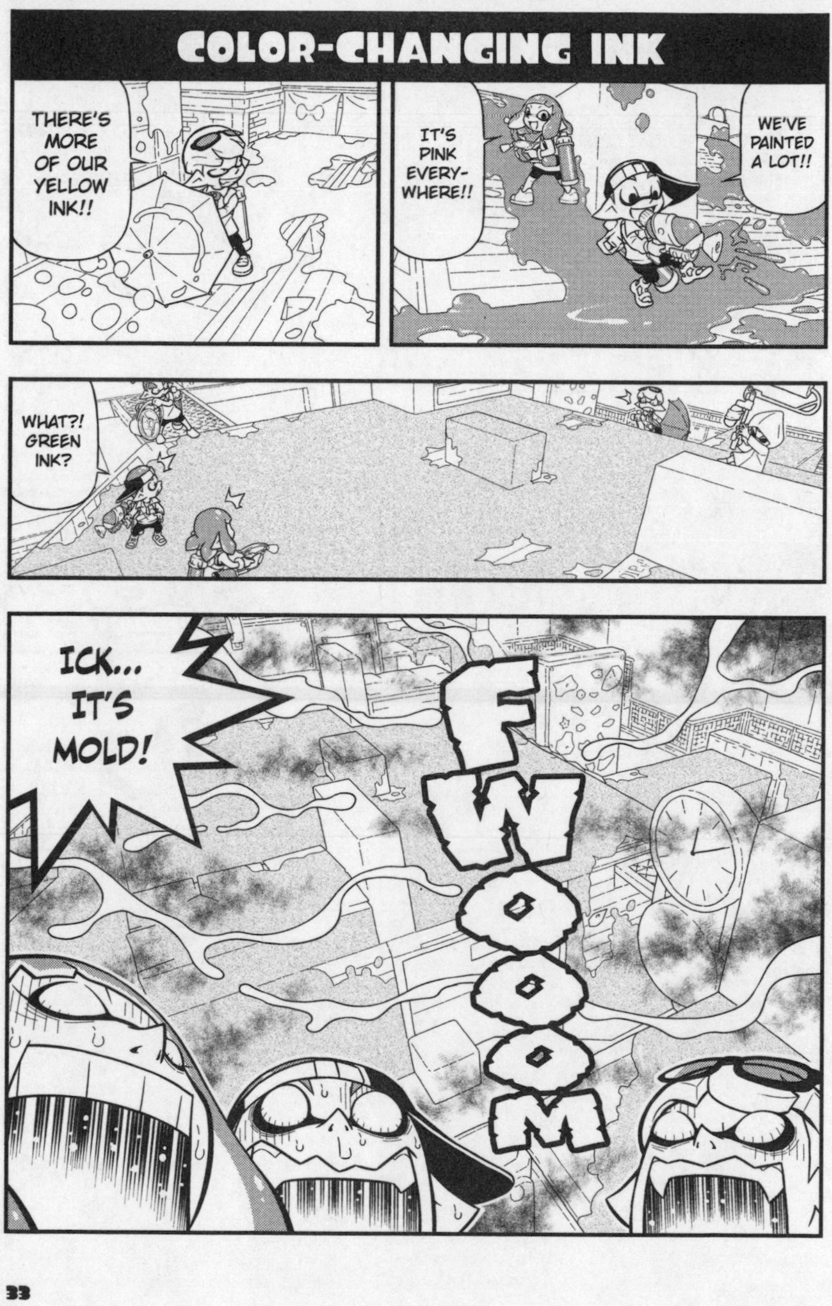
WE'VE PAINTED A LOT!!
IT'S PINK EVERY-WHERE!!
THERE'S MORE OF OUR YELLOW INK!!
WHAT?! GREEN INK?
ICK... IT'S MOLD!
FWOOOOM

AIR FRESHENER

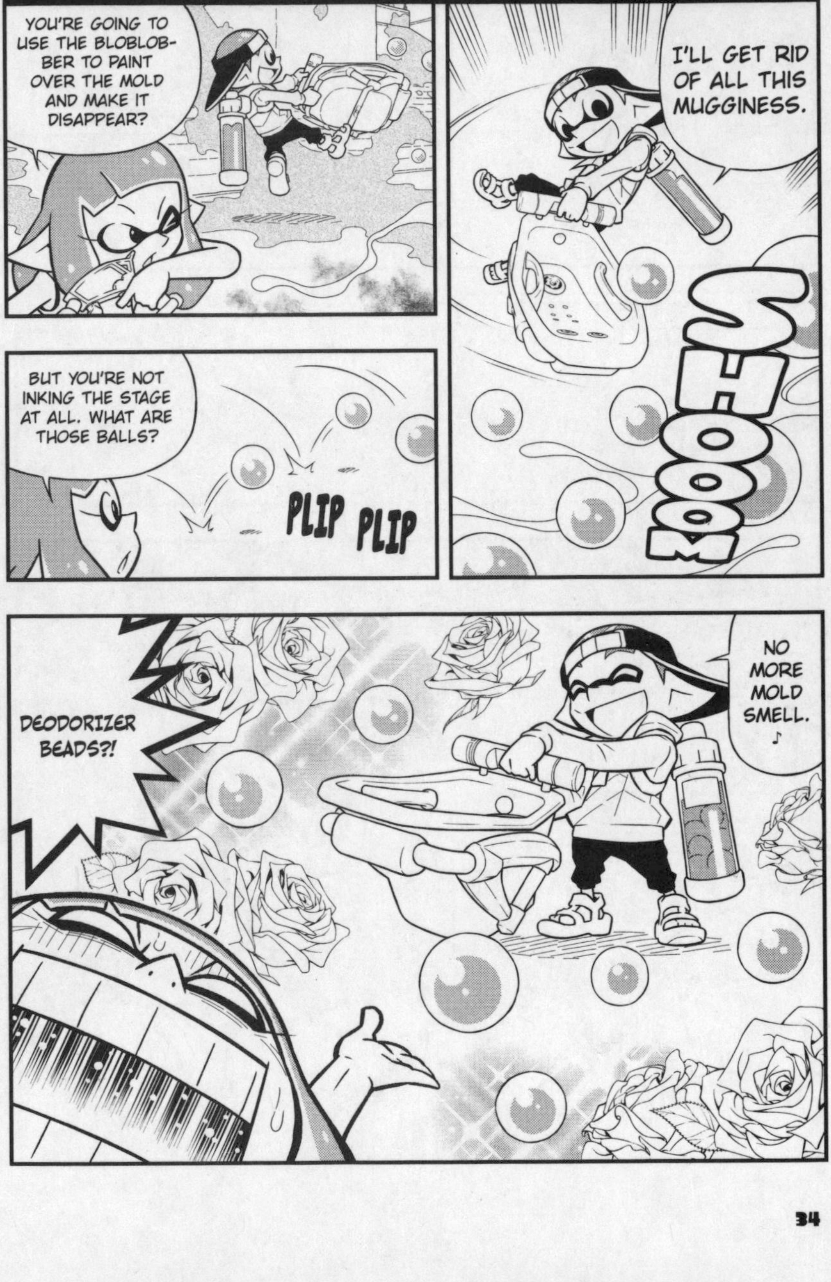
I'LL GET RID OF ALL THIS MUGGINESS.
SHOOOOM
YOU'RE GOING TO USE THE BLOBLOBBER TO PAINT OVER THE MOLD AND MAKE IT DISAPPEAR?
BUT YOU'RE NOT INKING THE STAGE AT ALL. WHAT ARE THOSE BALLS?
PLIP PLIP
NO MORE MOLD SMELL. ♪
DEODORIZER BEADS?!

DEHUMIDIFIED FITNESS CLUB

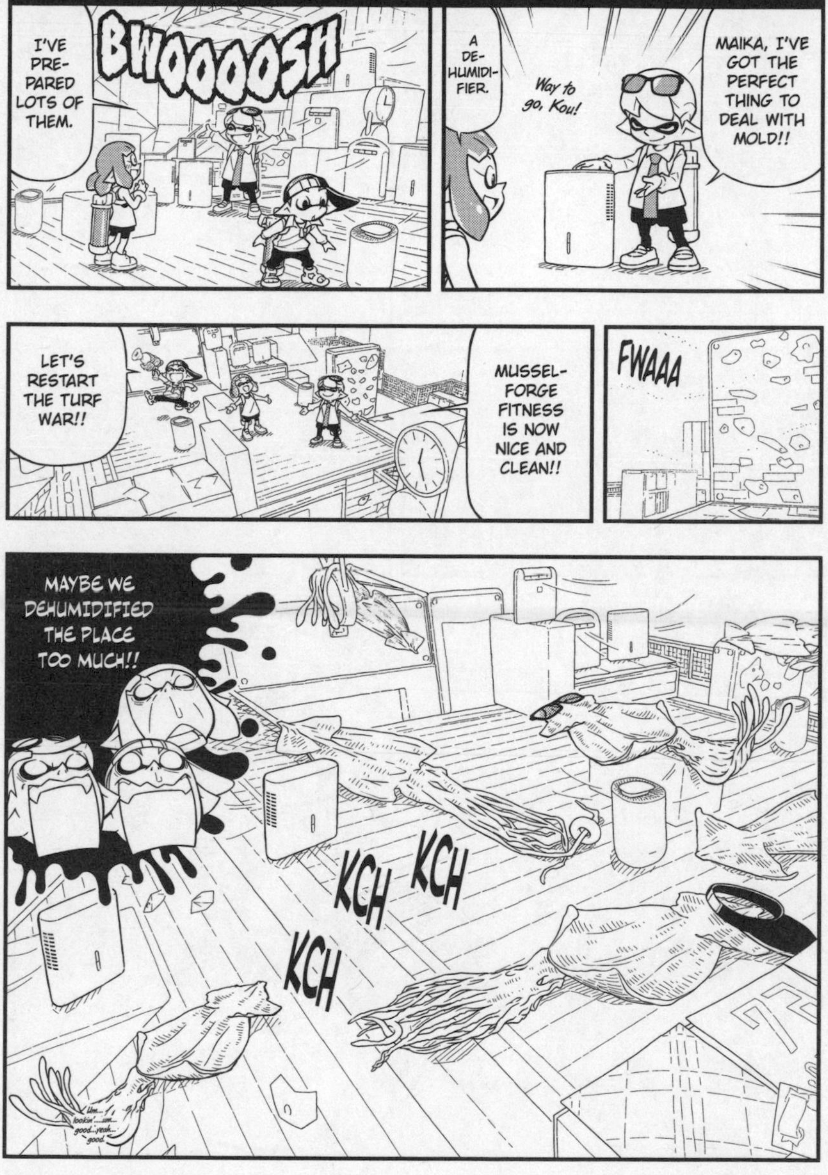

MAIKA, I'VE GOT THE PERFECT THING TO DEAL WITH MOLD!!
Way to go, Kou!
A DE-HUMIDIFIER.
BWOOOOOSH
I'VE PRE-PARED LOTS OF THEM.
FWAAA
MUSSEL-FORGE FITNESS IS NOW NICE AND CLEAN!!
LET'S RESTART THE TURF WAR!!
MAYBE WE DEHUMIDIFIED THE PLACE TOO MUCH!!
KCH
KCH
KCH
Um... lookin'...um... good...yeah... good.

Splatoon SQUID KIDS COMEDY SHOW

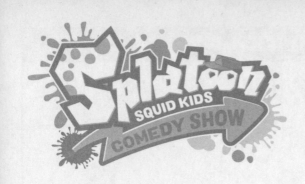

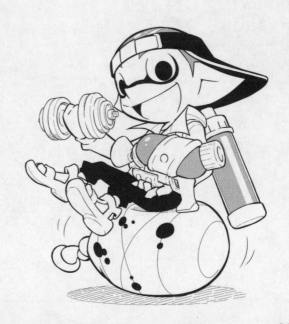

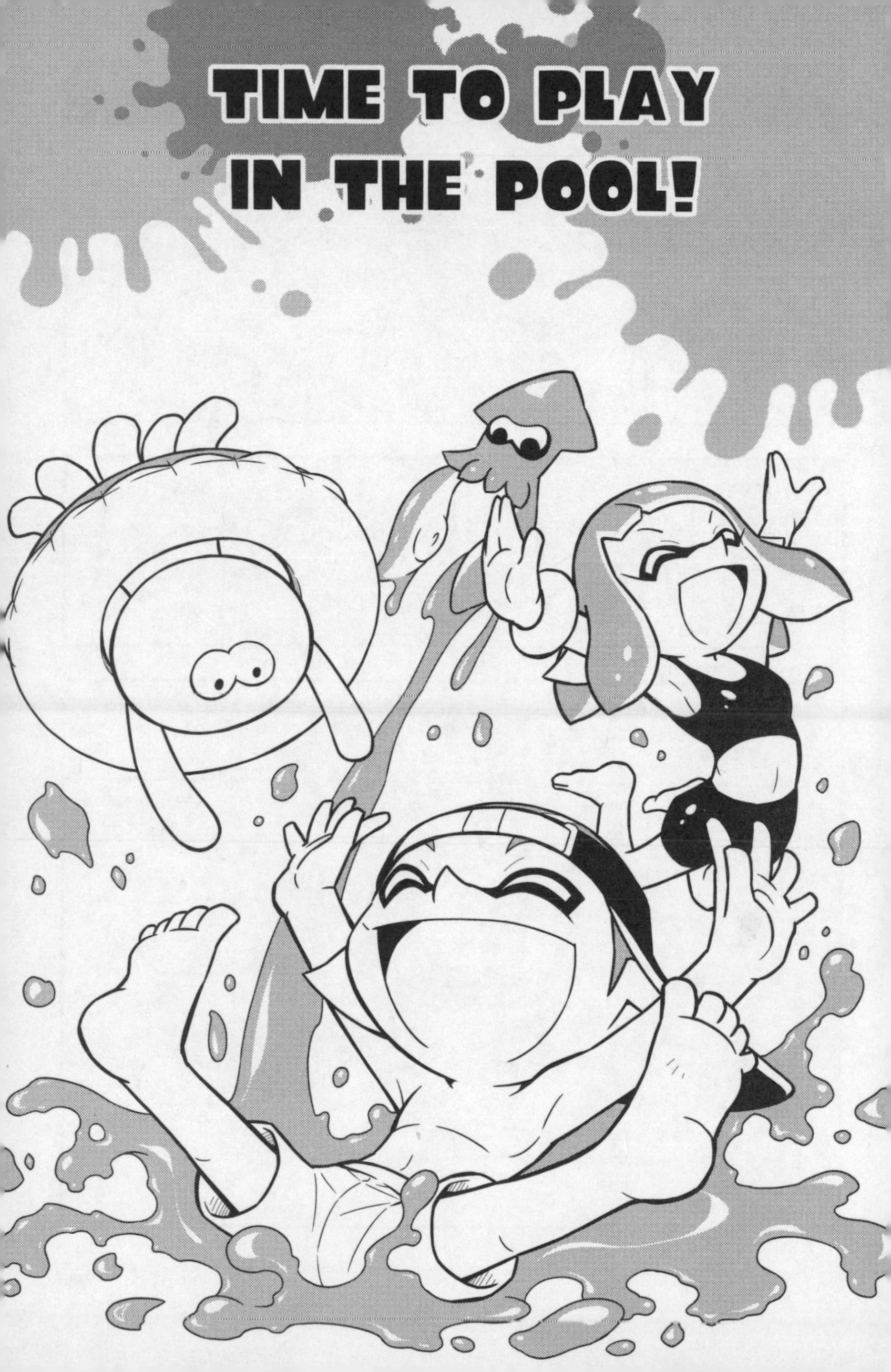
TIME TO PLAY IN THE POOL!

SUPER POPULAR POOL

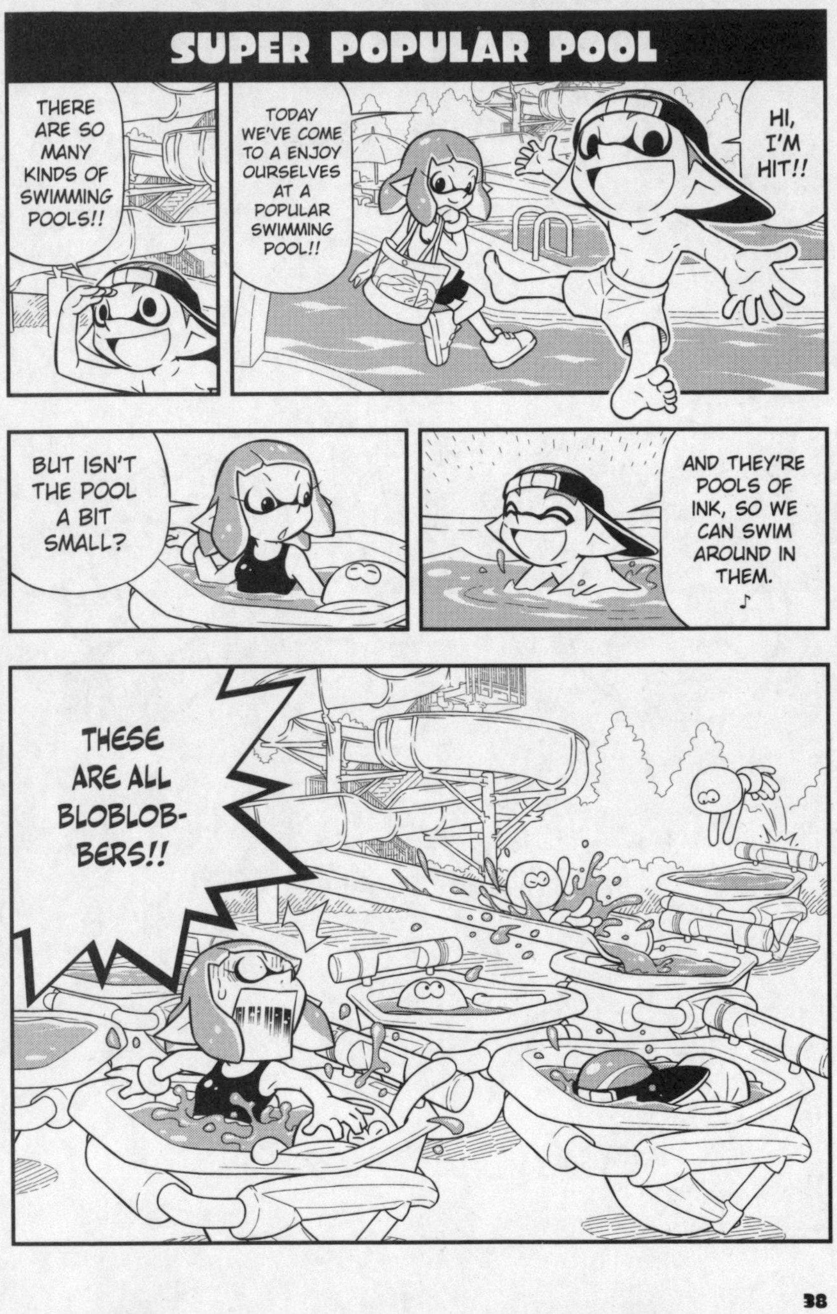
HI, I'M HIT!!
TODAY WE'VE COME TO A ENJOY OURSELVES AT A POPULAR SWIMMING POOL!!
THERE ARE SO MANY KINDS OF SWIMMING POOLS!!
AND THEY'RE POOLS OF INK, SO WE CAN SWIM AROUND IN THEM. ♪
BUT ISN'T THE POOL A BIT SMALL?
THESE ARE ALL BLOBLOB-BERS!!

OFF LIMITS

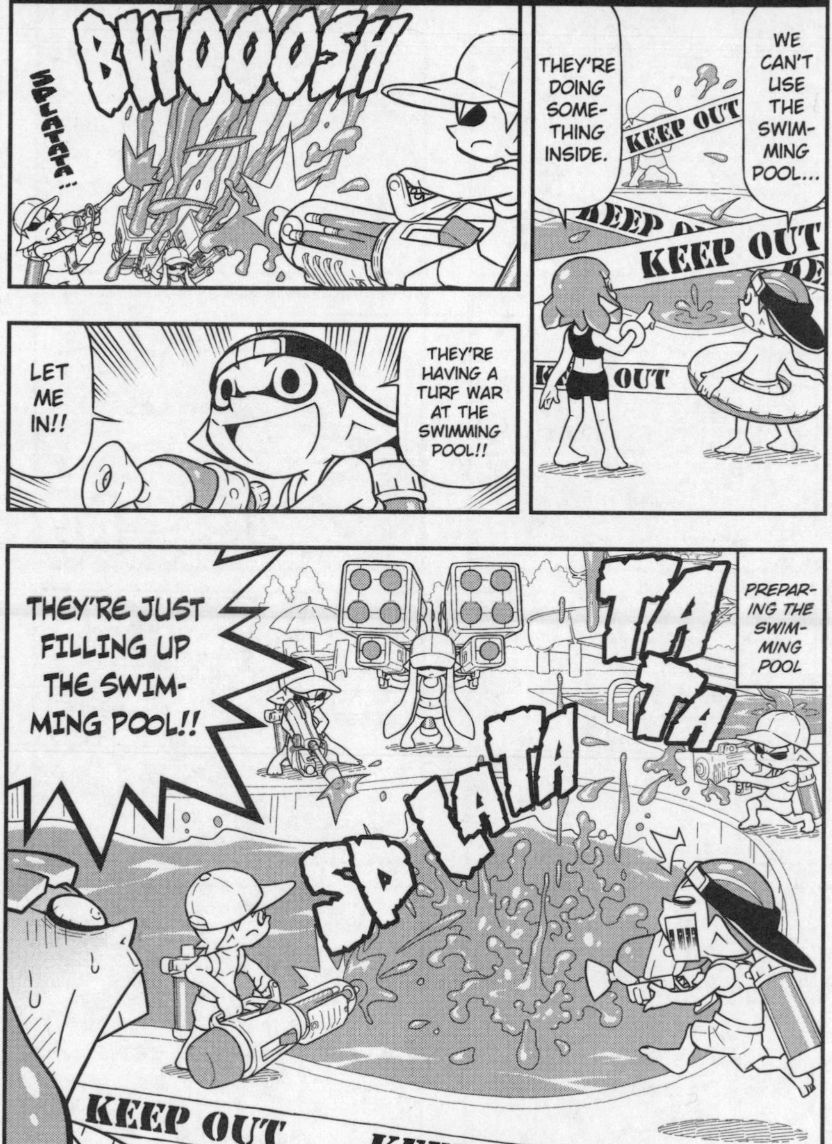
WE CAN'T USE THE SWIM-MING POOL...
KEEP OUT
THEY'RE DOING SOME-THING INSIDE.
KEEP OUT
BWOOOSH
SPLATATA...
THEY'RE HAVING A TURF WAR AT THE SWIMMING POOL!!
LET ME IN!!
PREPAR-ING THE SWIM-MING POOL
TA TA
SPLATA
THEY'RE JUST FILLING UP THE SWIM-MING POOL!!
KEEP OUT

WATERSLIDE

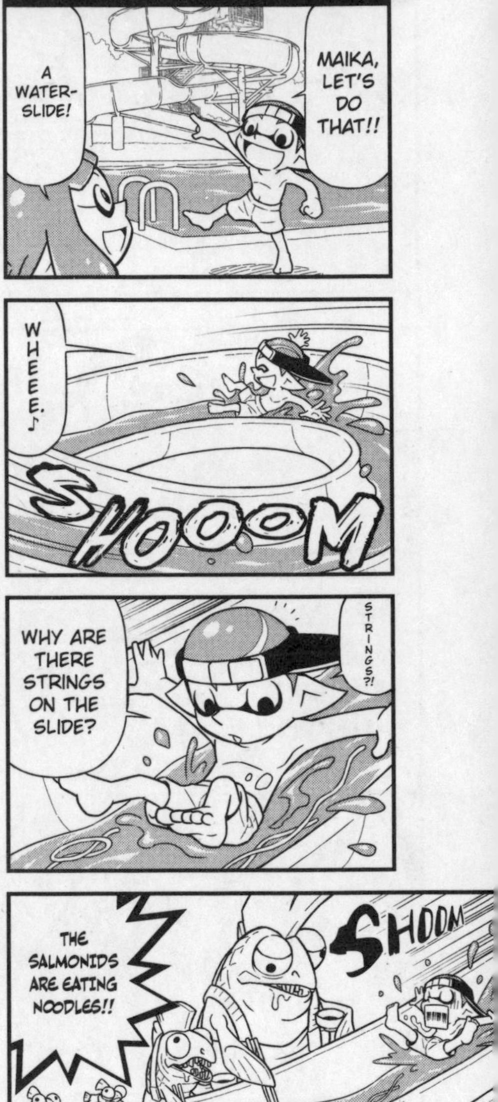
MAIKA, LET'S DO THAT!!
A WATER-SLIDE!
WHEEEE. ♪
SHOOOM
STRINGS?!
WHY ARE THERE STRINGS ON THE SLIDE?
SHOOM
THE SALMONIDS ARE EATING NOODLES!!

GRATED

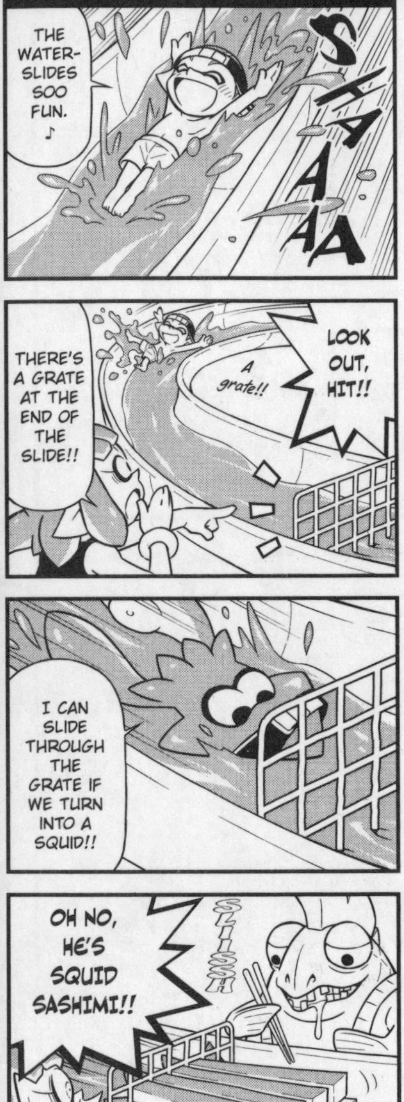
SHAAAAA
THE WATER-SLIDES SOO FUN. ♪
LOOK OUT, HIT!!
A grate!!
THERE'S A GRATE AT THE END OF THE SLIDE!!
I CAN SLIDE THROUGH THE GRATE IF WE TURN INTO A SQUID!!
OH NO, HE'S SQUID SASHIMI!!

MAXIMUM-DANGER WATERSLIDE

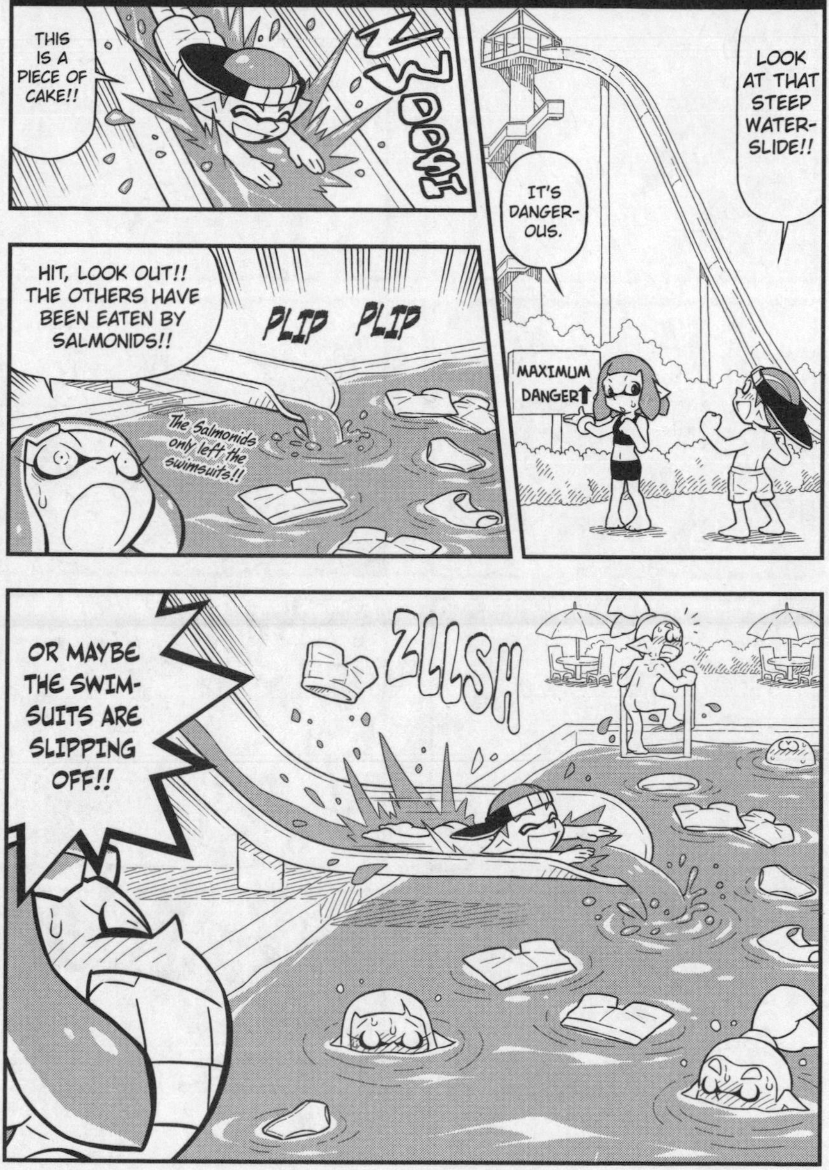

LOOK AT THAT STEEP WATER-SLIDE!!
IT'S DANGER-OUS.
MAXIMUM DANGER
THIS IS A PIECE OF CAKE!!
ZWOOSH
HIT, LOOK OUT!! THE OTHERS HAVE BEEN EATEN BY SALMONIDS!!
PLIP PLIP
The Salmonids only left the swimsuits!!
OR MAYBE THE SWIM-SUITS ARE SLIPPING OFF!!
ZLLSH

AIR PUMP

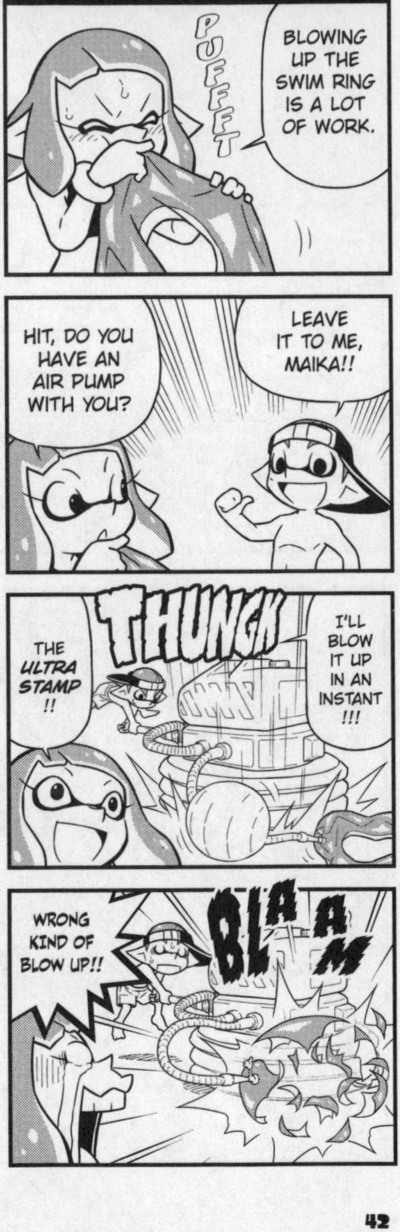
BLOWING UP THE SWIM RING IS A LOT OF WORK.
PUFFFT
LEAVE IT TO ME, MAIKA!!
HIT, DO YOU HAVE AN AIR PUMP WITH YOU?
THUNCK
I'LL BLOW IT UP IN AN INSTANT!!!
THE *ULTRA STAMP*!!
BLAAM
WRONG KIND OF BLOW UP!!

SQUID DIVE

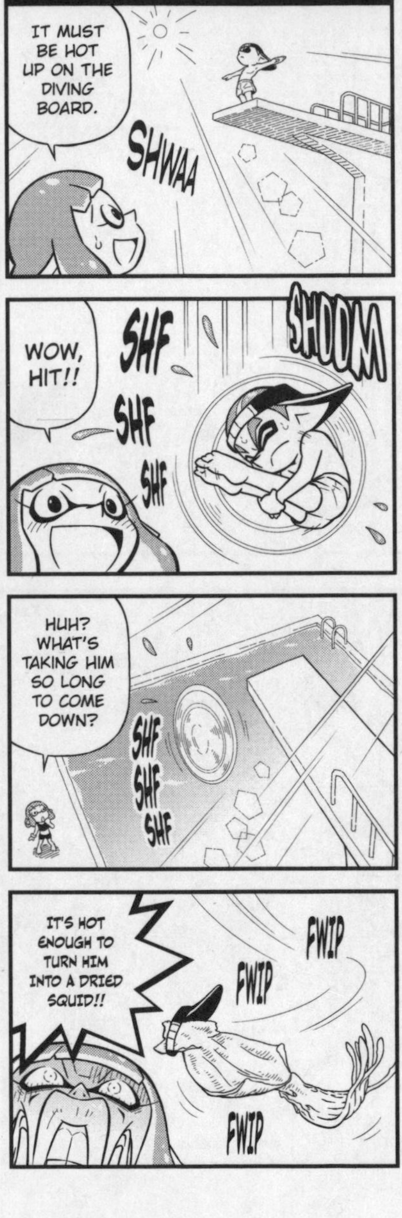
IT MUST BE HOT UP ON THE DIVING BOARD.
SHWAA
SHOOM
SHF
WOW, HIT!!
SHF
SHF
HUH? WHAT'S TAKING HIM SO LONG TO COME DOWN?
SHF
SHF
SHF
FWIP
FWIP
IT'S HOT ENOUGH TO TURN HIM INTO A DRIED SQUID!!
FWIP

BEACH VOLLEYBALL

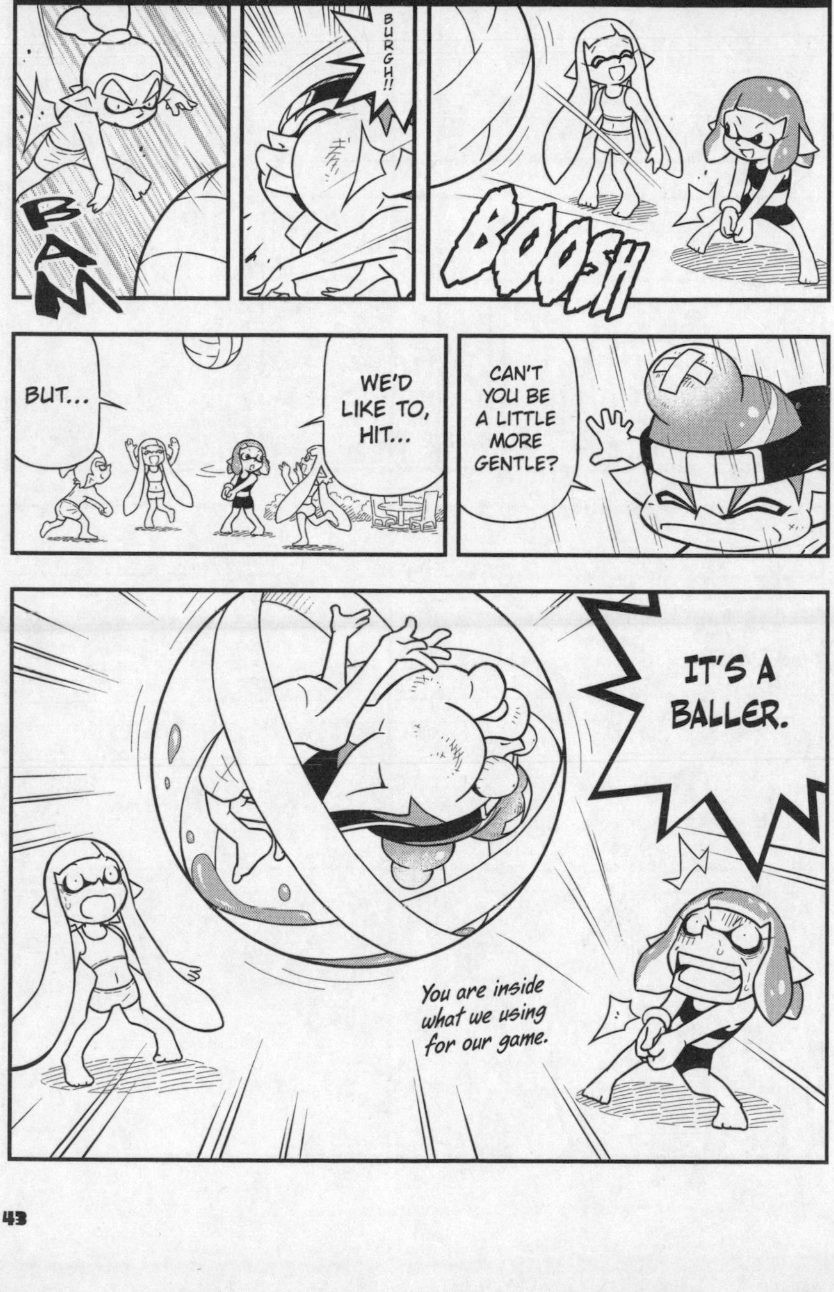
BOOSH
BURGH!!
BAM
CAN'T YOU BE A LITTLE MORE GENTLE?
WE'D LIKE TO, HIT...
BUT...
IT'S A BALLER.
You are inside what we using for our game.

DROWINING JELLYFISH

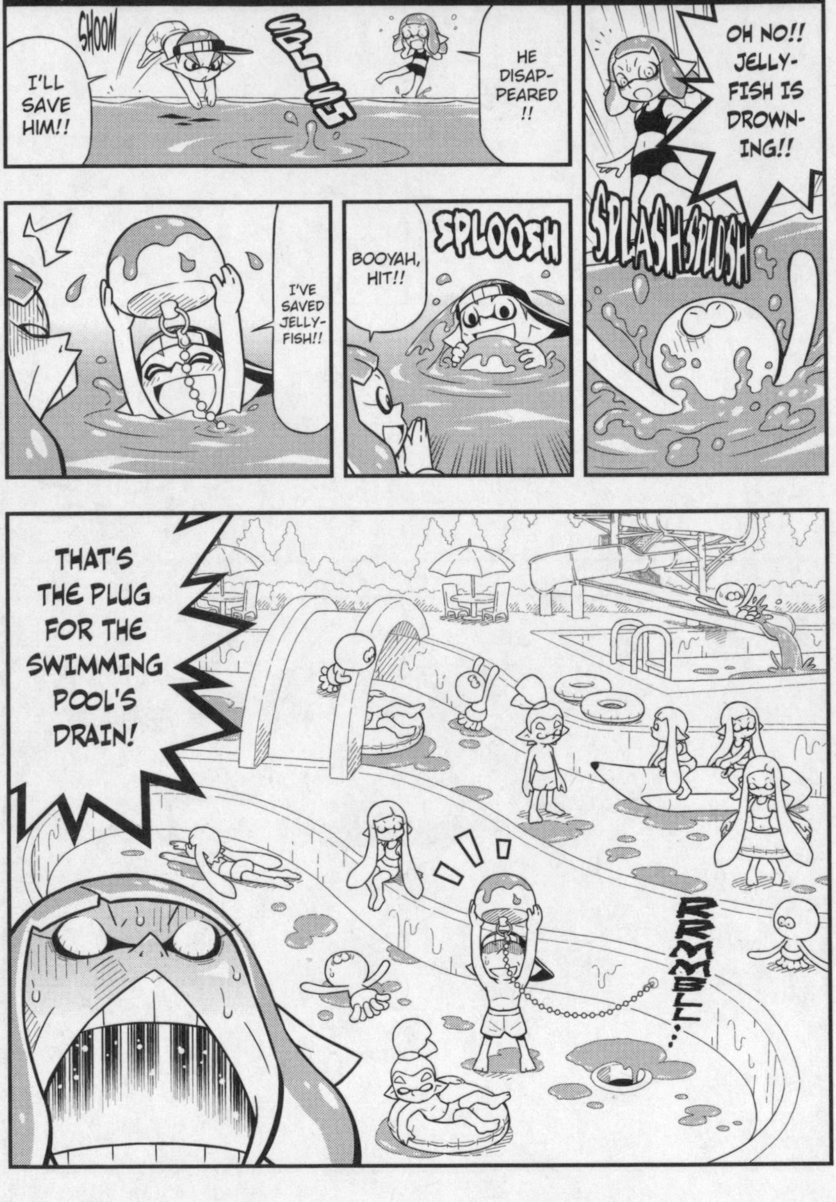
OH NO!! JELLY-FISH IS DROWN-ING!!
SPLASH SPLOSH
HE DISAP-PEARED!!
SPLISH
SHOOM
I'LL SAVE HIM!!
SPLOOSH
BOOYAH, HIT!!
I'VE SAVED JELLY-FISH!!
THAT'S THE PLUG FOR THE SWIMMING POOL'S DRAIN!
RRMMBLL...

Splatoon SQUID KIDS COMEDY SHOW

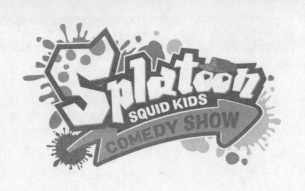

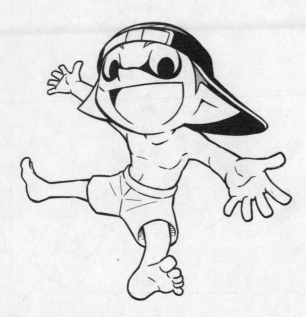

Splatoon
SQUID KIDS
COMEDY SHOW

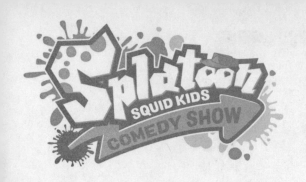

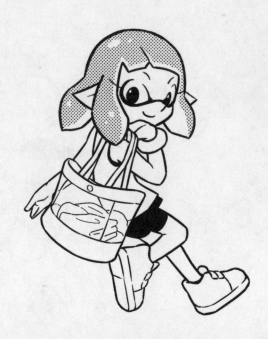

TIME TO ENJOY THE SCHOOL FESTIVAL!

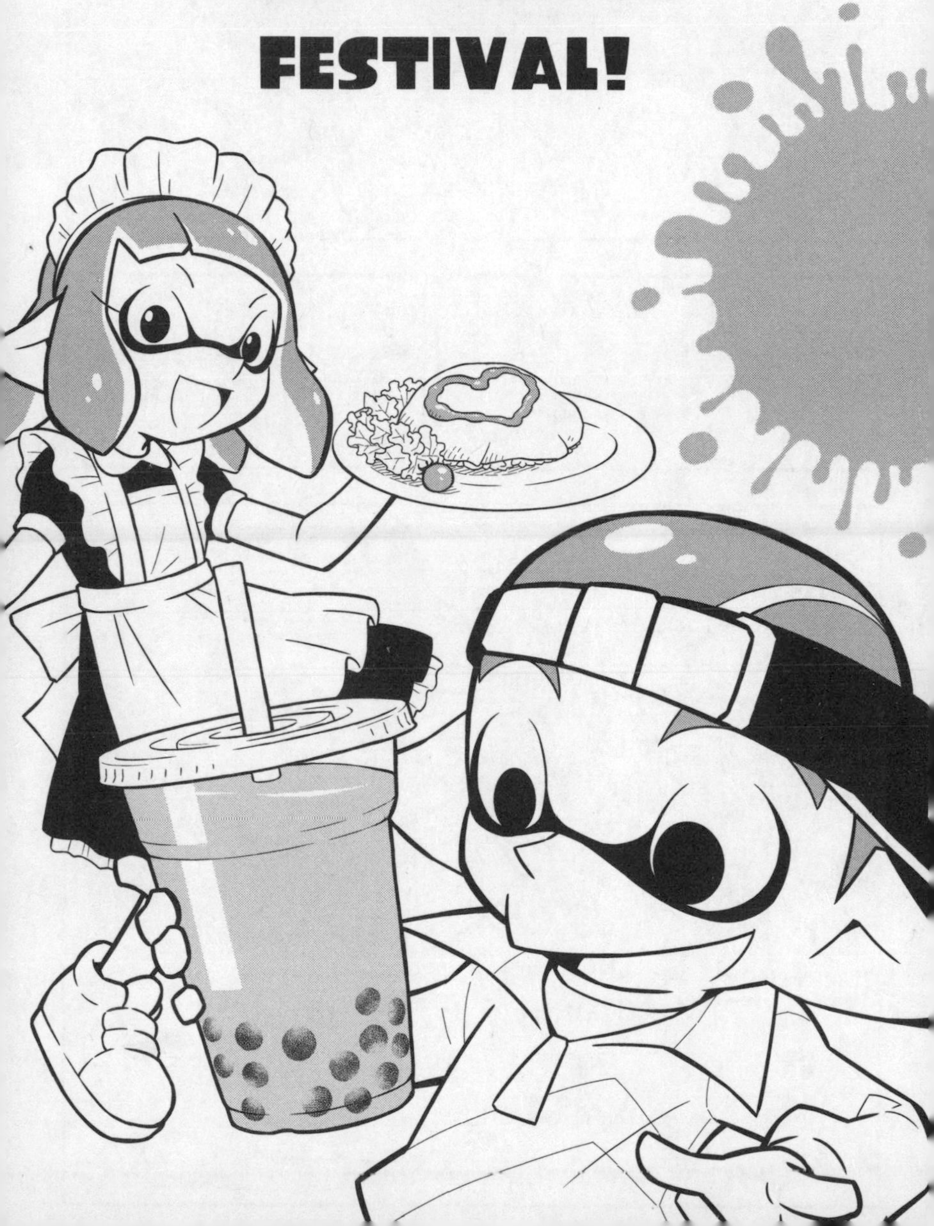

SCHOOL-FESTIVAL LINE

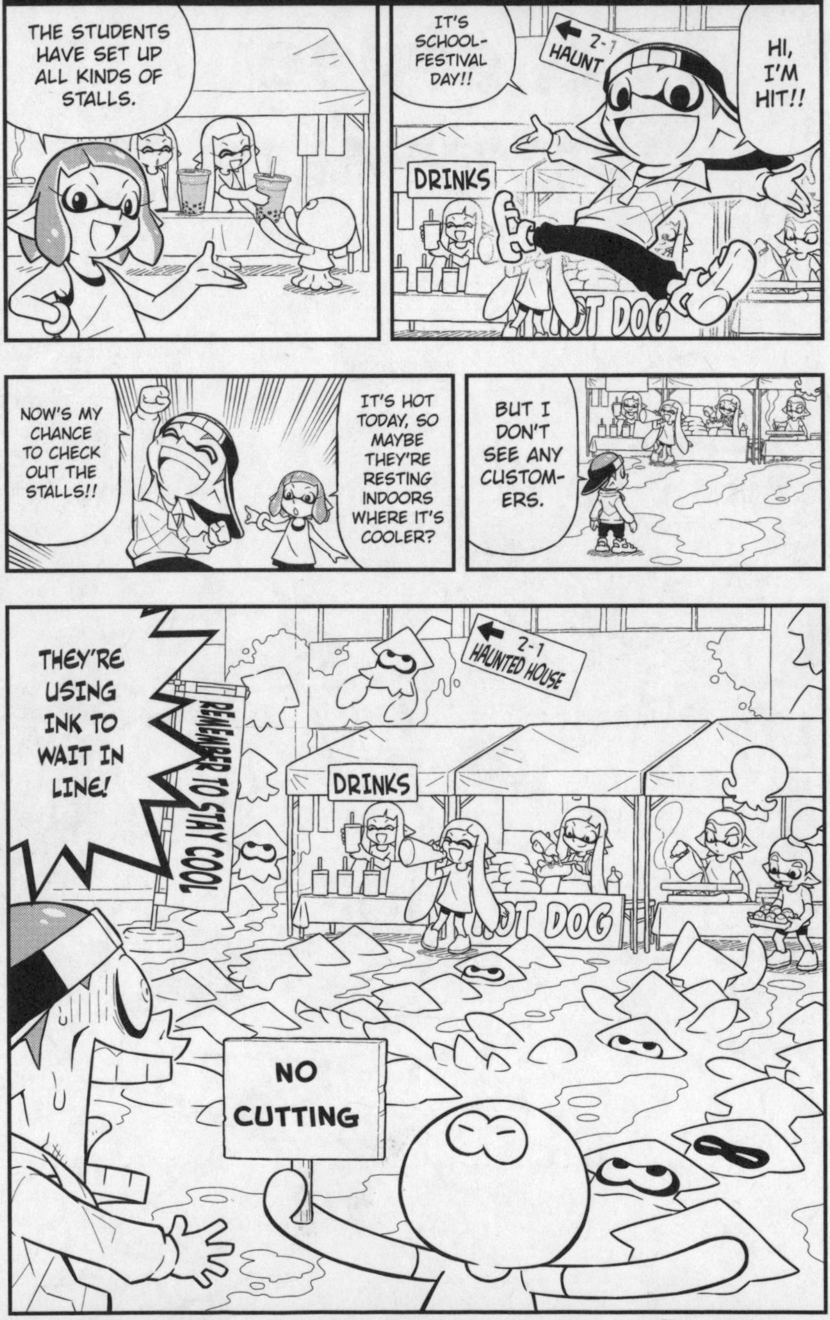
HI, I'M HIT!!
IT'S SCHOOL-FESTIVAL DAY!!
2-1 HAUNT
DRINKS
HOT DOG
THE STUDENTS HAVE SET UP ALL KINDS OF STALLS.
BUT I DON'T SEE ANY CUSTOM-ERS.
IT'S HOT TODAY, SO MAYBE THEY'RE RESTING INDOORS WHERE IT'S COOLER?
NOW'S MY CHANCE TO CHECK OUT THE STALLS!!
2-1 HAUNTED HOUSE
REMEMBER TO STAY COOL
DRINKS
HOT DOG
THEY'RE USING INK TO WAIT IN LINE!
NO CUTTING

FULL STOMACH

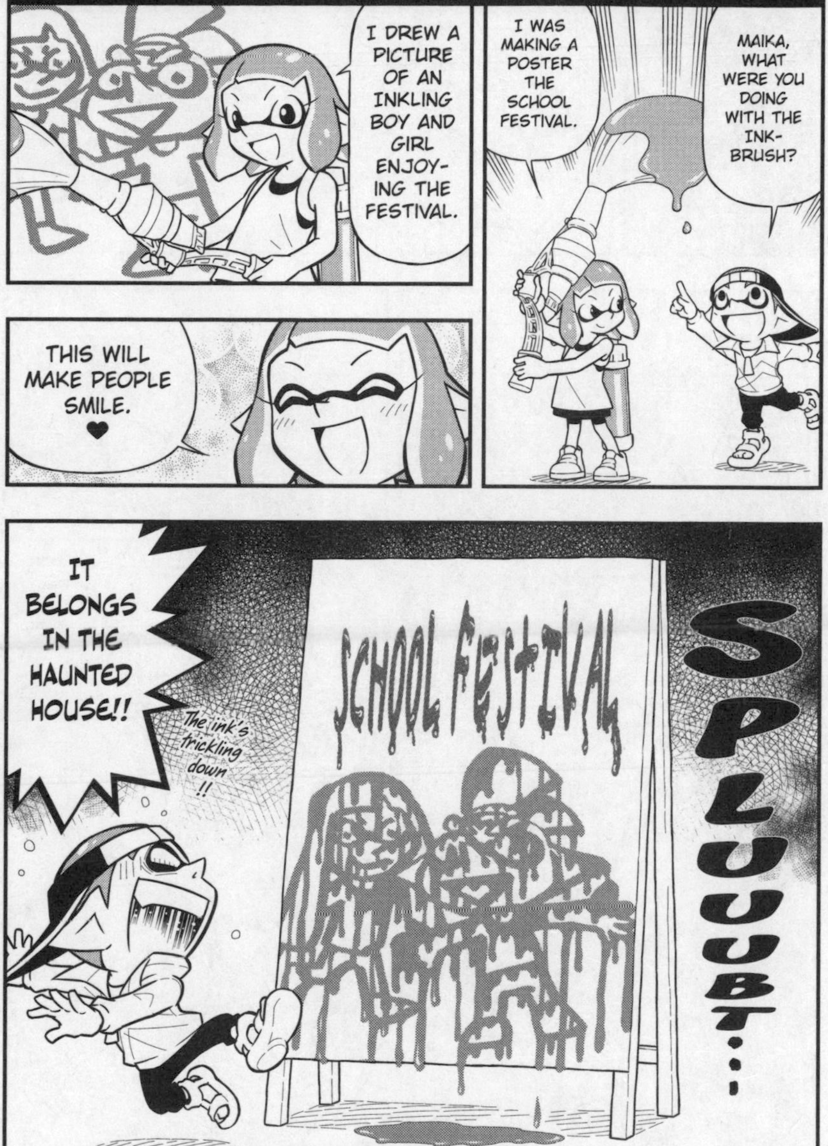
MAIKA, WHAT WERE YOU DOING WITH THE INK-BRUSH?
I WAS MAKING A POSTER THE SCHOOL FESTIVAL.
I DREW A PICTURE OF AN INKLING BOY AND GIRL ENJOYING THE FESTIVAL.
THIS WILL MAKE PEOPLE SMILE. ♥
SPLUUUBT...
SCHOOL FESTIVAL
IT BELONGS IN THE HAUNTED HOUSE!!
The ink's trickling down!!

BUBBLE TEA

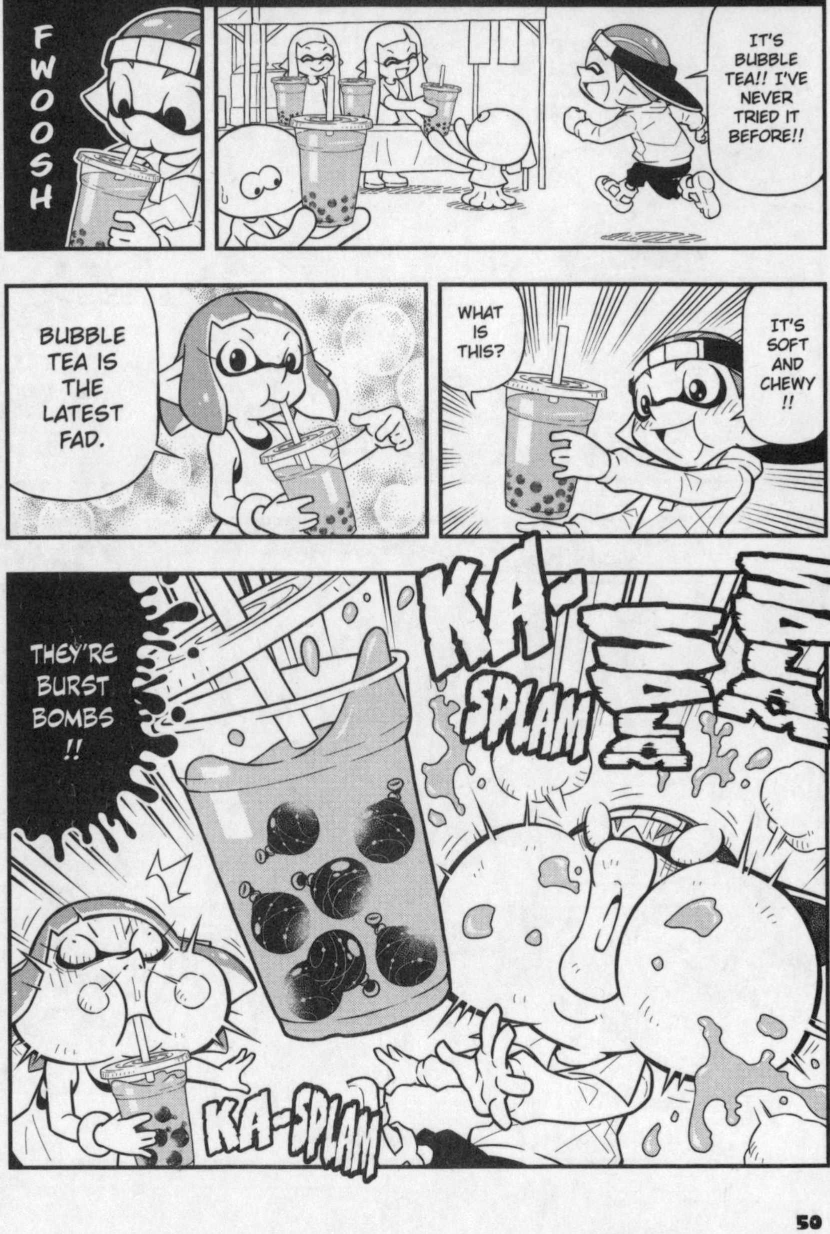
IT'S BUBBLE TEA!! I'VE NEVER TRIED IT BEFORE!!
FWOOSH
IT'S SOFT AND CHEWY!!
WHAT IS THIS?
BUBBLE TEA IS THE LATEST FAD.
KA-SPLAM
THEY'RE BURST BOMBS!!
KA-SPLAM

MAID CAFE

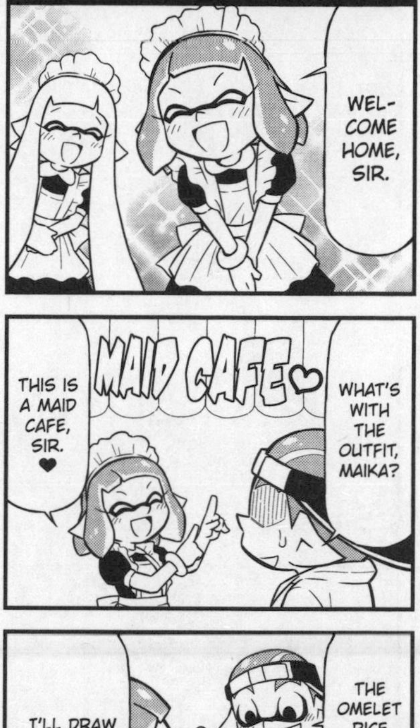
WEL-COME HOME, SIR.
WHAT'S WITH THE OUTFIT, MAIKA?
MAID CAFE♥
THIS IS A MAID CAFE, SIR. ♥
THE OMELET RICE LOOKS GOOD!!
I'LL DRAW A HEART ON IT FOR YOU WITH KETCHUP. ♥
SPLATATA...
AIYEEE!!
KETCHUP

STAMP♥

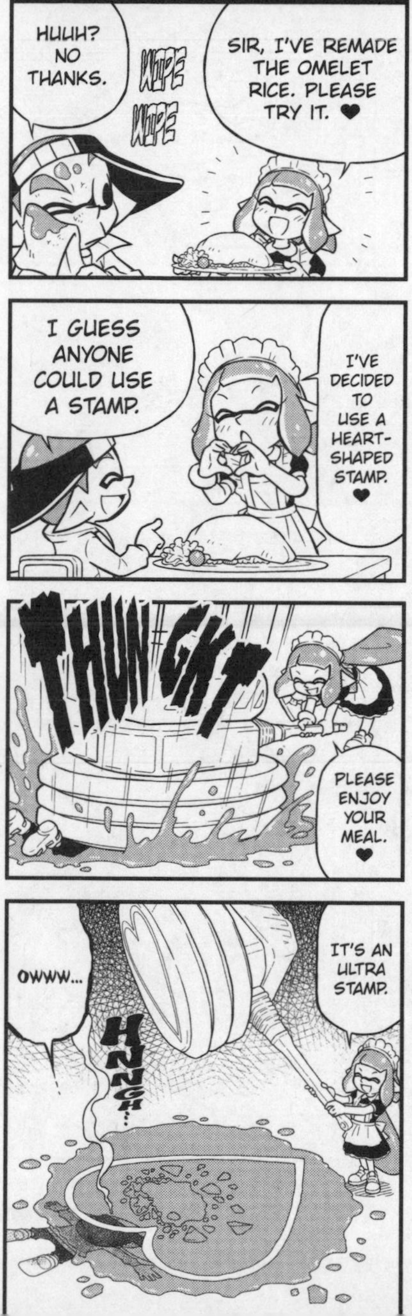
SIR, I'VE REMADE THE OMELET RICE. PLEASE TRY IT. ♥
WIPE WIPE
HUUH? NO THANKS.
I'VE DECIDED TO USE A HEART-SHAPED STAMP. ♥
I GUESS ANYONE COULD USE A STAMP.
THUNGKT
PLEASE ENJOY YOUR MEAL. ♥
IT'S AN ULTRA STAMP.
OWWW...
HNNGH...

SQUID SHOP

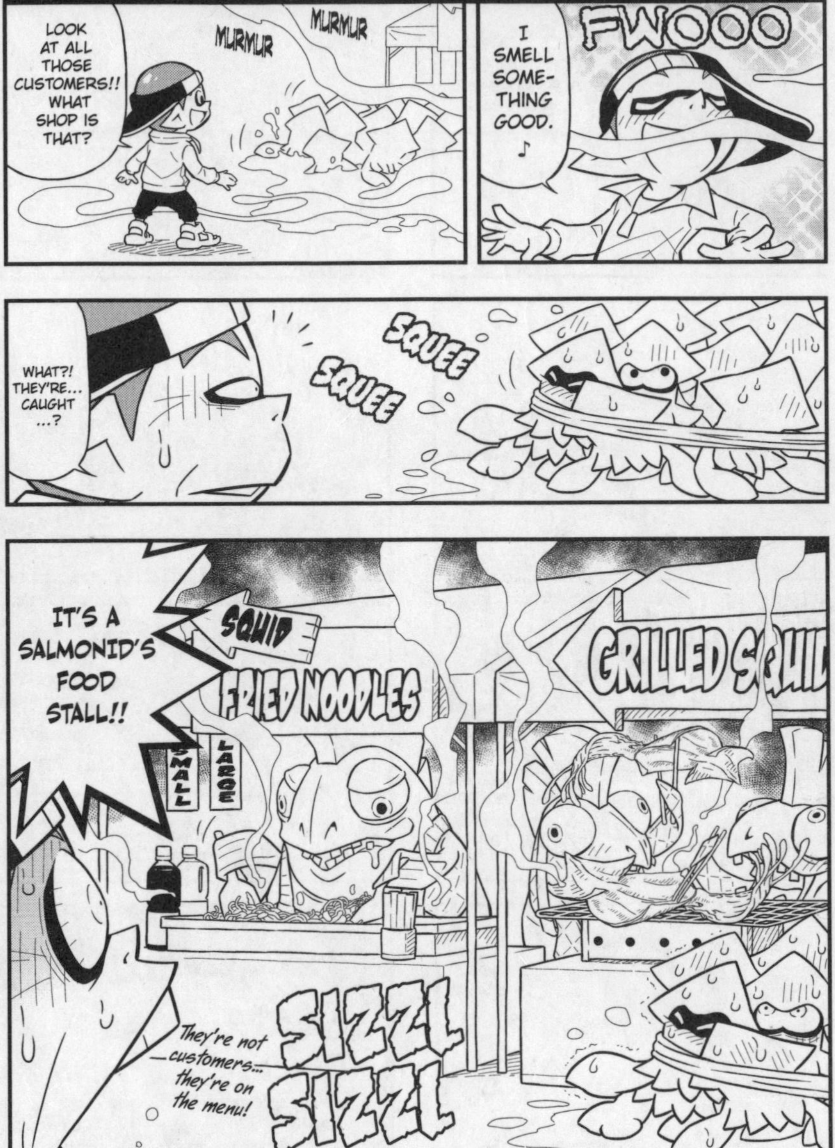
FWOOO
I SMELL SOME-THING GOOD. ♪
MURMUR
MURMUR
LOOK AT ALL THOSE CUSTOMERS!! WHAT SHOP IS THAT?
SQUEE
SQUEE
WHAT?! THEY'RE... CAUGHT ...?
GRILLED SQUI
SQUID
FRIED NOODLES
IT'S A SALMONID'S FOOD STALL!!
LARGE
SMALL
SIZZL
SIZZL
They're not customers... they're on the menu!

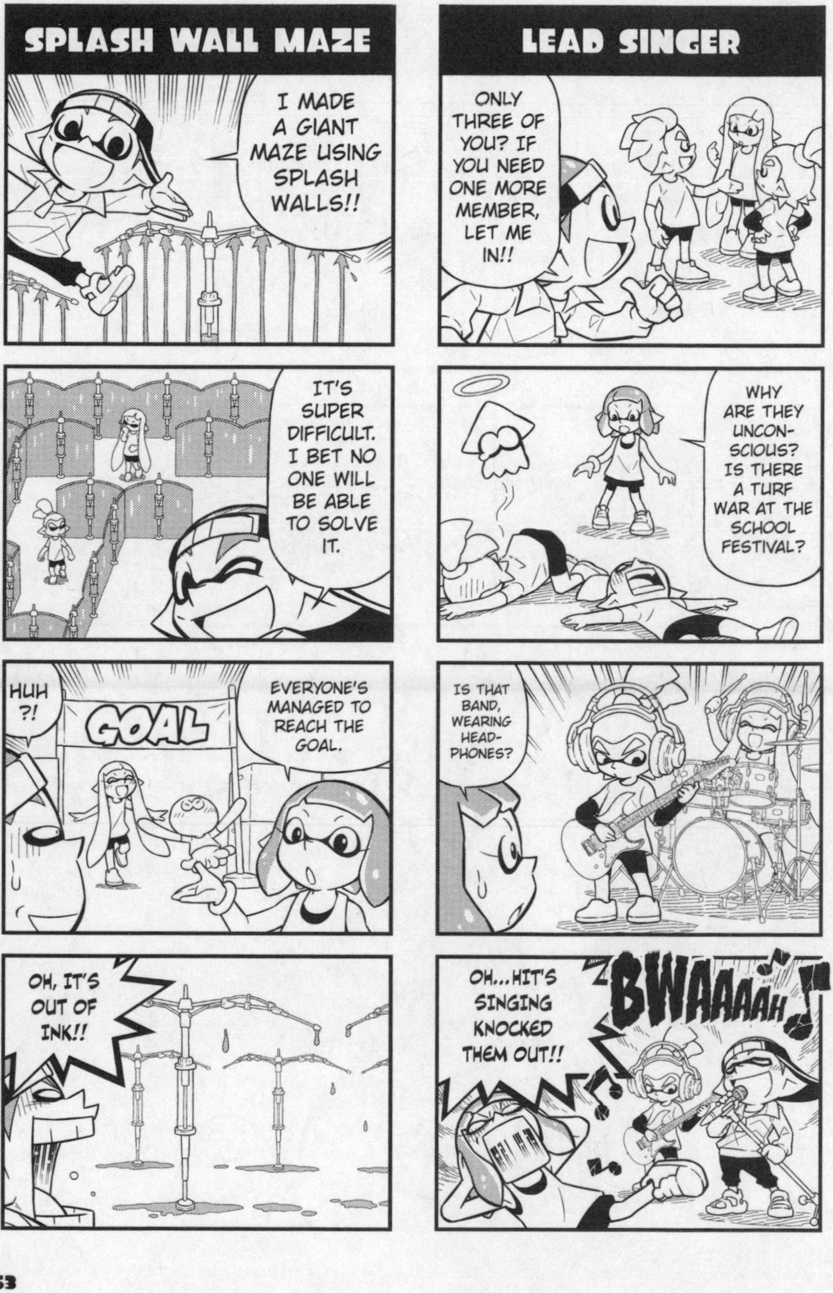
LEAD SINGER
ONLY THREE OF YOU? IF YOU NEED ONE MORE MEMBER, LET ME IN!!
WHY ARE THEY UNCON-SCIOUS? IS THERE A TURF WAR AT THE SCHOOL FESTIVAL?
IS THAT BAND, WEARING HEAD-PHONES?
BWAAAAH
OH...HIT'S SINGING KNOCKED THEM OUT!!
SPLASH WALL MAZE
I MADE A GIANT MAZE USING SPLASH WALLS!!
IT'S SUPER DIFFICULT. I BET NO ONE WILL BE ABLE TO SOLVE IT.
EVERYONE'S MANAGED TO REACH THE GOAL.
GOAL
HUH?!
OH, IT'S OUT OF INK!!

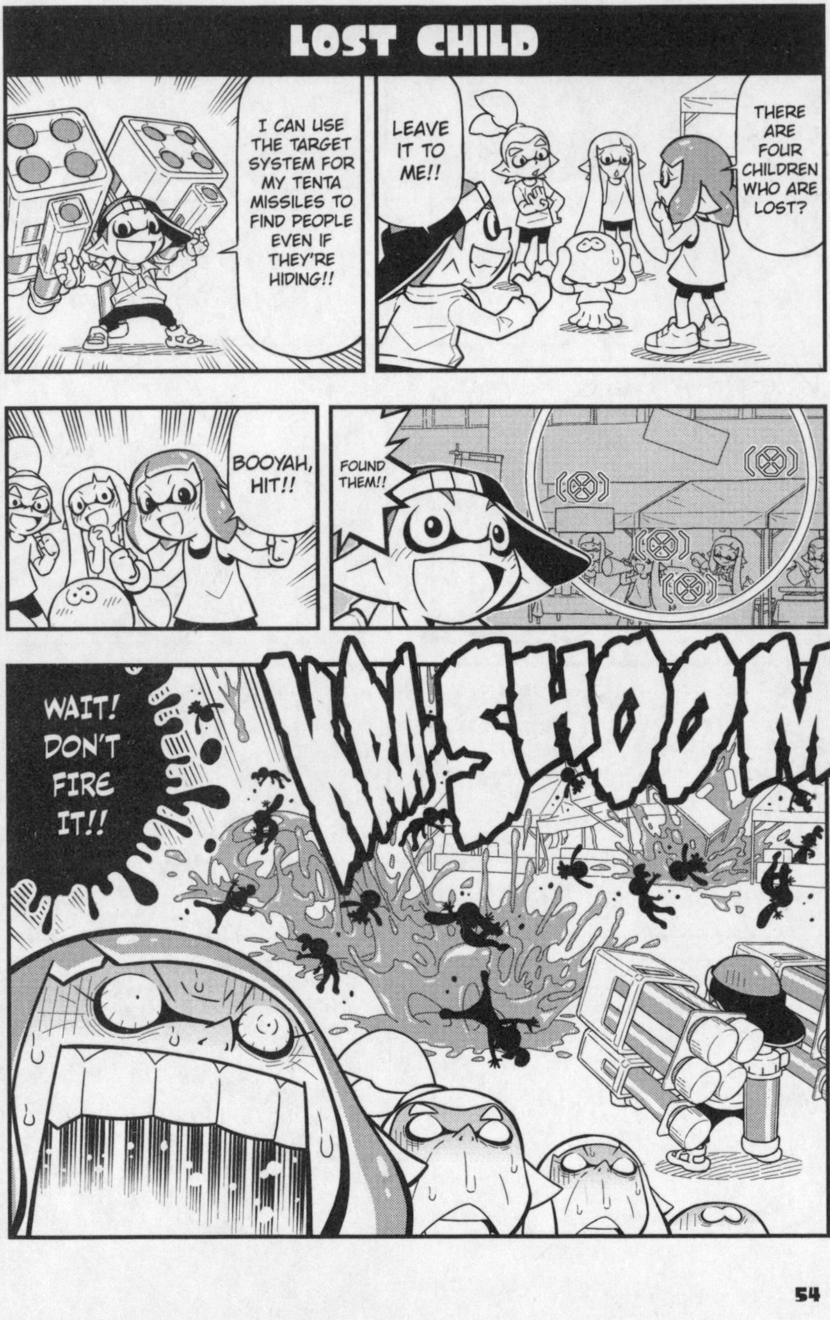
LOST CHILD
THERE ARE FOUR CHILDREN WHO ARE LOST?
LEAVE IT TO ME!!
I CAN USE THE TARGET SYSTEM FOR MY TENTA MISSILES TO FIND PEOPLE EVEN IF THEY'RE HIDING!!
FOUND THEM!!
BOOYAH, HIT!!
WA-SHOOM
WAIT! DON'T FIRE IT!!

IT'S SAMURAI TIME!

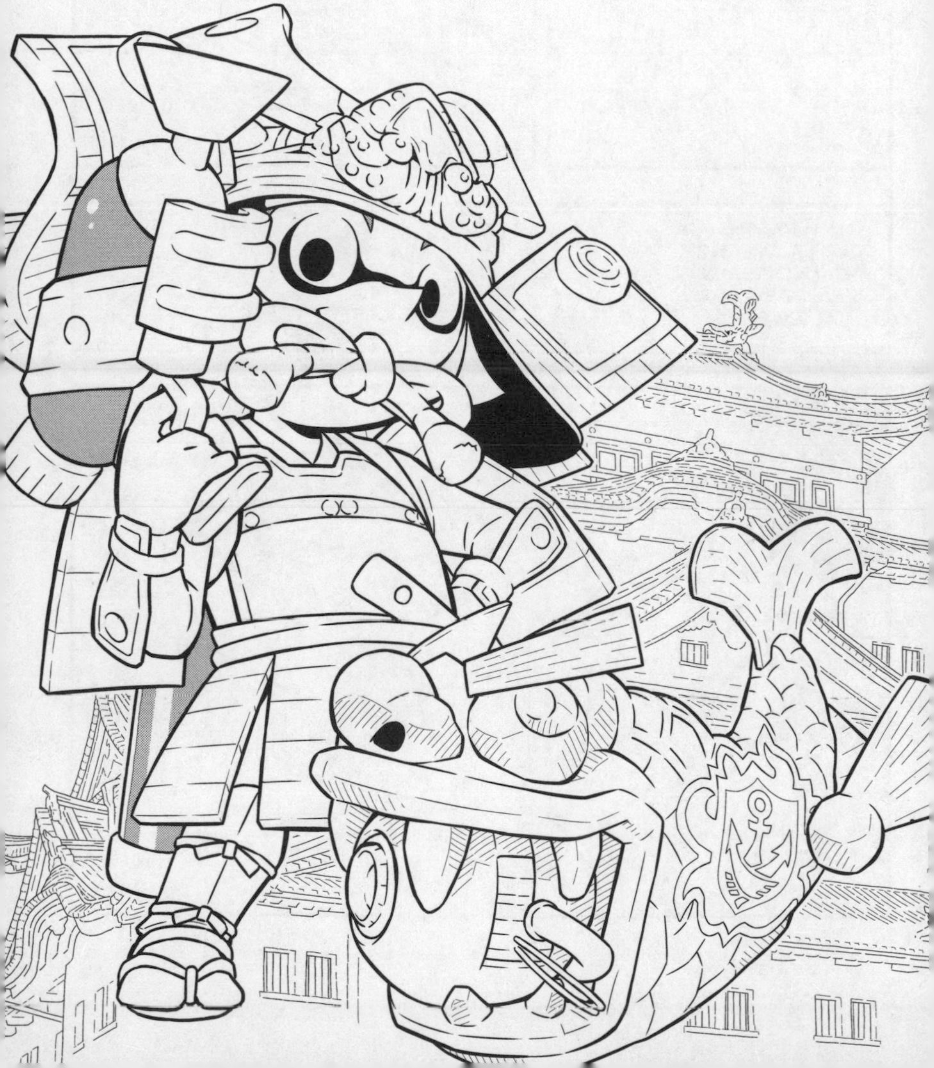

SAMURAI GEAR

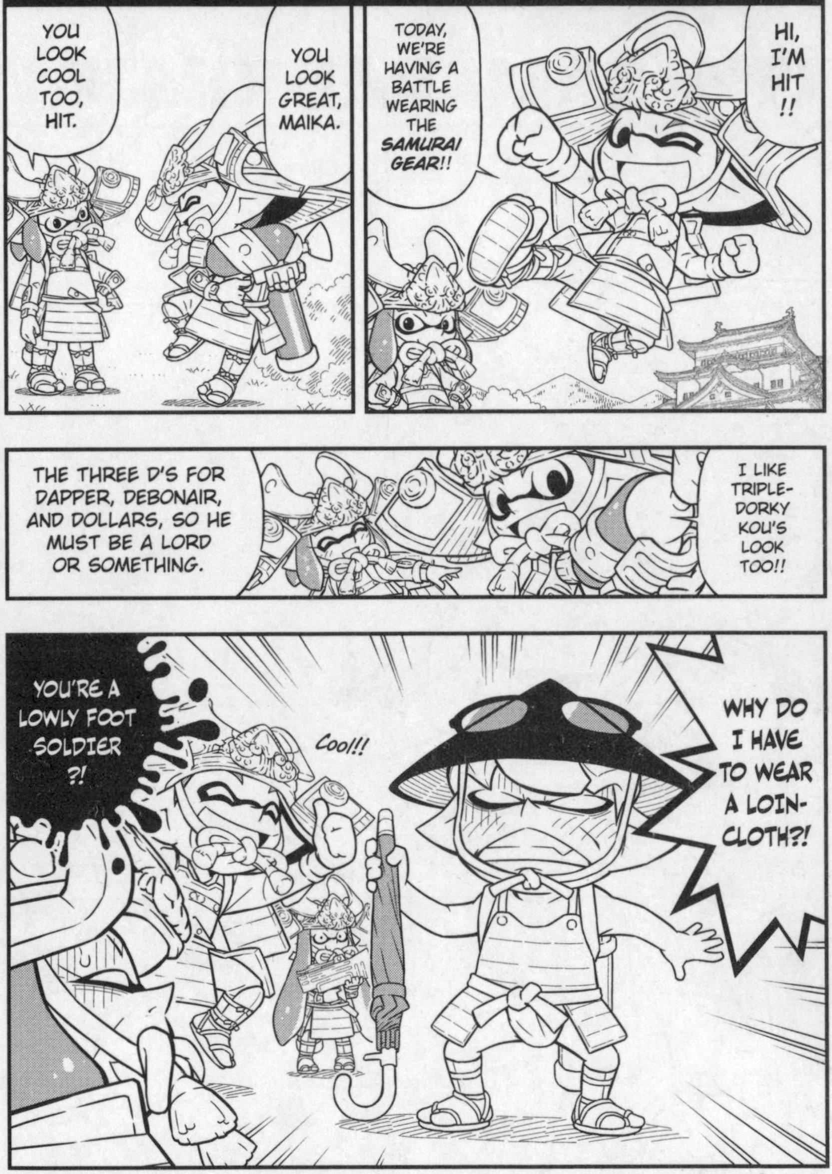

HI, I'M HIT !!
TODAY, WE'RE HAVING A BATTLE WEARING THE *SAMURAI GEAR*!!
YOU LOOK GREAT, MAIKA.
YOU LOOK COOL TOO, HIT.
I LIKE TRIPLE-DORKY KOU'S LOOK TOO!!
THE THREE D'S FOR DAPPER, DEBONAIR, AND DOLLARS, SO HE MUST BE A LORD OR SOMETHING.
WHY DO I HAVE TO WEAR A LOIN-CLOTH?!
Cool!!
YOU'RE A LOWLY FOOT SOLDIER ?!

RAINMAKER

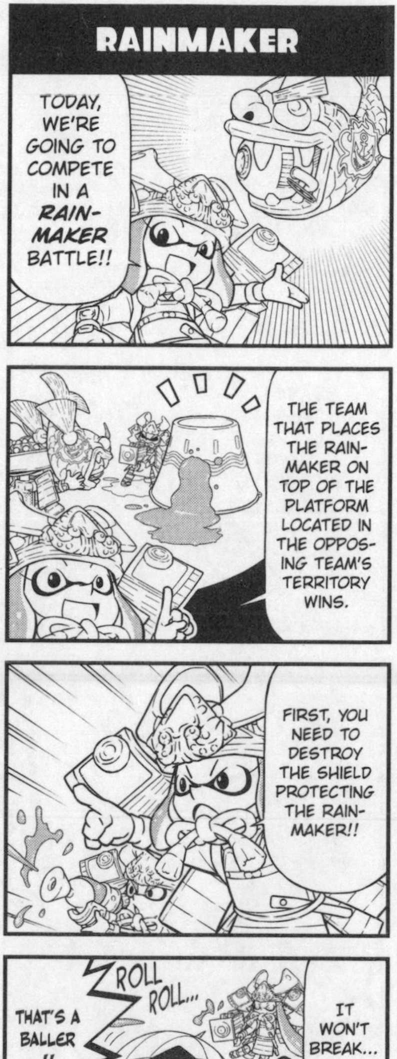
TODAY, WE'RE GOING TO COMPETE IN A *RAIN-MAKER* BATTLE!!
THE TEAM THAT PLACES THE RAIN-MAKER ON TOP OF THE PLATFORM LOCATED IN THE OPPOS-ING TEAM'S TERRITORY WINS.
FIRST, YOU NEED TO DESTROY THE SHIELD PROTECTING THE RAIN-MAKER!!
IT WON'T BREAK...
ROLL ROLL...
THAT'S A BALLER !!
SPLAT...
SPLATATA...

WHERE'S THE RAINMAKER?

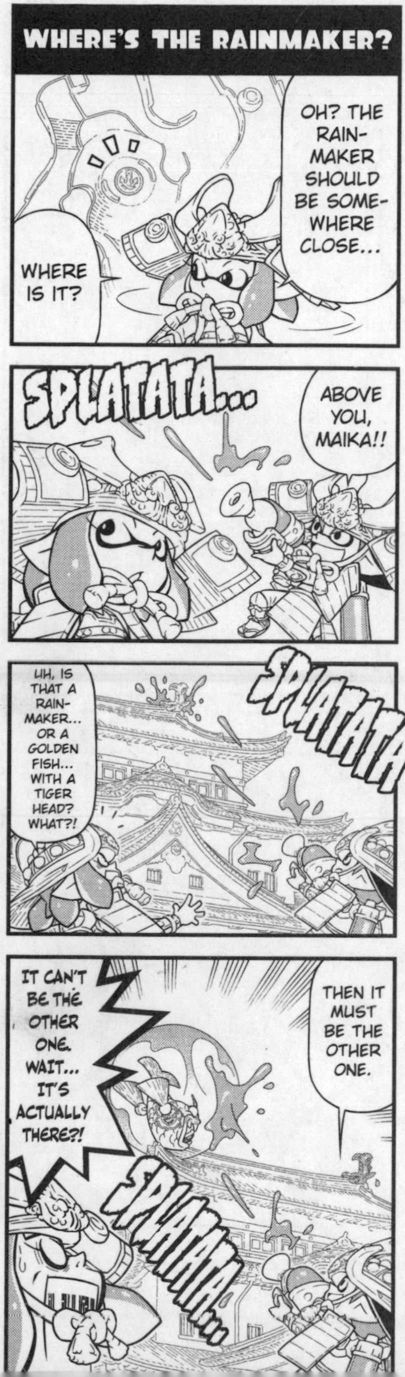
OH? THE RAIN-MAKER SHOULD BE SOME-WHERE CLOSE...
WHERE IS IT?
ABOVE YOU, MAIKA!!
SPLATATA...
SPLATATA
UH, IS THAT A RAIN-MAKER... OR A GOLDEN FISH... WITH A TIGER HEAD? WHAT?!
THEN IT MUST BE THE OTHER ONE.
IT CAN'T BE THE OTHER ONE. WAIT... IT'S ACTUALLY THERE?!
SPLATATA...

AIM FOR THE RAIN MAKER

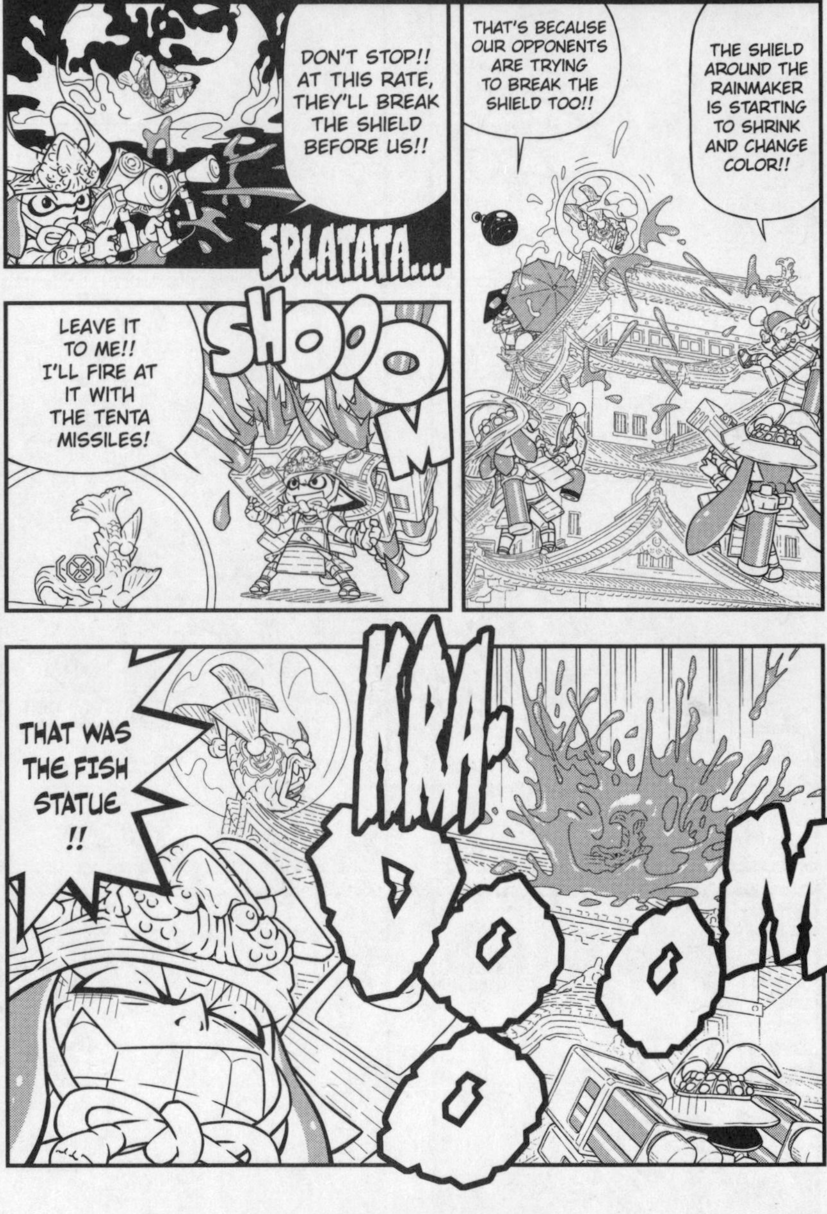
THE SHIELD AROUND THE RAINMAKER IS STARTING TO SHRINK AND CHANGE COLOR!!
THAT'S BECAUSE OUR OPPONENTS ARE TRYING TO BREAK THE SHIELD TOO!!
DON'T STOP!! AT THIS RATE, THEY'LL BREAK THE SHIELD BEFORE US!!
SPLATATA...
LEAVE IT TO ME!! I'LL FIRE AT IT WITH THE TENTA MISSILES!
SHOOOOM
KRA-DOOOOM
THAT WAS THE FISH STATUE!!

SMASH IT OPEN!!

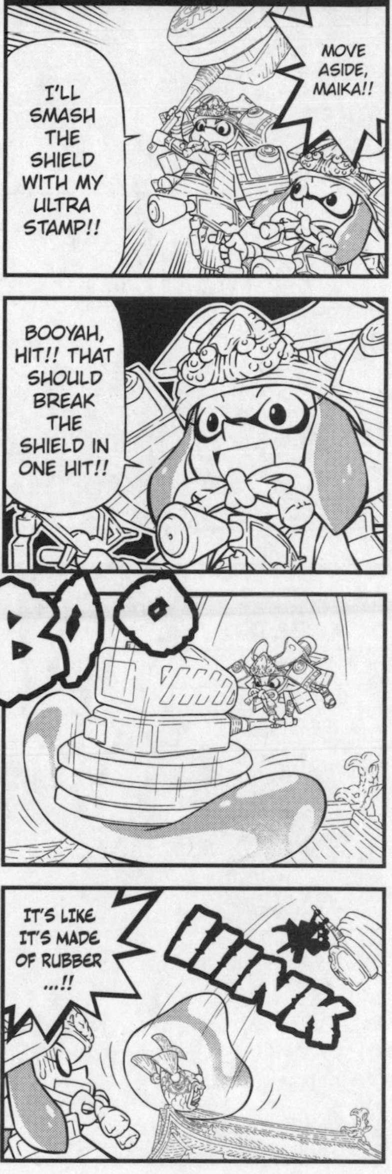
MOVE ASIDE, MAIKA!!
I'LL SMASH THE SHIELD WITH MY ULTRA STAMP!!
BOOYAH, HIT!! THAT SHOULD BREAK THE SHIELD IN ONE HIT!!
IIINK
IT'S LIKE IT'S MADE OF RUBBER ...!!

BOMB RUSH BATTLE

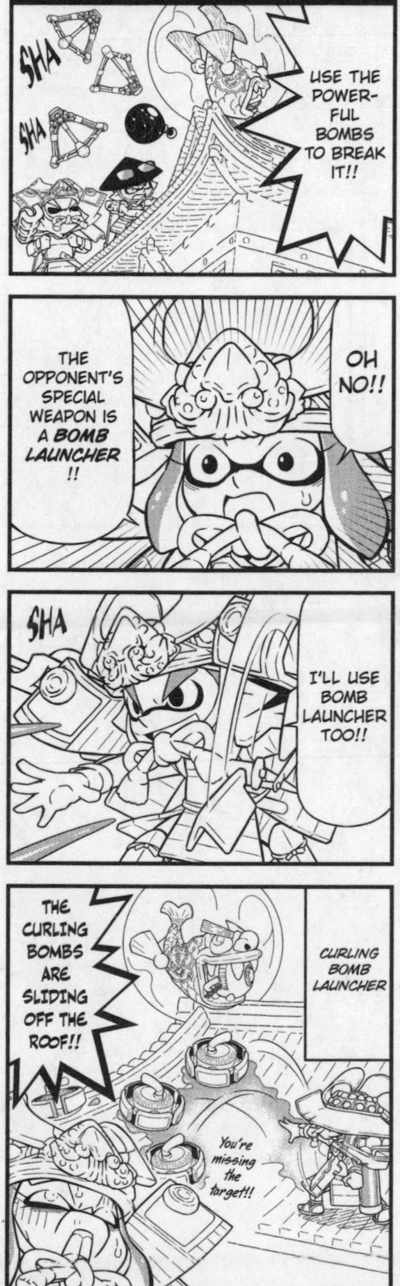
USE THE POWER-FUL BOMBS TO BREAK IT!!
SHA
SHA
OH NO!!
THE OPPONENT'S SPECIAL WEAPON IS A ***BOMB LAUNCHER***!!
I'LL USE BOMB LAUNCHER TOO!!
SHA
CURLING BOMB LAUNCHER
THE CURLING BOMBS ARE SLIDING OFF THE ROOF!!
You're missing the target!!

RAINMAKER EXPLOSION

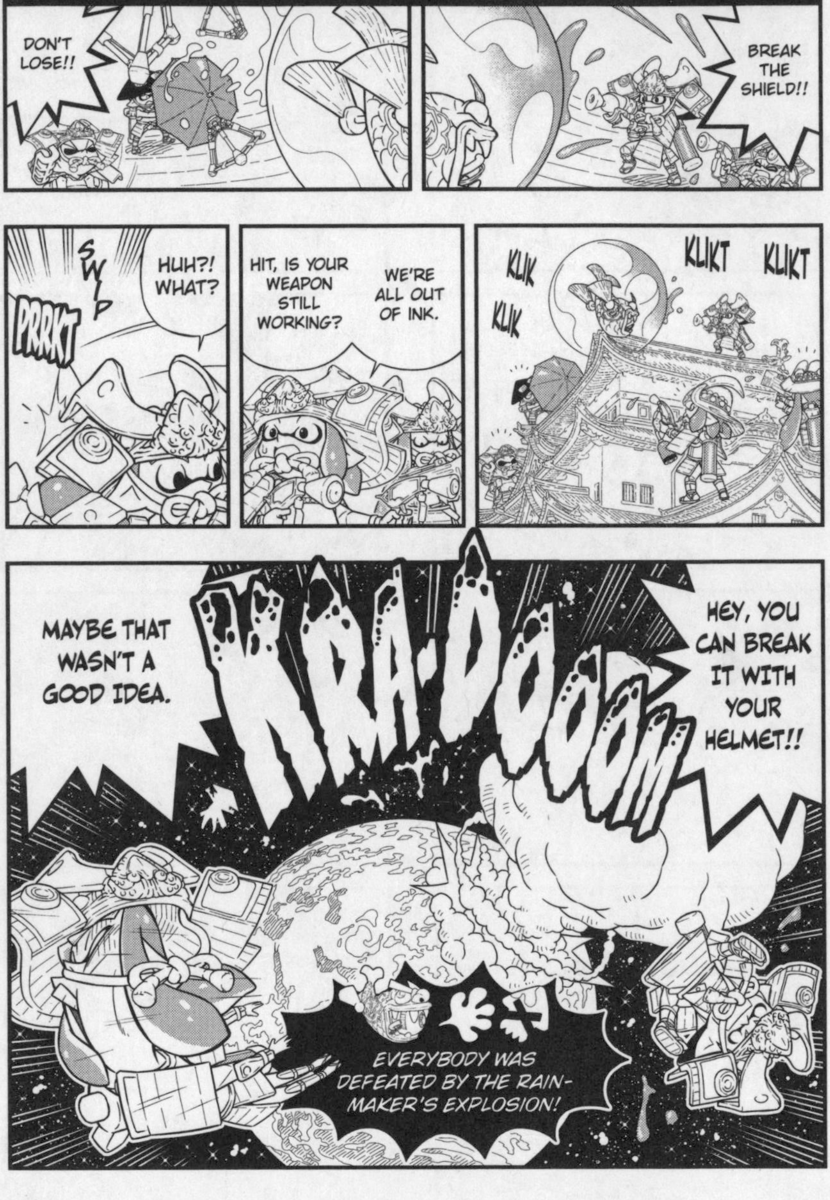
BREAK THE SHIELD!!
DON'T LOSE!!
KLIKT
KLIKT
KLIK
KLIK
WE'RE ALL OUT OF INK.
HIT, IS YOUR WEAPON STILL WORKING?
HUH?! WHAT?
SWIP
PRRKT
HEY, YOU CAN BREAK IT WITH YOUR HELMET!!
KRA-DOOM
MAYBE THAT WASN'T A GOOD IDEA.
EVERYBODY WAS DEFEATED BY THE RAIN-MAKER'S EXPLOSION!

Splatoon SQUID KIDS COMEDY SHOW

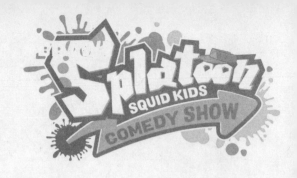

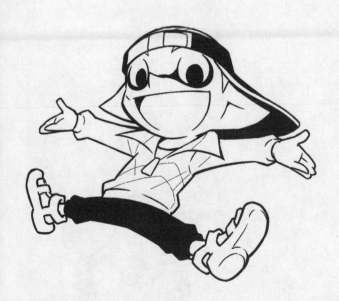

Splatoon
SQUID KIDS
COMEDY SHOW

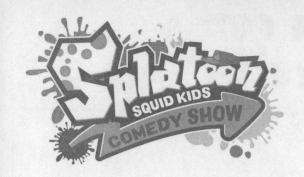

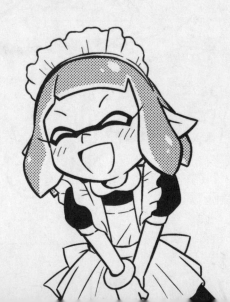

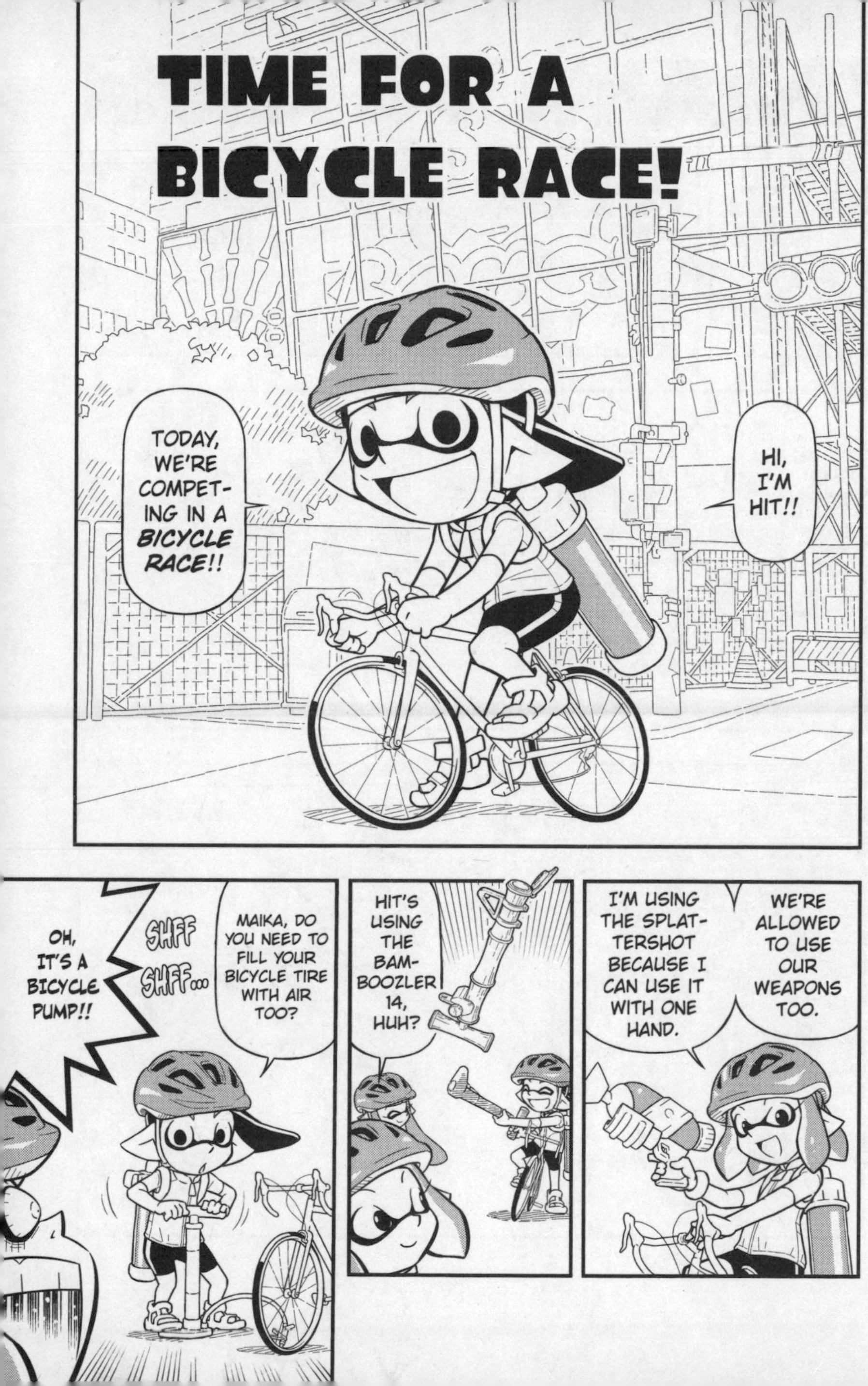
TIME FOR A BICYCLE RACE!
HI, I'M HIT!!
TODAY, WE'RE COMPET-ING IN A *BICYCLE RACE!!*
WE'RE ALLOWED TO USE OUR WEAPONS TOO.
I'M USING THE SPLAT-TERSHOT BECAUSE I CAN USE IT WITH ONE HAND.
HIT'S USING THE BAM-BOOZLER 14, HUH?
MAIKA, DO YOU NEED TO FILL YOUR BICYCLE TIRE WITH AIR TOO?
SHFF SHFF...
OH, IT'S A BICYCLE PUMP!!

WINDSHIELD

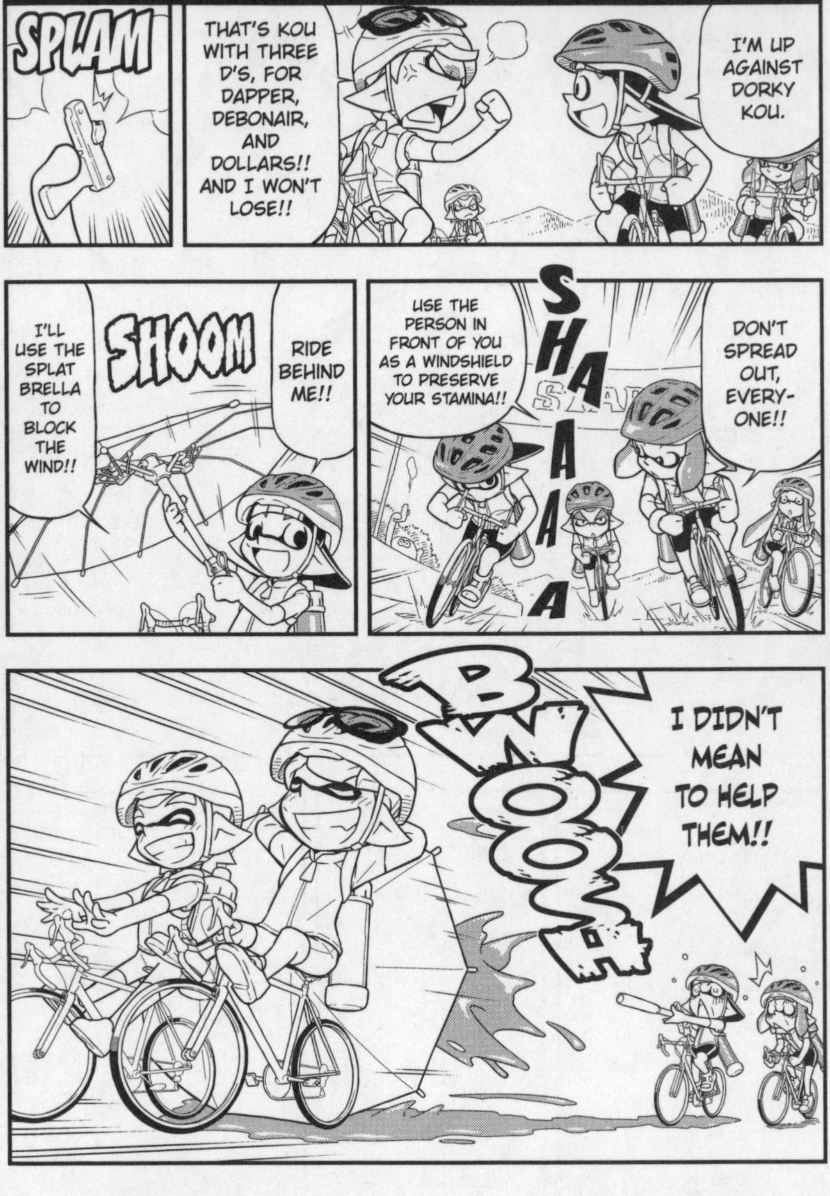
I'M UP AGAINST DORKY KOU.
THAT'S KOU WITH THREE D'S, FOR DAPPER, DEBONAIR, AND DOLLARS!! AND I WON'T LOSE!!
SPLAM
DON'T SPREAD OUT, EVERY-ONE!!
USE THE PERSON IN FRONT OF YOU AS A WINDSHIELD TO PRESERVE YOUR STAMINA!!
SHAAAA
RIDE BEHIND ME!!
SHOOM
I'LL USE THE SPLAT BRELLA TO BLOCK THE WIND!!
I DIDN'T MEAN TO HELP THEM!!
BWOOSH

TRAIN

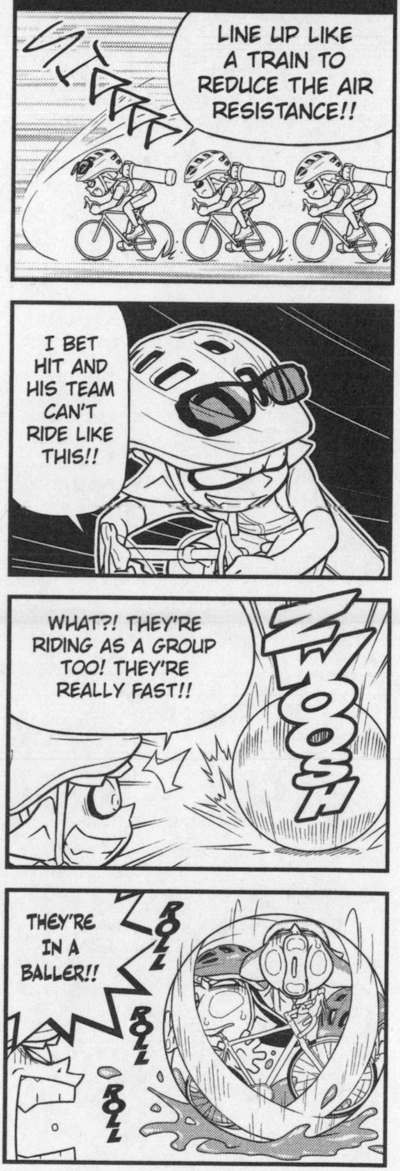
LINE UP LIKE A TRAIN TO REDUCE THE AIR RESISTANCE!!
I BET HIT AND HIS TEAM CAN'T RIDE LIKE THIS!!
ZWOOSH
WHAT?! THEY'RE RIDING AS A GROUP TOO! THEY'RE REALLY FAST!!
ROLL ROLL ROLL
THEY'RE IN A BALLER!!

DUD

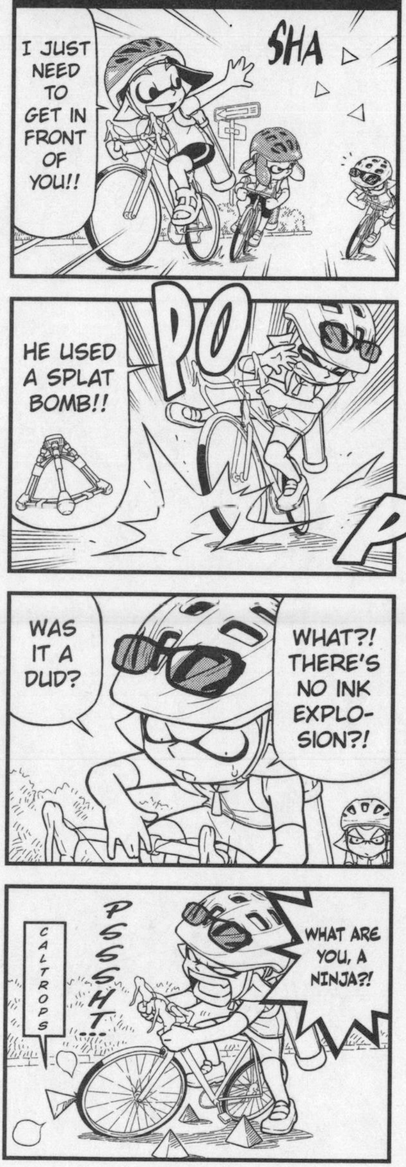
SHA
I JUST NEED TO GET IN FRONT OF YOU!!
PO P
HE USED A SPLAT BOMB!!
WHAT?! THERE'S NO INK EXPLOSION?!
WAS IT A DUD?
WHAT ARE YOU, A NINJA?!
PSSSHT...
CALTROPS

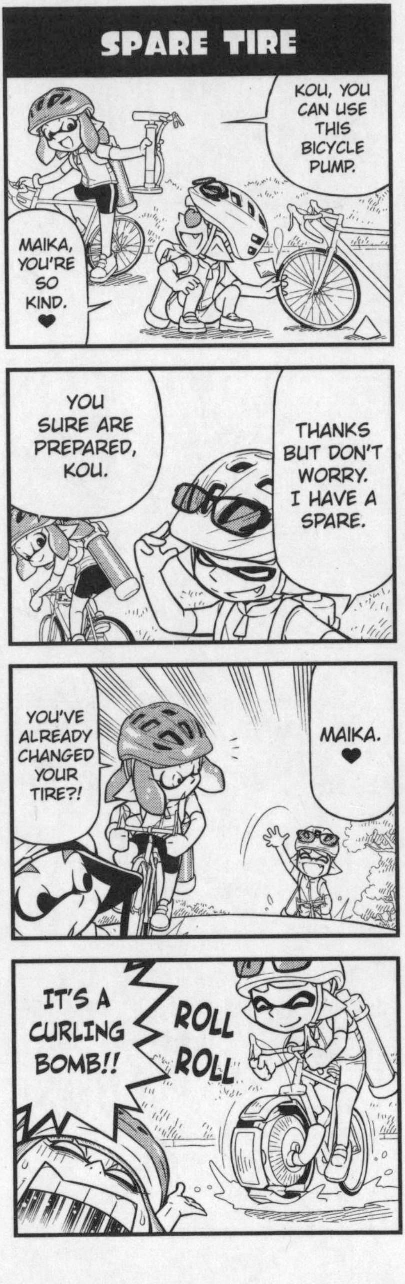
SPARE TIRE
KOU, YOU CAN USE THIS BICYCLE PUMP.
MAIKA, YOU'RE SO KIND. ♥
THANKS BUT DON'T WORRY. I HAVE A SPARE.
YOU SURE ARE PREPARED, KOU.
MAIKA. ♥
YOU'VE ALREADY CHANGED YOUR TIRE?!
ROLL ROLL
IT'S A CURLING BOMB!!

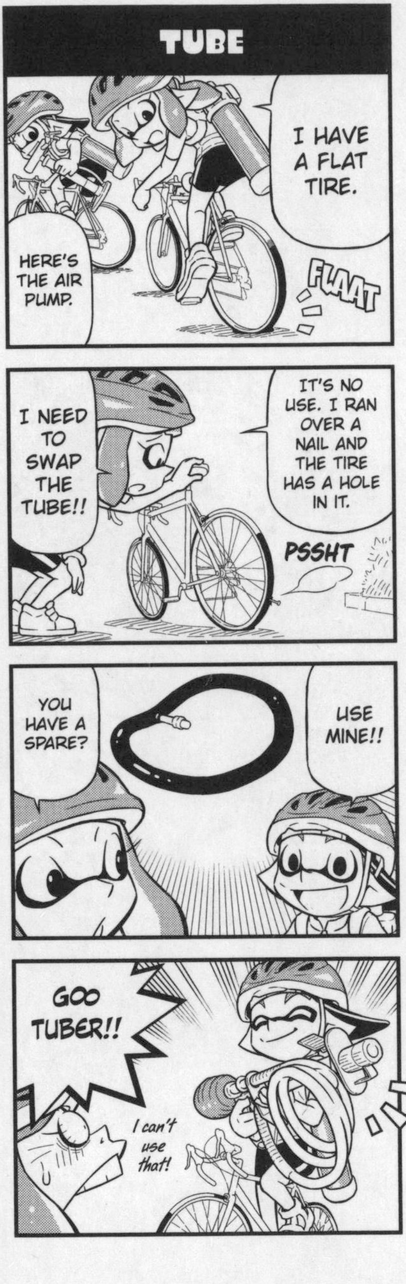
TUBE
I HAVE A FLAT TIRE.
FLAAAT
HERE'S THE AIR PUMP.
IT'S NO USE. I RAN OVER A NAIL AND THE TIRE HAS A HOLE IN IT.
PSSHT
I NEED TO SWAP THE TUBE!!
USE MINE!!
YOU HAVE A SPARE?
GOO TUBER!!
I can't use that!

TRAINING WHEELS

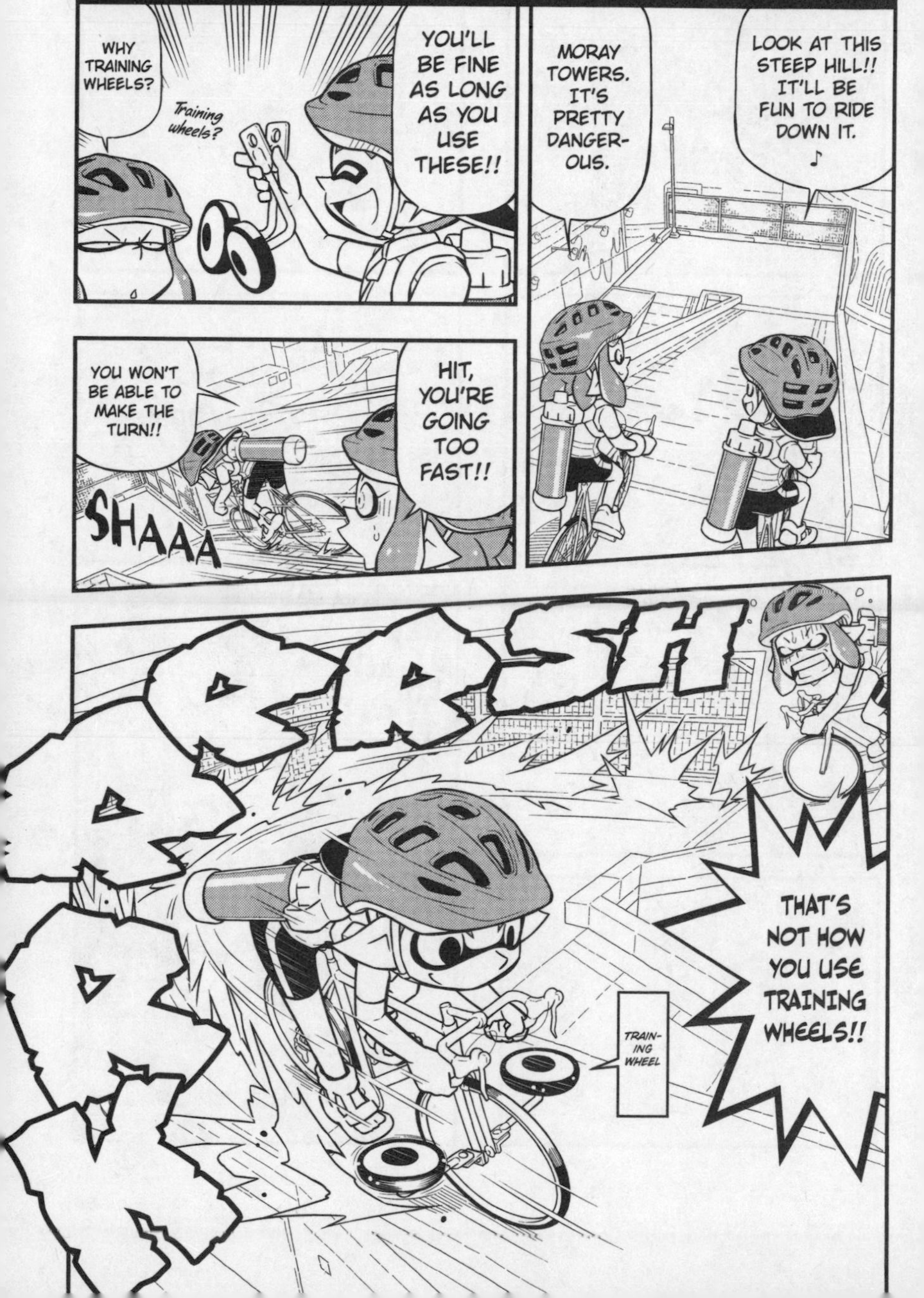
LOOK AT THIS STEEP HILL!! IT'LL BE FUN TO RIDE DOWN IT. ♪
MORAY TOWERS. IT'S PRETTY DANGER-OUS.
YOU'LL BE FINE AS LONG AS YOU USE THESE!!
WHY TRAINING WHEELS?
Training wheels?
HIT, YOU'RE GOING TOO FAST!!
YOU WON'T BE ABLE TO MAKE THE TURN!!
SHAAA
THAT'S NOT HOW YOU USE TRAINING WHEELS!!
TRAIN-ING WHEEL

AID STATION

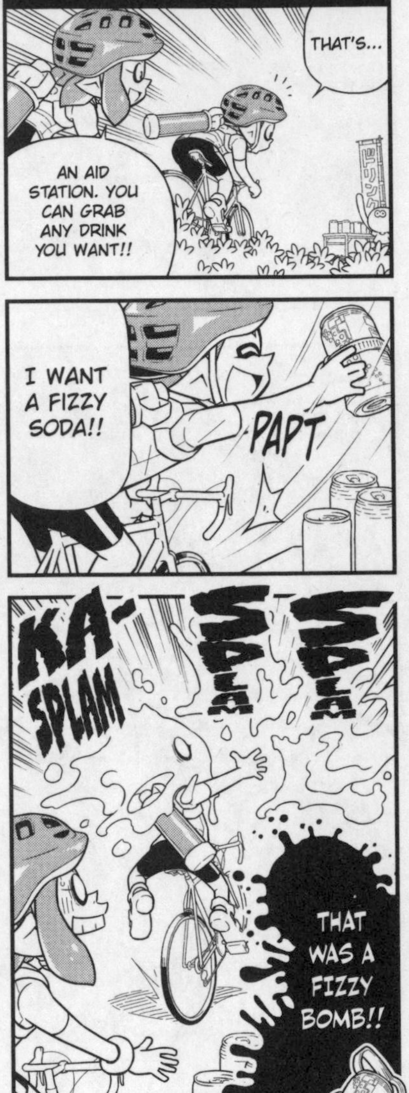
THAT'S...
AN AID STATION. YOU CAN GRAB ANY DRINK YOU WANT!!
I WANT A FIZZY SODA!!
PAPT
KA-SPLAM
THAT WAS A FIZZY BOMB!!

PAINT OBSTRUCTION

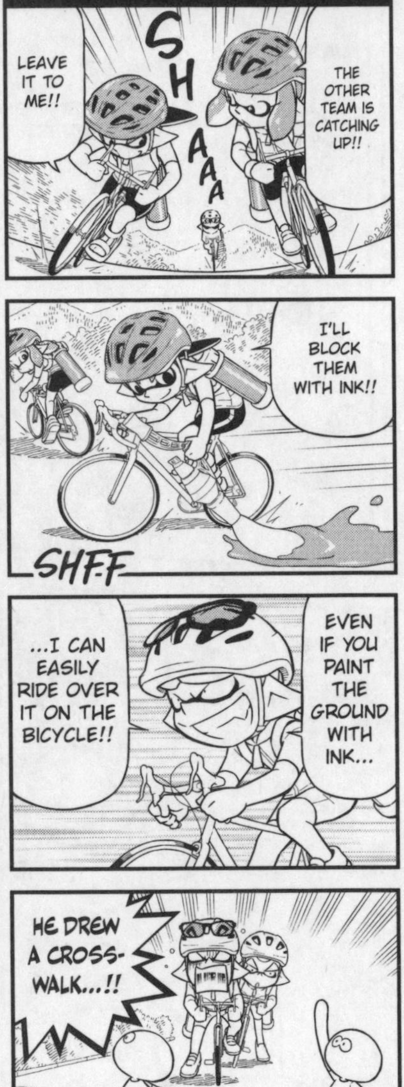
THE OTHER TEAM IS CATCHING UP!!
SHAAA
LEAVE IT TO ME!!
I'LL BLOCK THEM WITH INK!!
SHF-F
EVEN IF YOU PAINT THE GROUND WITH INK...
...I CAN EASILY RIDE OVER IT ON THE BICYCLE!!
HE DREW A CROSS-WALK...!!

JET ENGINE

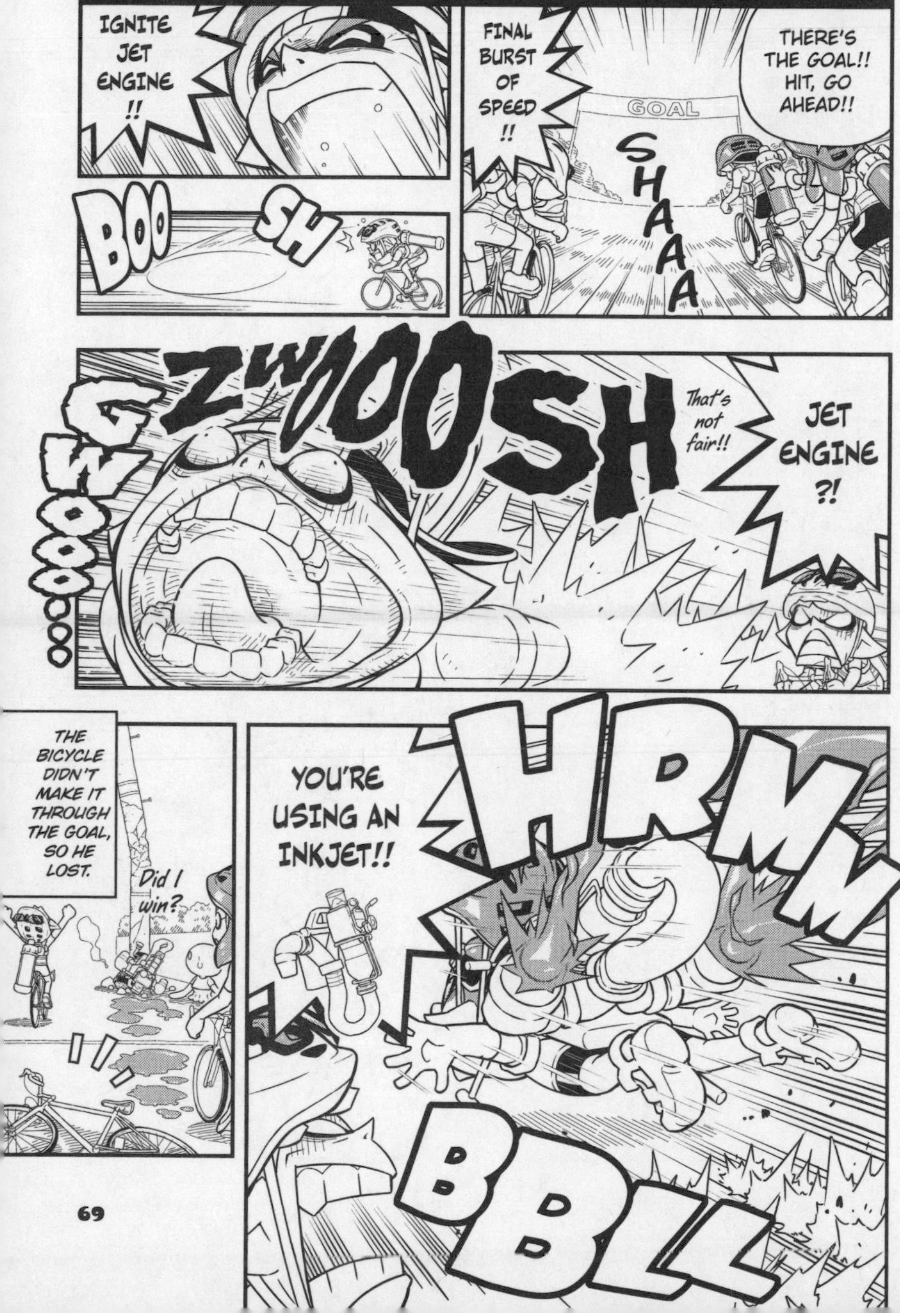
THERE'S THE GOAL!! HIT, GO AHEAD!!
FINAL BURST OF SPEED !!
GOAL
SHAAAA
IGNITE JET ENGINE !!
BOOSH
JET ENGINE ?!
That's not fair!!
GZWOOSH
WOOOOOOO
HRMM
YOU'RE USING AN INKJET!!
BBLL
THE BICYCLE DIDN'T MAKE IT THROUGH THE GOAL, SO HE LOST.
Did I win?

Splatoon
SQUID KIDS COMEDY SHOW

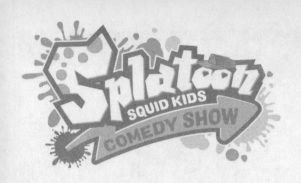

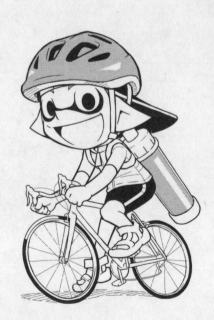

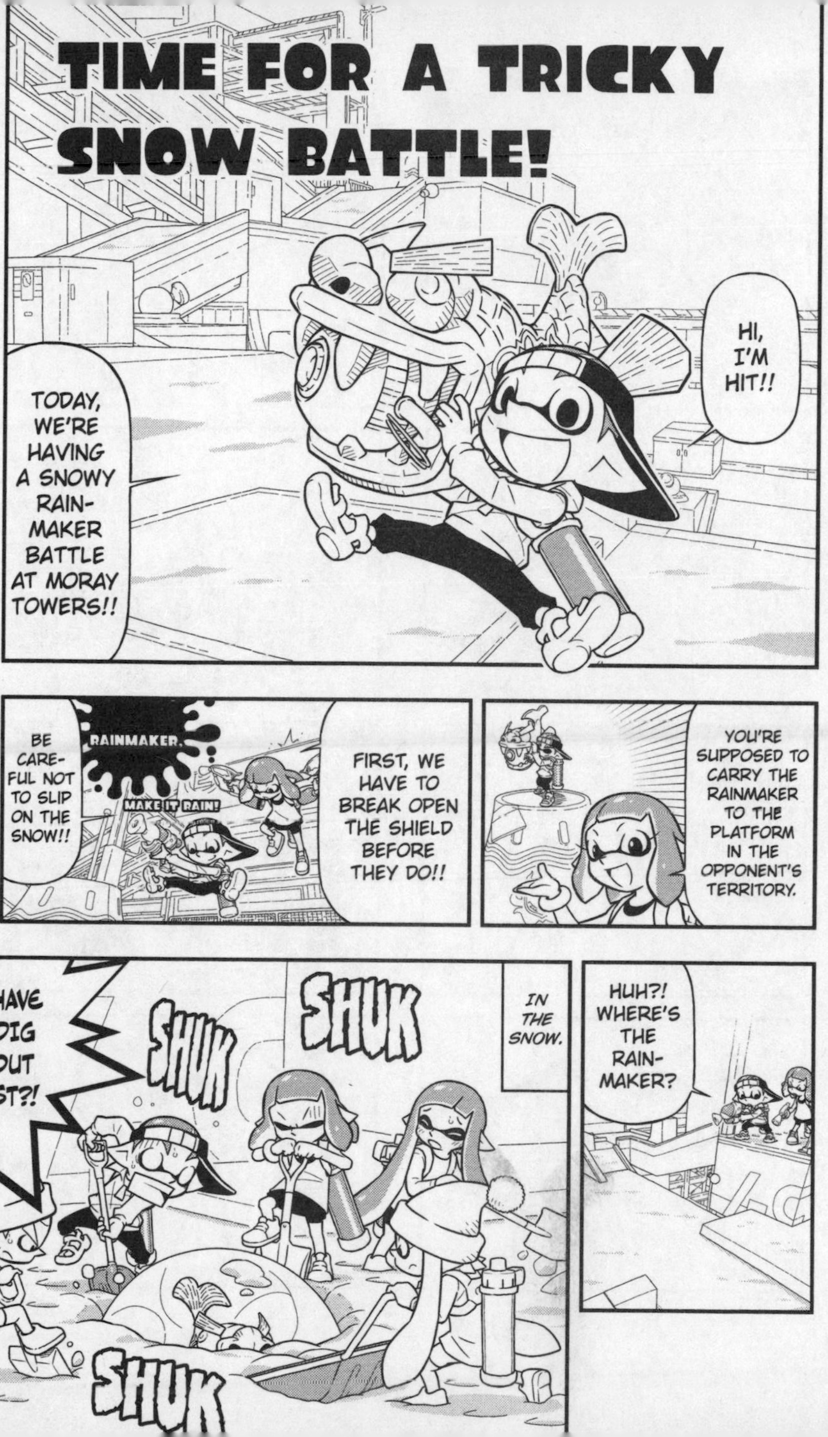
TIME FOR A TRICKY SNOW BATTLE!
HI, I'M HIT!!
TODAY, WE'RE HAVING A SNOWY RAIN-MAKER BATTLE AT MORAY TOWERS!!
YOU'RE SUPPOSED TO CARRY THE RAINMAKER TO THE PLATFORM IN THE OPPONENT'S TERRITORY.
FIRST, WE HAVE TO BREAK OPEN THE SHIELD BEFORE THEY DO!!
RAINMAKER
MAKE IT RAIN!
BE CARE-FUL NOT TO SLIP ON THE SNOW!!
HUH?! WHERE'S THE RAIN-MAKER?
IN THE SNOW.
SHUK
SHUK
WE HAVE TO DIG IT OUT FIRST?!
SHUK

SHATTER THE SHIELD

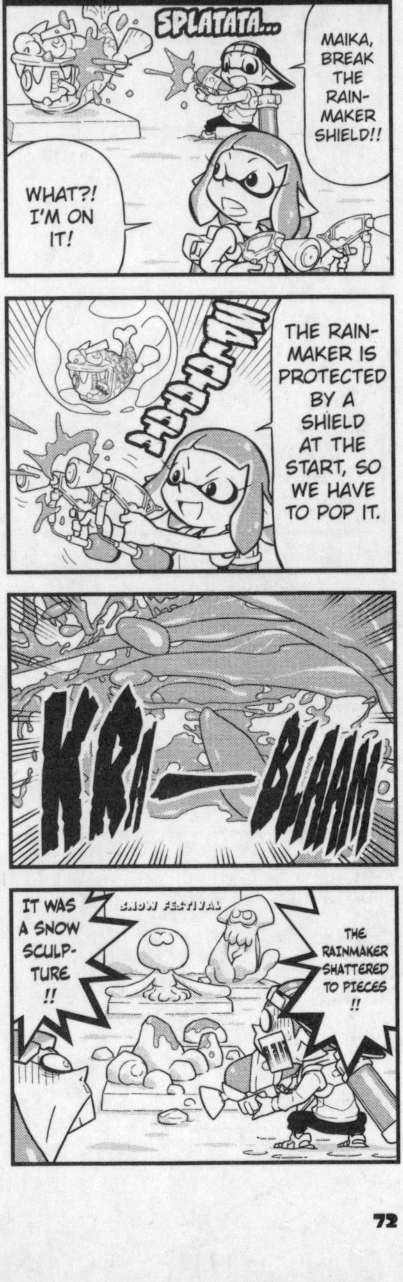
MAIKA, BREAK THE RAIN-MAKER SHIELD!!
SPLATATA...
WHAT?! I'M ON IT!
THE RAIN-MAKER IS PROTECTED BY A SHIELD AT THE START, SO WE HAVE TO POP IT.
KRA—BLAAM
THE RAINMAKER SHATTERED TO PIECES !!
SNOW FESTIVAL
IT WAS A SNOW SCULP-TURE !!

WINTER INK

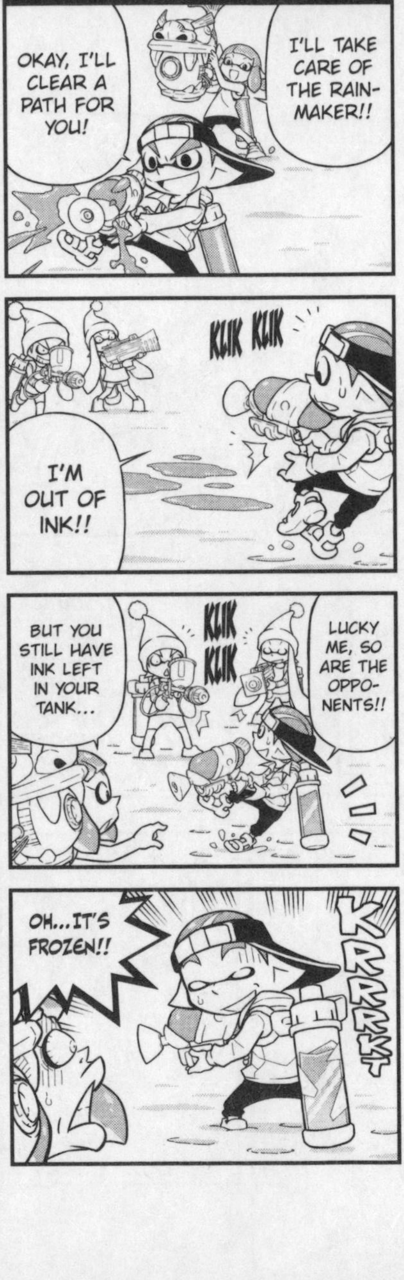
I'LL TAKE CARE OF THE RAIN-MAKER!!
OKAY, I'LL CLEAR A PATH FOR YOU!
KLIK KLIK
I'M OUT OF INK!!
LUCKY ME, SO ARE THE OPPO-NENTS!!
KLIK KLIK
BUT YOU STILL HAVE INK LEFT IN YOUR TANK...
KRRRKT
OH...IT'S FROZEN!!

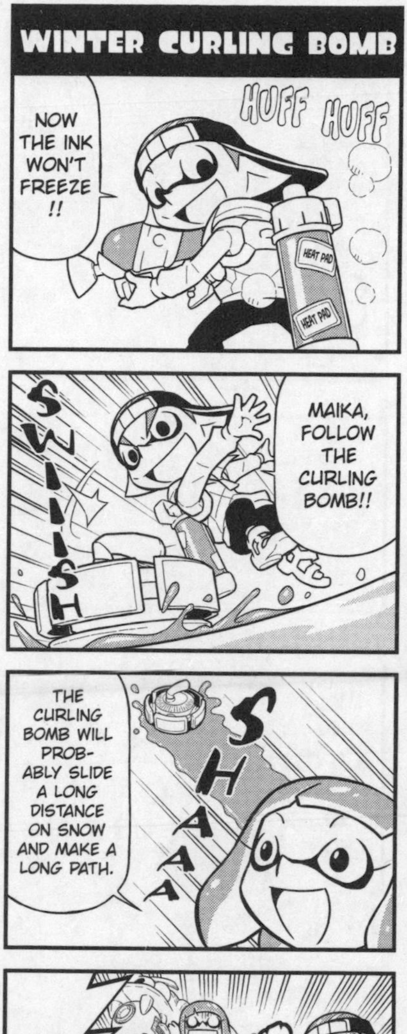
WINTER CURLING BOMB
HUFF HUFF
NOW THE INK WON'T FREEZE !!
MAIKA, FOLLOW THE CURLING BOMB!!
SWIIISH
SHAAAA
THE CURLING BOMB WILL PROB- ABLY SLIDE A LONG DISTANCE ON SNOW AND MAKE A LONG PATH.
FWUMP
UNLESS IT GETS STUCK!!

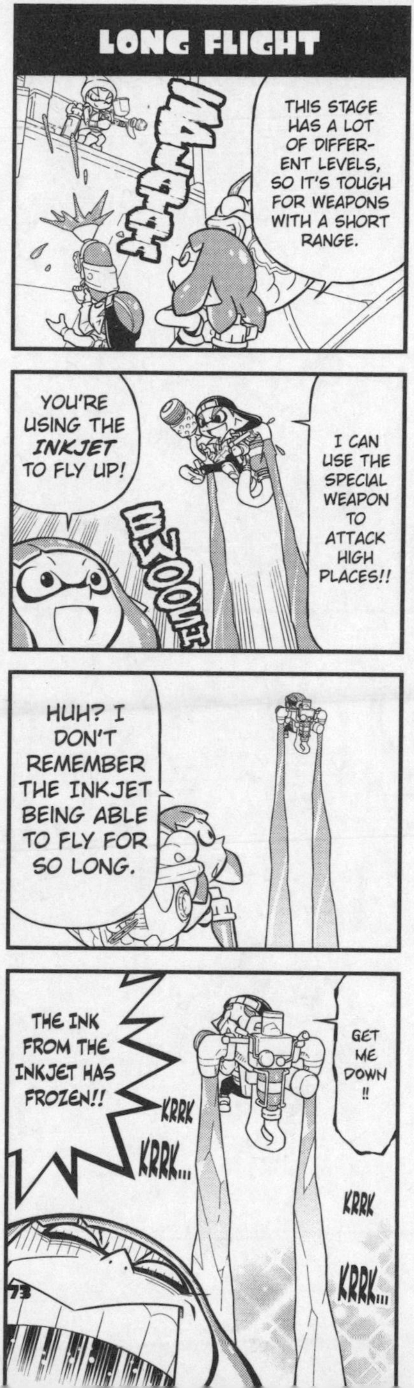
LONG FLIGHT
THIS STAGE HAS A LOT OF DIFFER- ENT LEVELS, SO IT'S TOUGH FOR WEAPONS WITH A SHORT RANGE.
I CAN USE THE SPECIAL WEAPON TO ATTACK HIGH PLACES!!
YOU'RE USING THE *INKJET* TO FLY UP!
HUH? I DON'T REMEMBER THE INKJET BEING ABLE TO FLY FOR SO LONG.
GET ME DOWN !!
THE INK FROM THE INKJET HAS FROZEN!!
KRRK
KRRK...
KRRK
KRRK...

STAMPING AND SHAKING

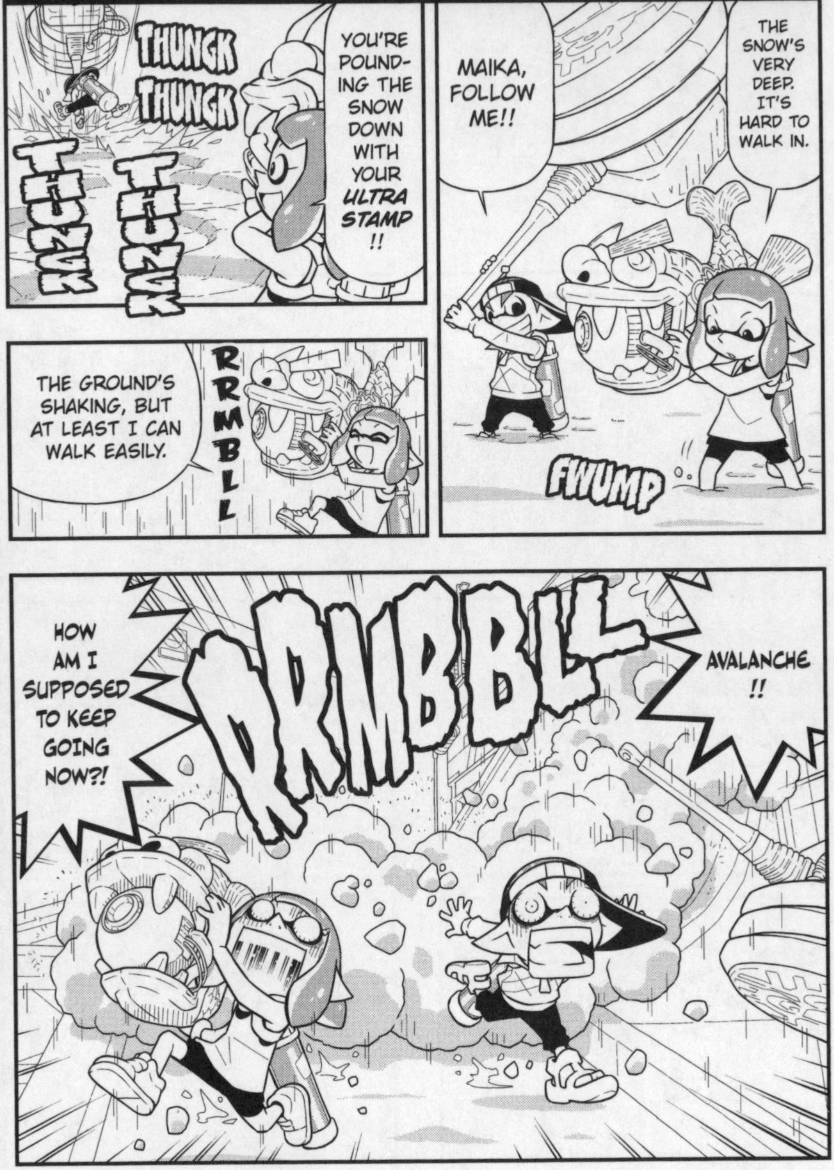

THE SNOW'S VERY DEEP. IT'S HARD TO WALK IN.
MAIKA, FOLLOW ME!!
FWUMP
YOU'RE POUNDING THE SNOW DOWN WITH YOUR *ULTRA STAMP* !!
THUNGK
THUNGK
THUNGK
THUNGK
RRMBLL
THE GROUND'S SHAKING, BUT AT LEAST I CAN WALK EASILY.
AVALANCHE !!
DRMBBLL
HOW AM I SUPPOSED TO KEEP GOING NOW?!

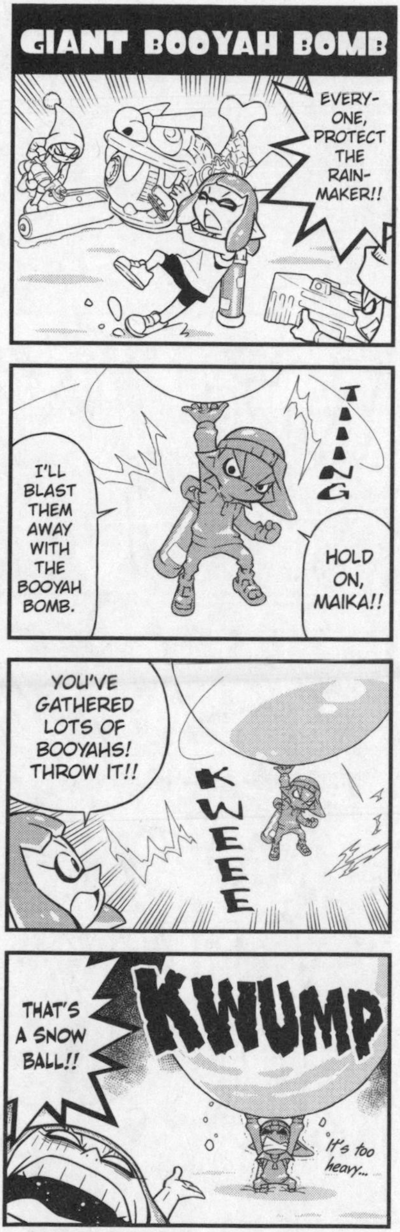
GIANT BOOYAH BOMB
EVERY-ONE, PROTECT THE RAIN-MAKER!!
TAAANG
I'LL BLAST THEM AWAY WITH THE BOOYAH BOMB.
HOLD ON, MAIKA!!
YOU'VE GATHERED LOTS OF BOOYAHS! THROW IT!!
KWEEE
KWUMP
THAT'S A SNOW BALL!!
It's too heavy...
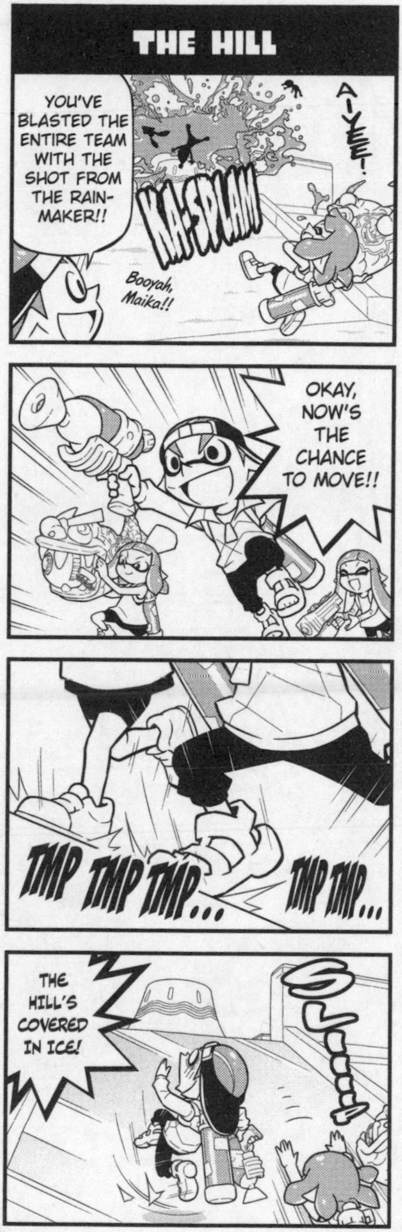
THE HILL
AIYEE!
YOU'VE BLASTED THE ENTIRE TEAM WITH THE SHOT FROM THE RAIN-MAKER!!
KA-SPLAM
Booyah, Maika!!
OKAY, NOW'S THE CHANCE TO MOVE!!
TMP TMP TMP... TMP TMP...
THE HILL'S COVERED IN ICE!

SNOW BALLER

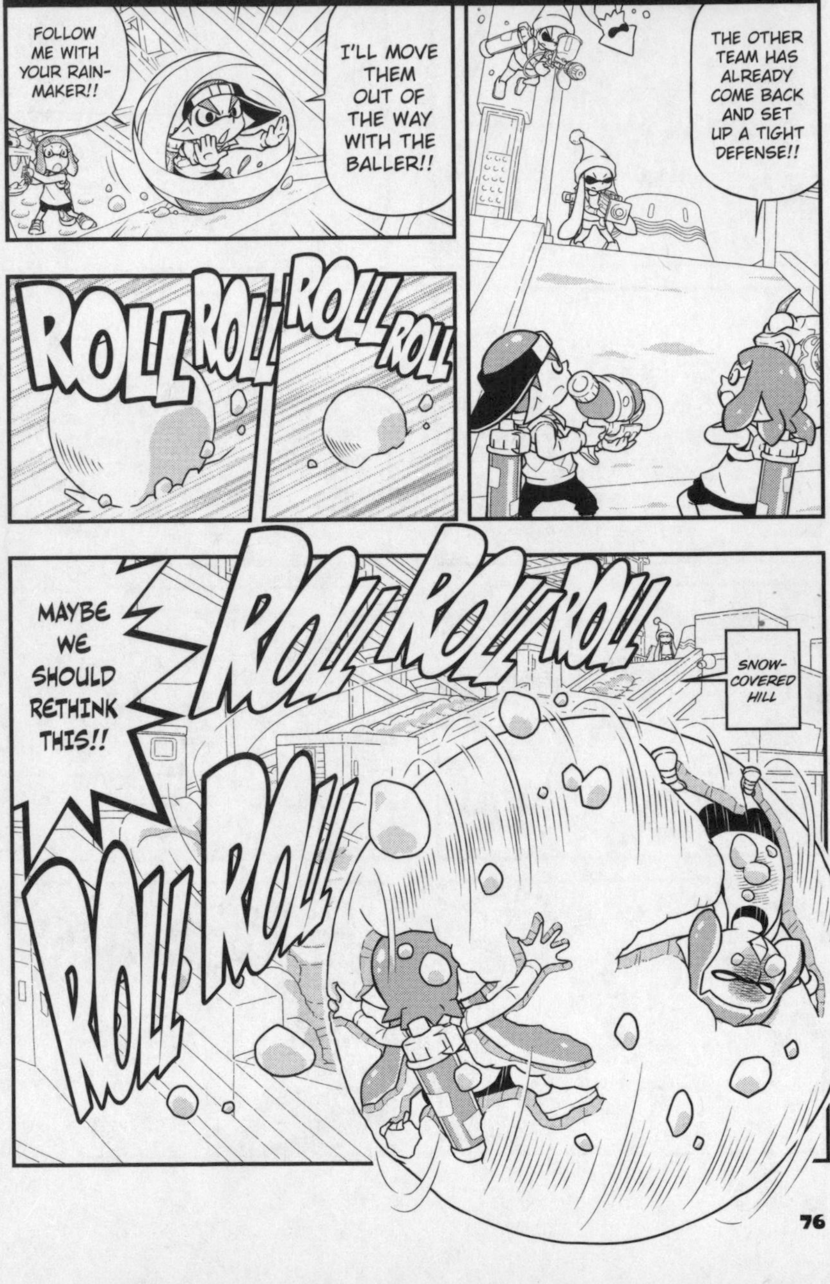
THE OTHER TEAM HAS ALREADY COME BACK AND SET UP A TIGHT DEFENSE!!
I'LL MOVE THEM OUT OF THE WAY WITH THE BALLER!!
FOLLOW ME WITH YOUR RAIN-MAKER!!
ROLL ROLL
ROLL ROLL
ROLL ROLL ROLL
SNOW-COVERED HILL
MAYBE WE SHOULD RETHINK THIS!!
ROLL ROLL

Splatoon
SQUID KIDS
COMEDY SHOW

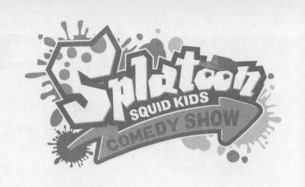

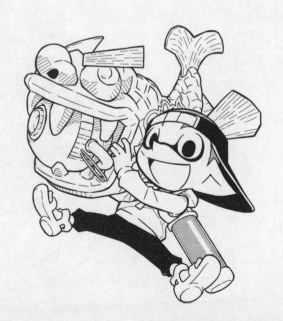

Splatoon
SQUID KIDS
COMEDY SHOW

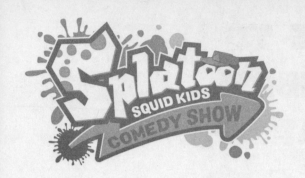

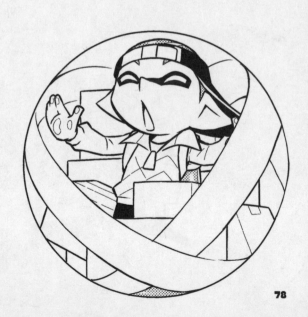

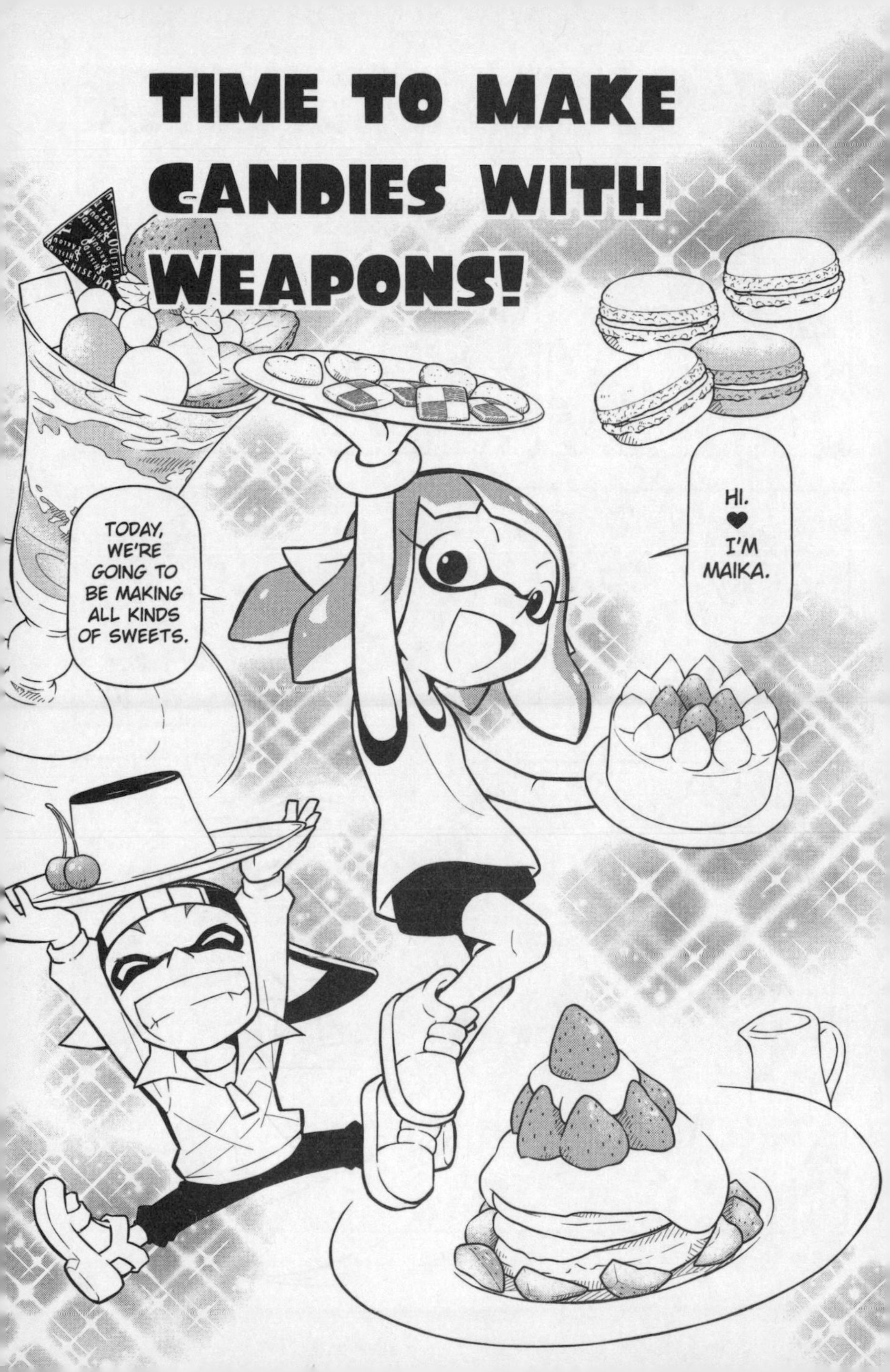
TIME TO MAKE CANDIES WITH WEAPONS!
HI. ♥ I'M MAIKA.
TODAY, WE'RE GOING TO BE MAKING ALL KINDS OF SWEETS.

MAKING SWEETS

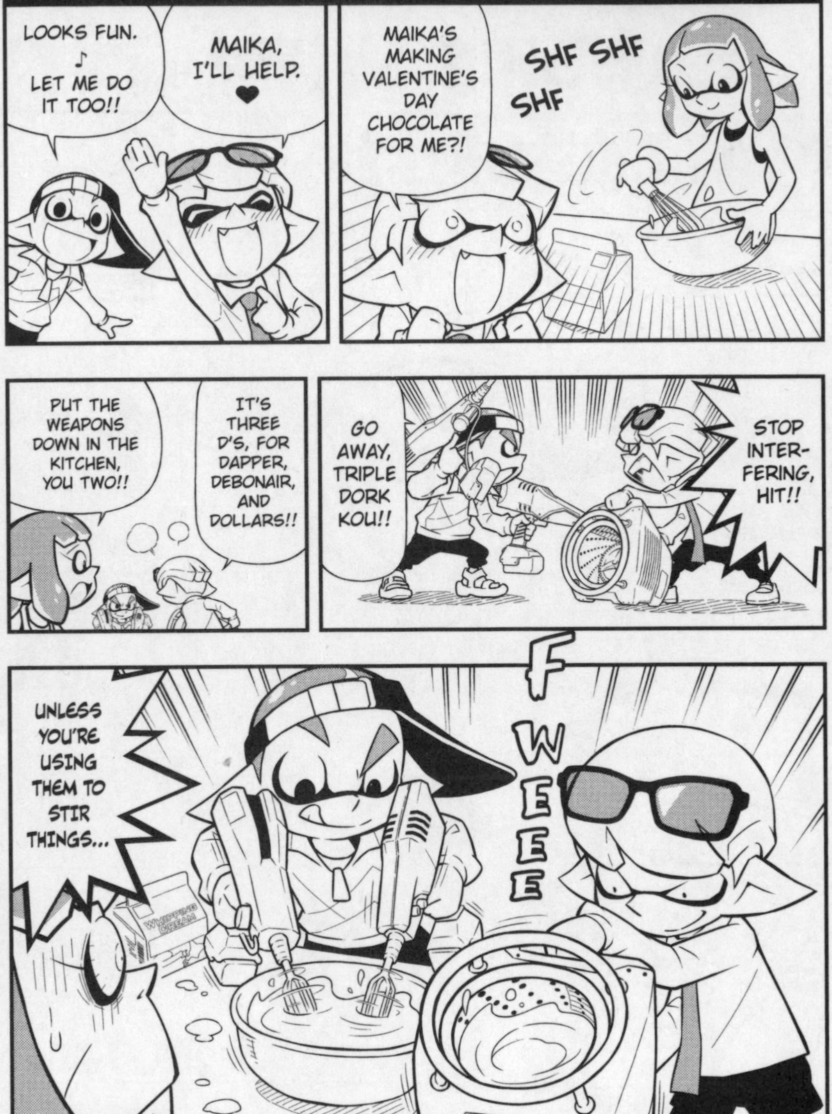

MAIKA'S MAKING VALENTINE'S DAY CHOCOLATE FOR ME?!
SHF SHF SHF
MAIKA, I'LL HELP. ♥
LOOKS FUN. ♪ LET ME DO IT TOO!!
STOP INTER-FERING, HIT!!
GO AWAY, TRIPLE DORK KOU!!
IT'S THREE D'S, FOR DAPPER, DEBONAIR, AND DOLLARS!!
PUT THE WEAPONS DOWN IN THE KITCHEN, YOU TWO!!
F WEEE
UNLESS YOU'RE USING THEM TO STIR THINGS...
WHIPPING CREAM

CHOCOLATE PEN

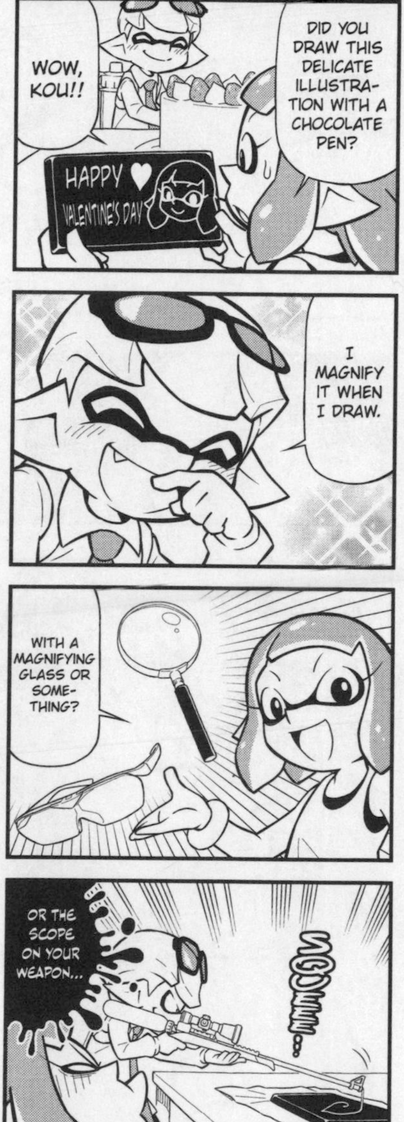
DID YOU DRAW THIS DELICATE ILLUSTRATION WITH A CHOCOLATE PEN?
WOW, KOU!!
HAPPY ♥ VALENTINE'S DAY
I MAGNIFY IT WHEN I DRAW.
WITH A MAGNIFYING GLASS OR SOMETHING?
OR THE SCOPE ON YOUR WEAPON...

UPSIDE-DOWN TRI-SLOSHER

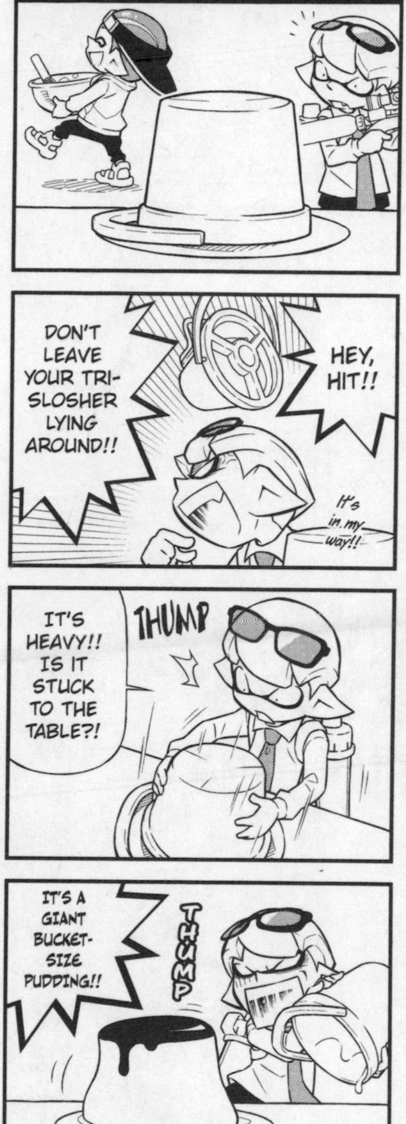
HEY, HIT!!
DON'T LEAVE YOUR TRI-SLOSHER LYING AROUND!!
It's in my way!!
THUMP
IT'S HEAVY!! IS IT STUCK TO THE TABLE?!
THUMP
IT'S A GIANT BUCKET-SIZE PUDDING!!

TIMER

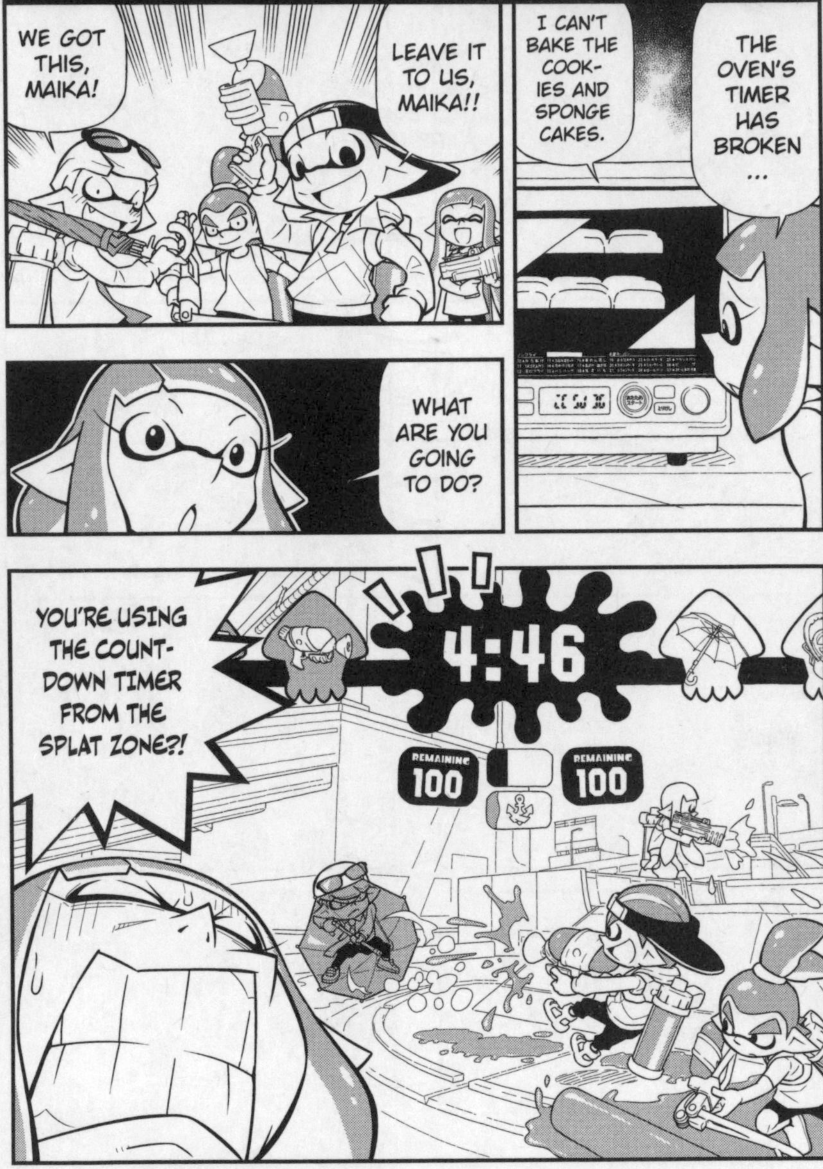

THE OVEN'S TIMER HAS BROKEN ...
I CAN'T BAKE THE COOK-IES AND SPONGE CAKES.
LEAVE IT TO US, MAIKA!!
WE GOT THIS, MAIKA!
WHAT ARE YOU GOING TO DO?
!!!
4:46
YOU'RE USING THE COUNT-DOWN TIMER FROM THE SPLAT ZONE?!
REMAINING 100
REMAINING 100

BUBBLING BOOYAH BOMB

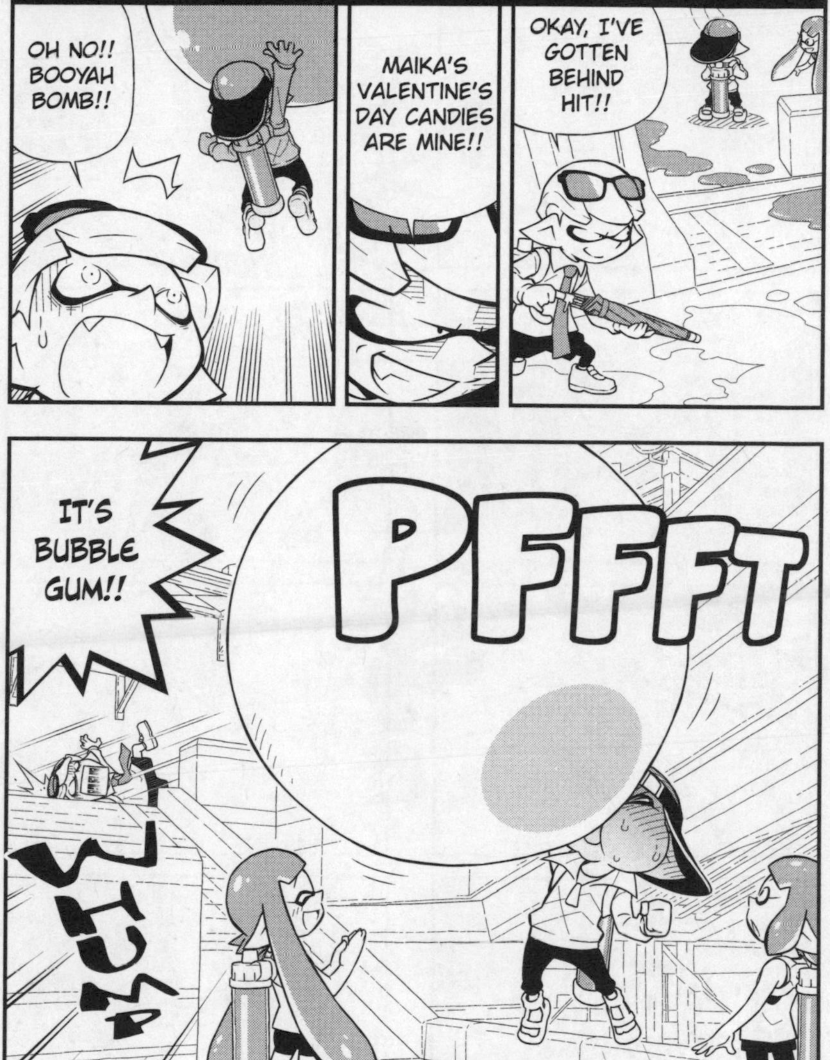

OKAY, I'VE GOTTEN BEHIND HIT!!
MAIKA'S VALENTINE'S DAY CANDIES ARE MINE!!
OH NO!! BOOYAH BOMB!!
PFFFT
IT'S BUBBLE GUM!!
SHLUMP

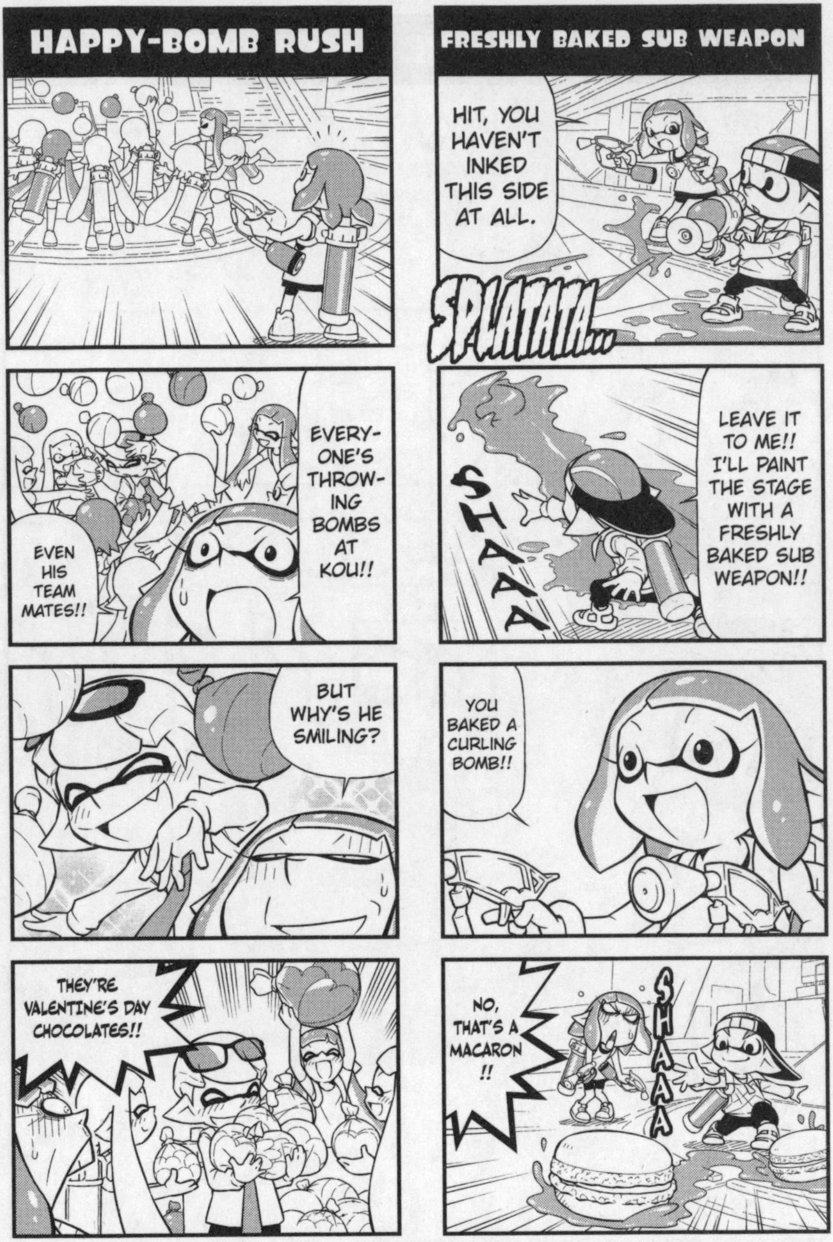
FRESHLY BAKED SUB WEAPON
HIT, YOU HAVEN'T INKED THIS SIDE AT ALL.
SPLATATA...
LEAVE IT TO ME!! I'LL PAINT THE STAGE WITH A FRESHLY BAKED SUB WEAPON!!
SHAAA
YOU BAKED A CURLING BOMB!!
SHAAA
NO, THAT'S A MACARON!!
HAPPY-BOMB RUSH
EVERY-ONE'S THROW-ING BOMBS AT KOU!!
EVEN HIS TEAM MATES!!
BUT WHY'S HE SMILING?
THEY'RE VALENTINE'S DAY CHOCOLATES!!

VALENTINE'S DAY ARMOR

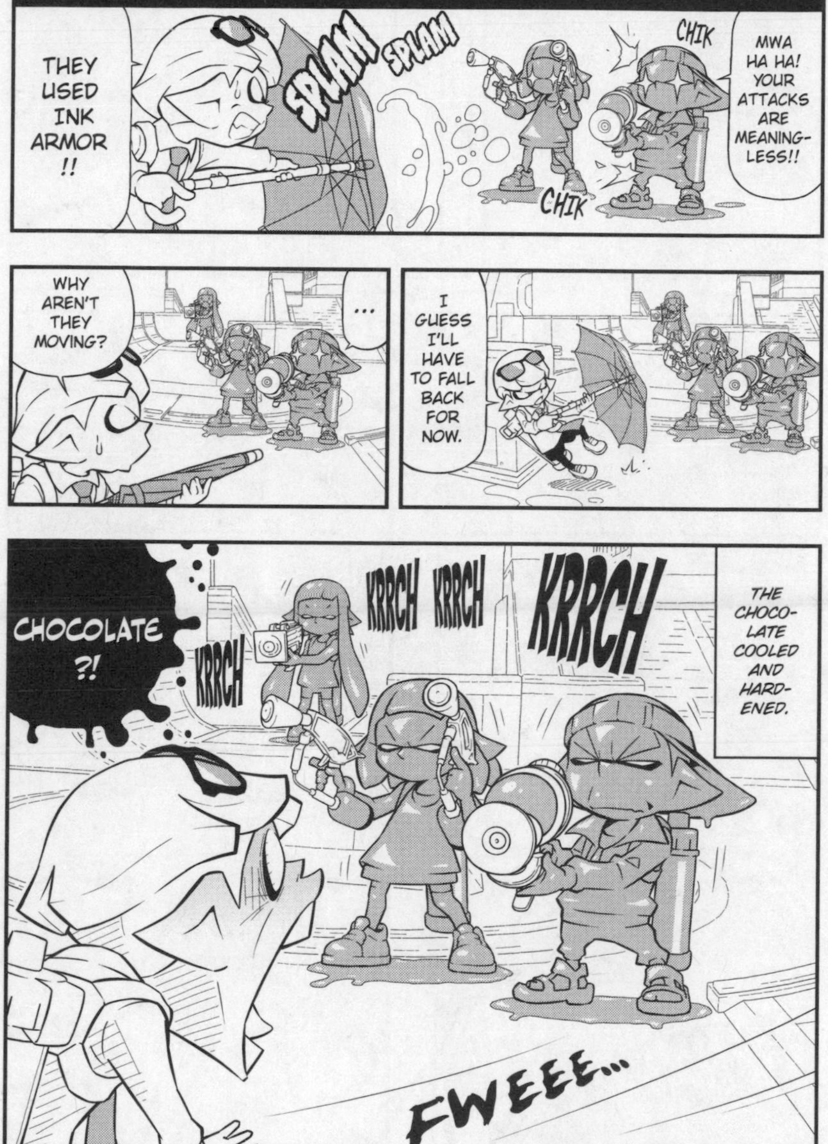

MWA HA HA! YOUR ATTACKS ARE MEANING-LESS!!
CHIK
CHIK
SPLAM
SPLAM
THEY USED INK ARMOR!!
I GUESS I'LL HAVE TO FALL BACK FOR NOW.
...
WHY AREN'T THEY MOVING?
THE CHOCO-LATE COOLED AND HARD-ENED.
KRRCH
KRRCH
KRRCH
KRRCH
CHOCOLATE ?!
FWEEE...

ENDLESS TIME

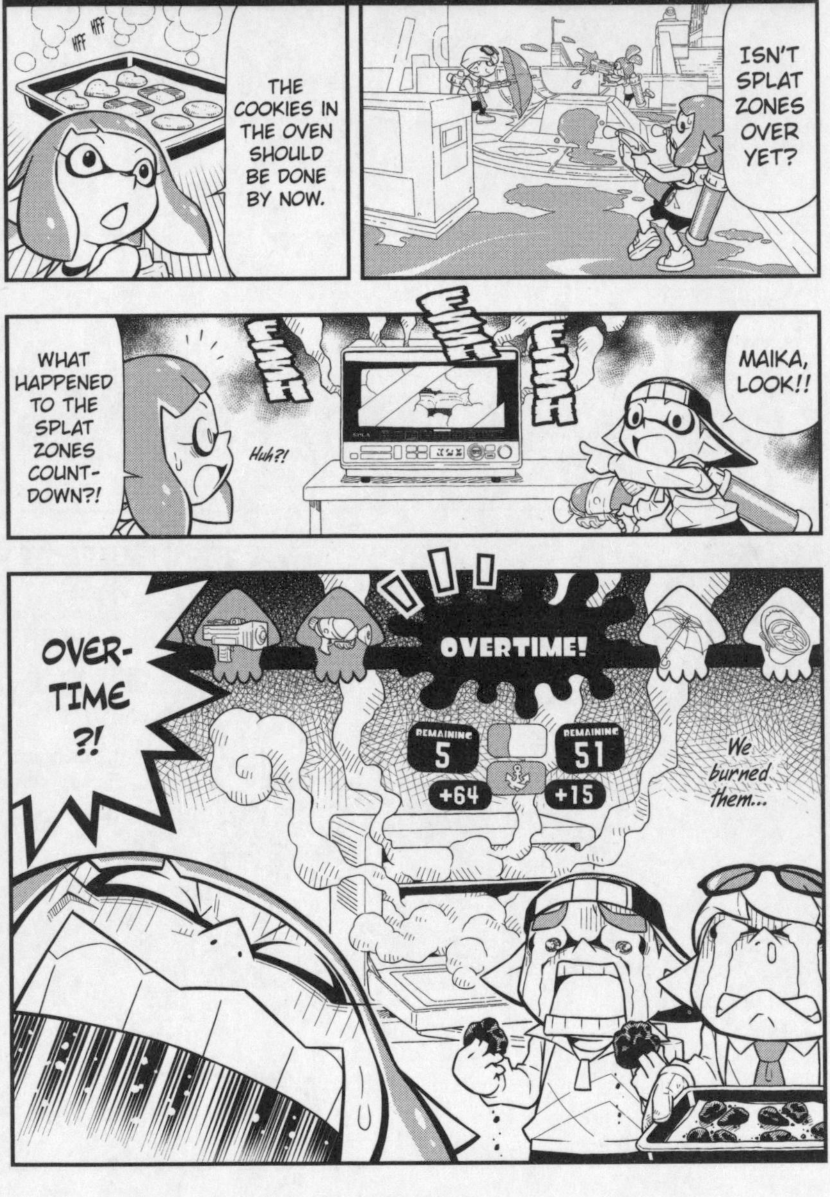
ISN'T SPLAT ZONES OVER YET?
HFF HFF
THE COOKIES IN THE OVEN SHOULD BE DONE BY NOW.
MAIKA, LOOK!!
FSSH
FSSH
FSSH
Huh?!
WHAT HAPPENED TO THE SPLAT ZONES COUNTDOWN?!
OVERTIME!
REMAINING 51
+15
REMAINING 5
+64
We burned them...
OVER-TIME?!

Splatoon SQUID KIDS COMEDY SHOW

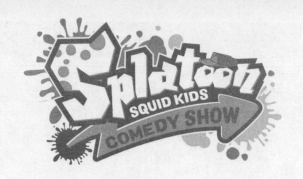

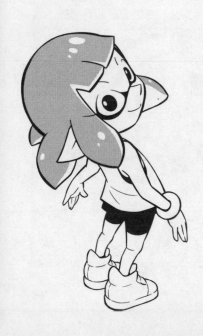

Splatoon
SQUID KIDS COMEDY SHOW

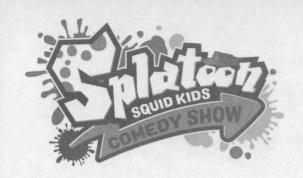

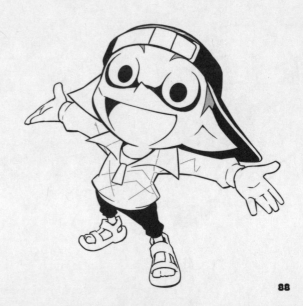

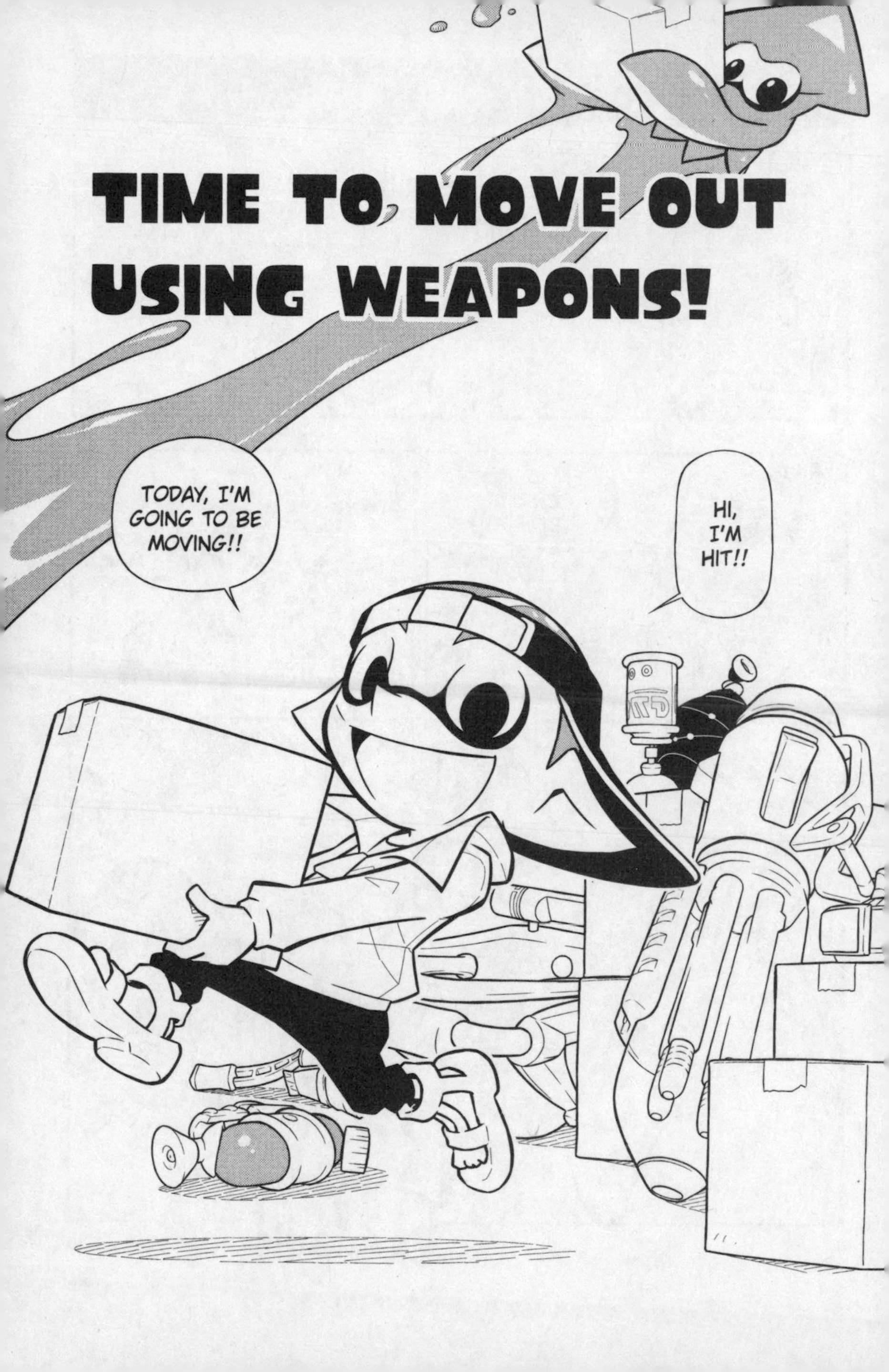
TIME TO MOVE OUT USING WEAPONS!
HI, I'M HIT!!
TODAY, I'M GOING TO BE MOVING!!

EASY MOVING

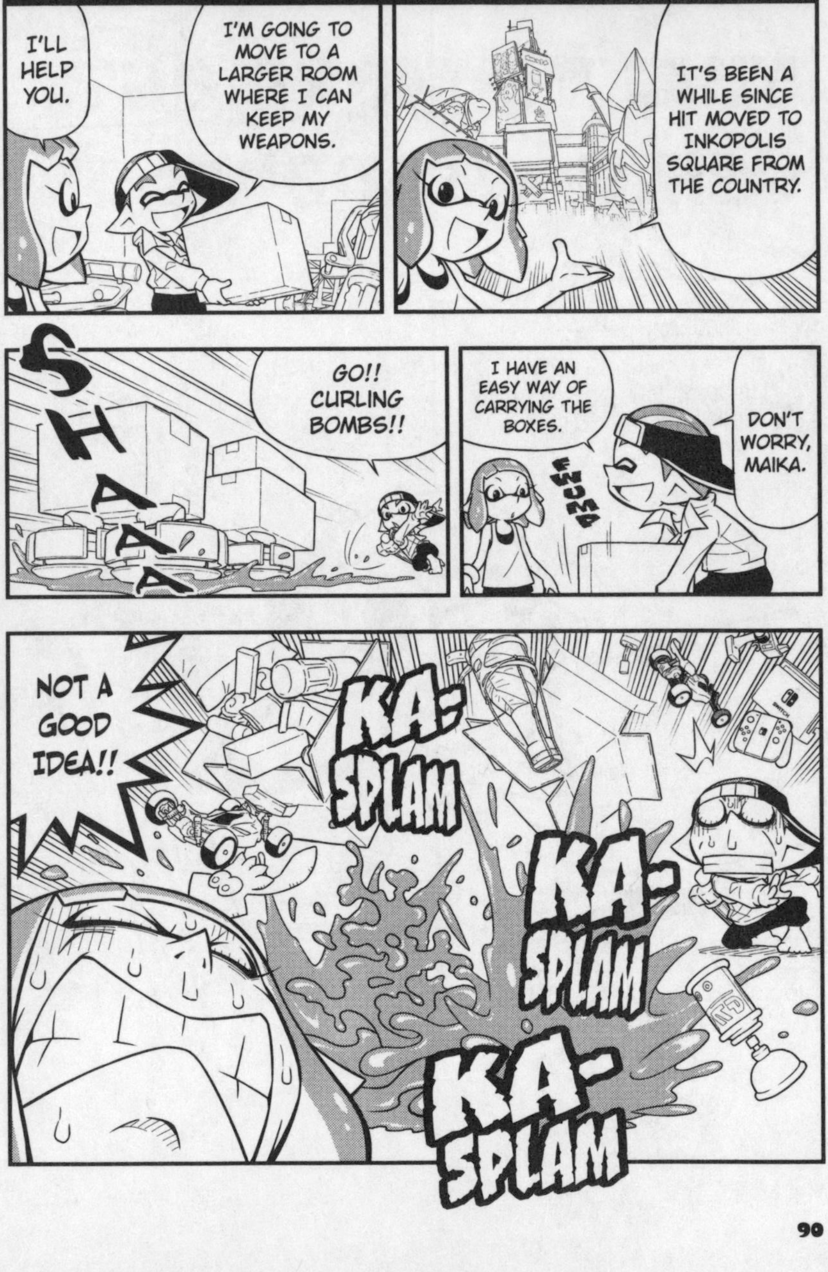
IT'S BEEN A WHILE SINCE HIT MOVED TO INKOPOLIS SQUARE FROM THE COUNTRY.
I'M GOING TO MOVE TO A LARGER ROOM WHERE I CAN KEEP MY WEAPONS.
I'LL HELP YOU.
DON'T WORRY, MAIKA.
I HAVE AN EASY WAY OF CARRYING THE BOXES.
FWUMP
GO!! CURLING BOMBS!!
SHAAAA
KA-SPLAM
KA-SPLAM
KA-SPLAM
NOT A GOOD IDEA!!

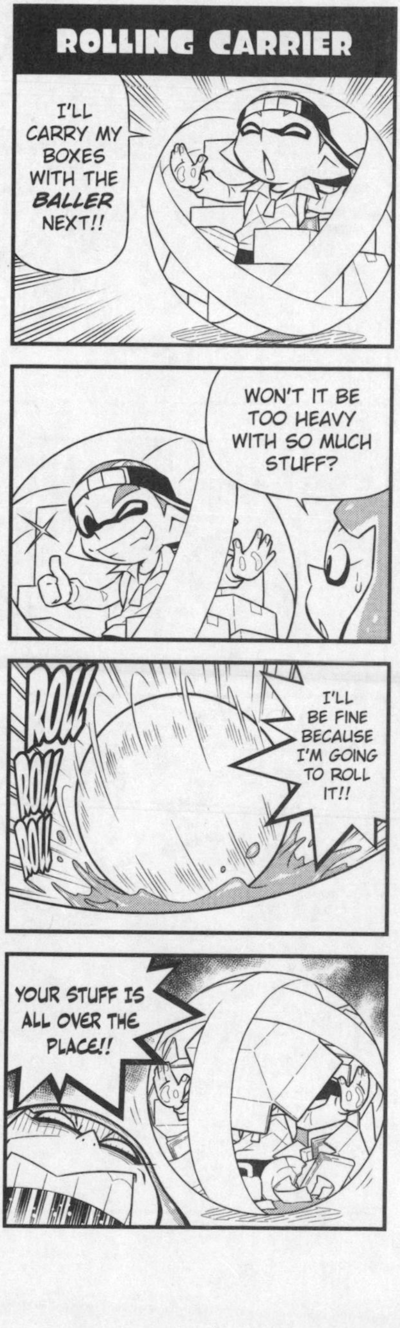
ROLLING CARRIER
I'LL CARRY MY BOXES WITH THE *BALLER* NEXT!!
WON'T IT BE TOO HEAVY WITH SO MUCH STUFF?
I'LL BE FINE BECAUSE I'M GOING TO ROLL IT!!
ROLL ROLL ROLL
YOUR STUFF IS ALL OVER THE PLACE!!

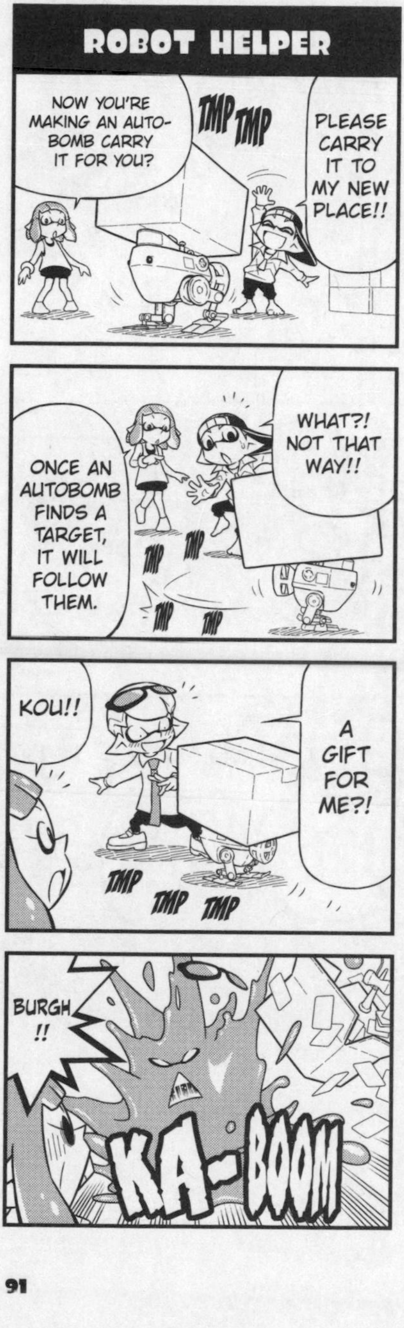
ROBOT HELPER
PLEASE CARRY IT TO MY NEW PLACE!!
TMP TMP
NOW YOU'RE MAKING AN AUTO-BOMB CARRY IT FOR YOU?
WHAT?! NOT THAT WAY!!
ONCE AN AUTOBOMB FINDS A TARGET, IT WILL FOLLOW THEM.
TMP TMP TMP TMP
A GIFT FOR ME?!
KOU!!
TMP TMP TMP
BURGH!!
KA-BOOM

MISSILE PACKAGE

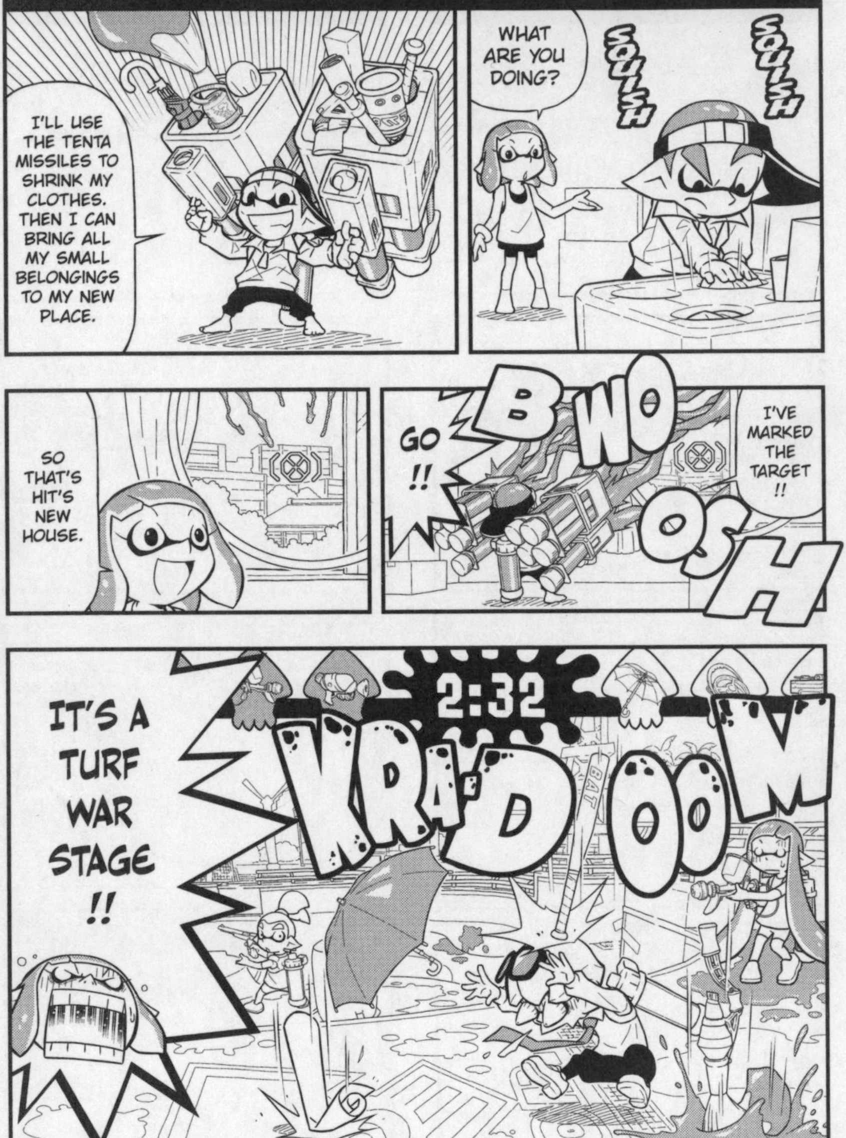
SQUISH
SQUISH
WHAT ARE YOU DOING?
I'LL USE THE TENTA MISSILES TO SHRINK MY CLOTHES. THEN I CAN BRING ALL MY SMALL BELONGINGS TO MY NEW PLACE.
I'VE MARKED THE TARGET!!
BWOOSH
GO!!
SO THAT'S HIT'S NEW HOUSE.
2:32
KRA-DOOOM
BAT
IT'S A TURF WAR STAGE!!

HIDING SCRATCHES

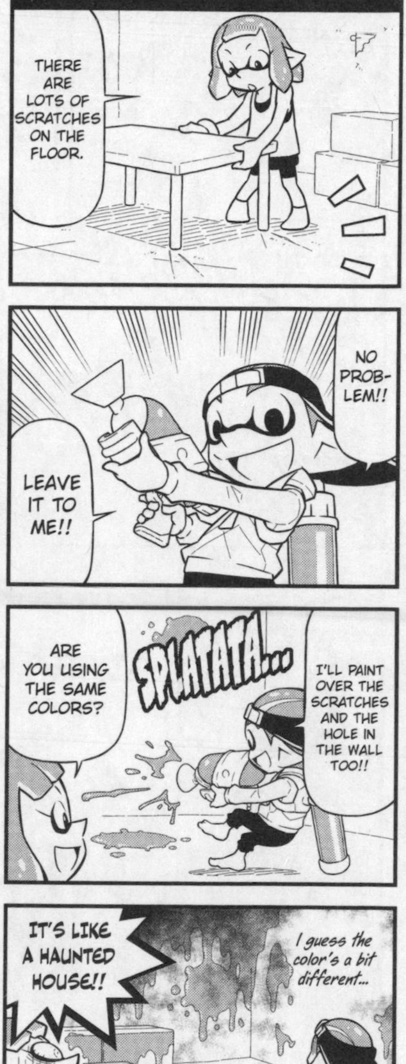
THERE ARE LOTS OF SCRATCHES ON THE FLOOR.
NO PROB-LEM!!
LEAVE IT TO ME!!
I'LL PAINT OVER THE SCRATCHES AND THE HOLE IN THE WALL TOO!!
SPLATATA...
ARE YOU USING THE SAME COLORS?
I guess the color's a bit different...
IT'S LIKE A HAUNTED HOUSE!!

MOVERS

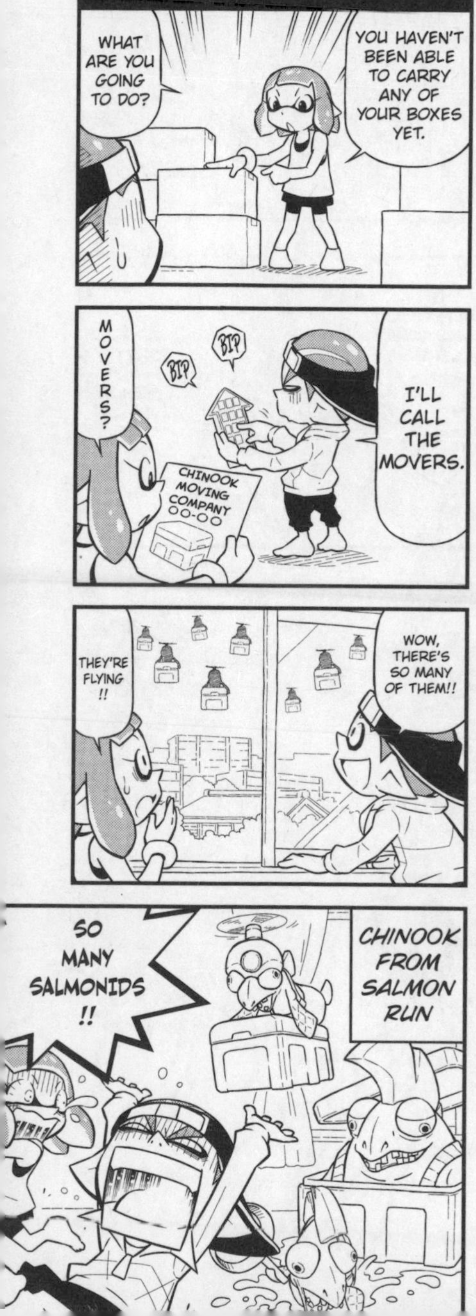
YOU HAVEN'T BEEN ABLE TO CARRY ANY OF YOUR BOXES YET.
WHAT ARE YOU GOING TO DO?
I'LL CALL THE MOVERS.
BIP
BIP
MOVERS?
CHINOOK MOVING COMPANY OO-OO
WOW, THERE'S SO MANY OF THEM!!
THEY'RE FLYING!!
CHINOOK FROM SALMON RUN
SO MANY SALMONIDS!!

A BEAKON IN THE NEW HOUSE

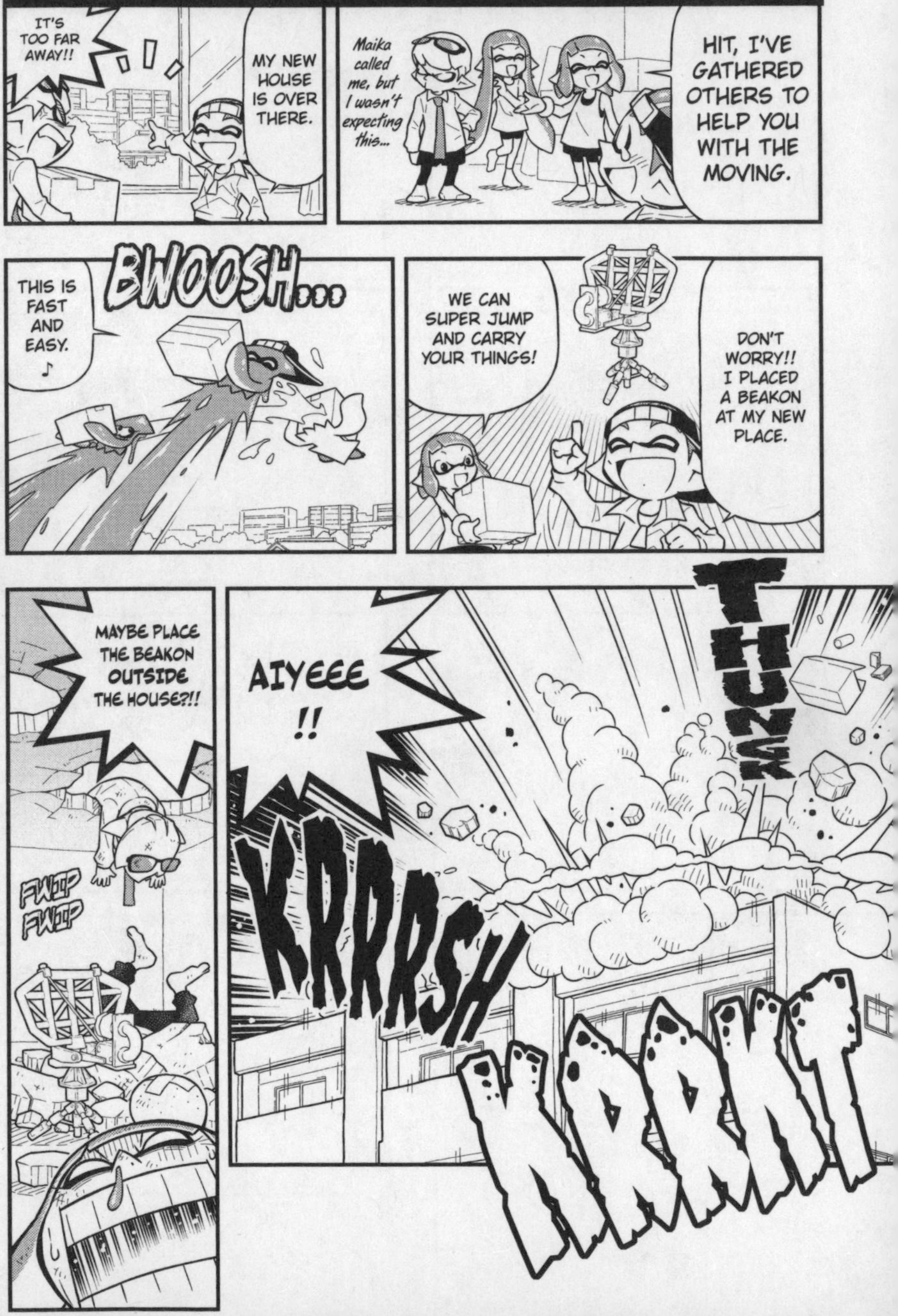
HIT, I'VE GATHERED OTHERS TO HELP YOU WITH THE MOVING.
Maika called me, but I wasn't expecting this...
MY NEW HOUSE IS OVER THERE.
IT'S TOO FAR AWAY!!
DON'T WORRY!! I PLACED A BEAKON AT MY NEW PLACE.
WE CAN SUPER JUMP AND CARRY YOUR THINGS!
BWOOSH...
THIS IS FAST AND EASY. ♪
THUNK
AIYEEE!!
KRRRSH
KRRKT
MAYBE PLACE THE BEAKON OUTSIDE THE HOUSE?!!
FWIP FWIP

TIME TO PLAY INDOORS!

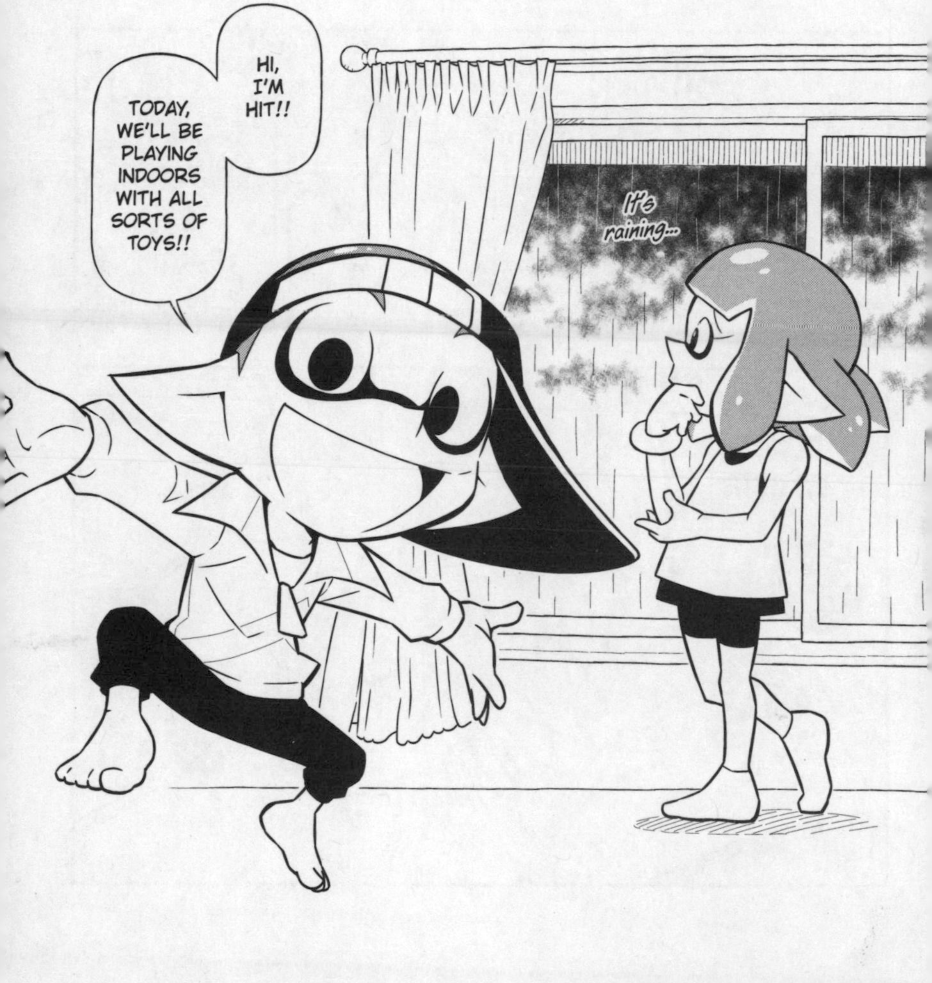
It's raining...
HI, I'M HIT!!
TODAY, WE'LL BE PLAYING INDOORS WITH ALL SORTS OF TOYS!!

SPLATTER KENDAMA

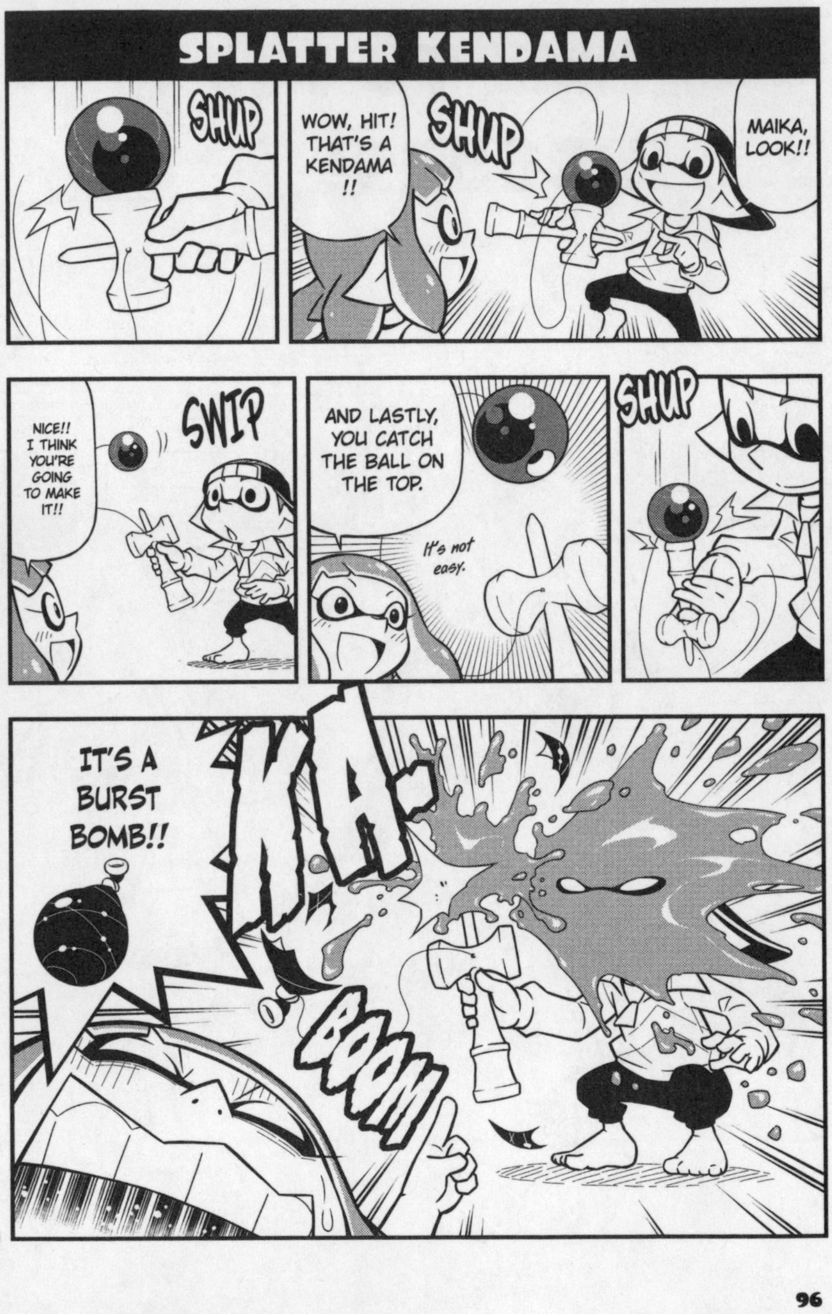

MAIKA, LOOK!!
SHUP
WOW, HIT! THAT'S A KENDAMA !!
SHUP
SHUP
AND LASTLY, YOU CATCH THE BALL ON THE TOP.
It's not easy.
SWIP
NICE!! I THINK YOU'RE GOING TO MAKE IT!!
KA
IT'S A BURST BOMB!!
BOOM

SPLATTER YO-YO

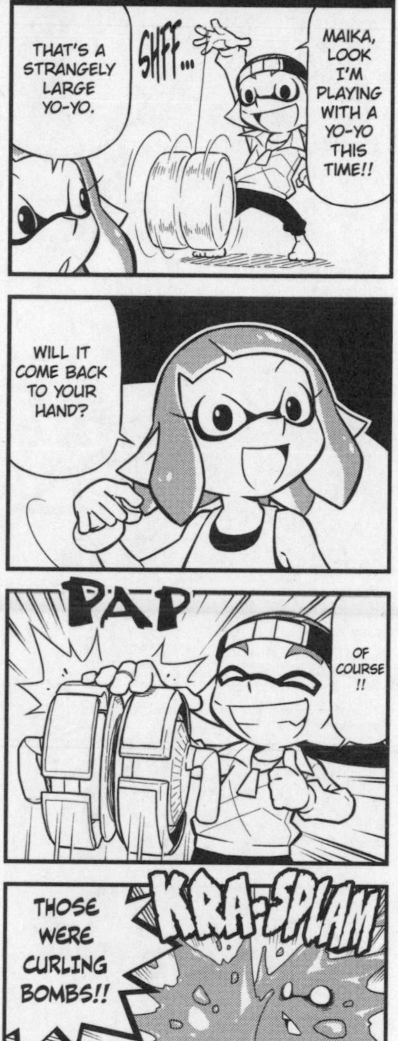
MAIKA, LOOK I'M PLAYING WITH A YO-YO THIS TIME!!
SHFF...
THAT'S A STRANGELY LARGE YO-YO.
WILL IT COME BACK TO YOUR HAND?
PAP
OF COURSE !!
KRA-SPLAM
THOSE WERE CURLING BOMBS!!

SPLATTER TIN-CAN TELEPHONE

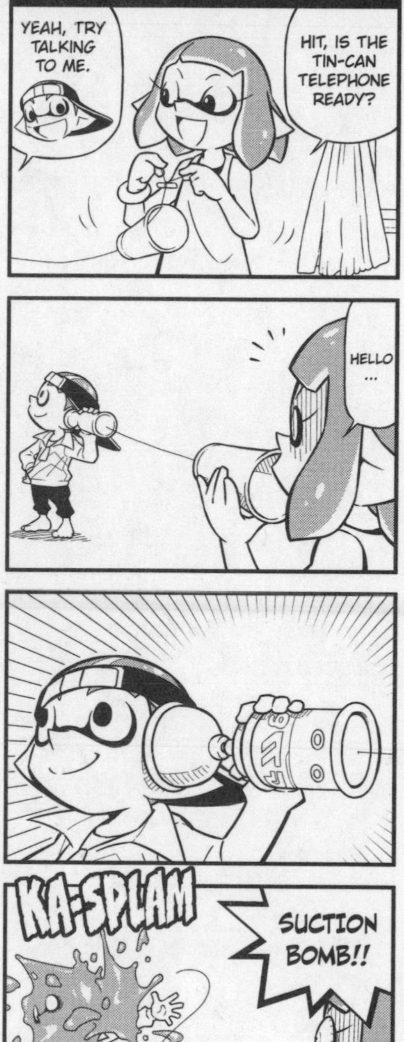
HIT, IS THE TIN-CAN TELEPHONE READY?
YEAH, TRY TALKING TO ME.
HELLO ...
KA-SPLAM
SUCTION BOMB!!

SPLATTER BOWLING

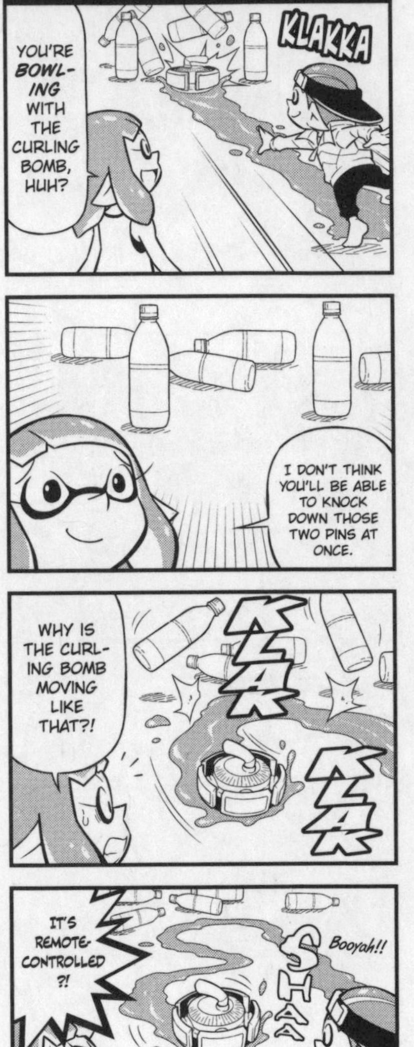
KLAKKA
YOU'RE BOWLING WITH THE CURLING BOMB, HUH?
I DON'T THINK YOU'LL BE ABLE TO KNOCK DOWN THOSE TWO PINS AT ONCE.
KLAK
KLAK
WHY IS THE CURLING BOMB MOVING LIKE THAT?!
Booyah!!
SHAA
IT'S REMOTE-CONTROLLED?!
SHF SHF

SPLATTER GIANT JUMP ROPE

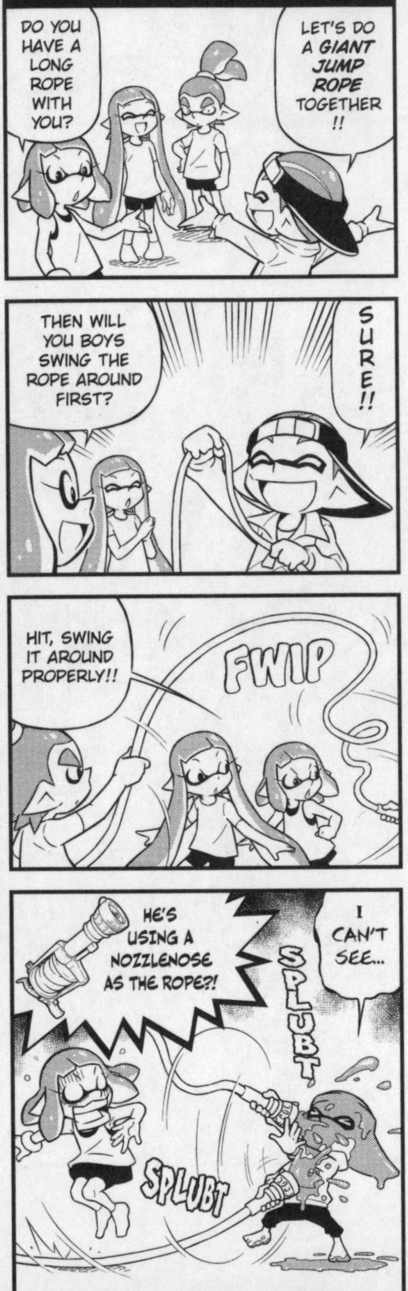
LET'S DO A GIANT JUMP ROPE TOGETHER!!
DO YOU HAVE A LONG ROPE WITH YOU?
SURE!!
THEN WILL YOU BOYS SWING THE ROPE AROUND FIRST?
FWIP
HIT, SWING IT AROUND PROPERLY!!
I CAN'T SEE...
SPLUBT
HE'S USING A NOZZLENOSE AS THE ROPE?!
SPLUBT

SPLATTER DOMINOES

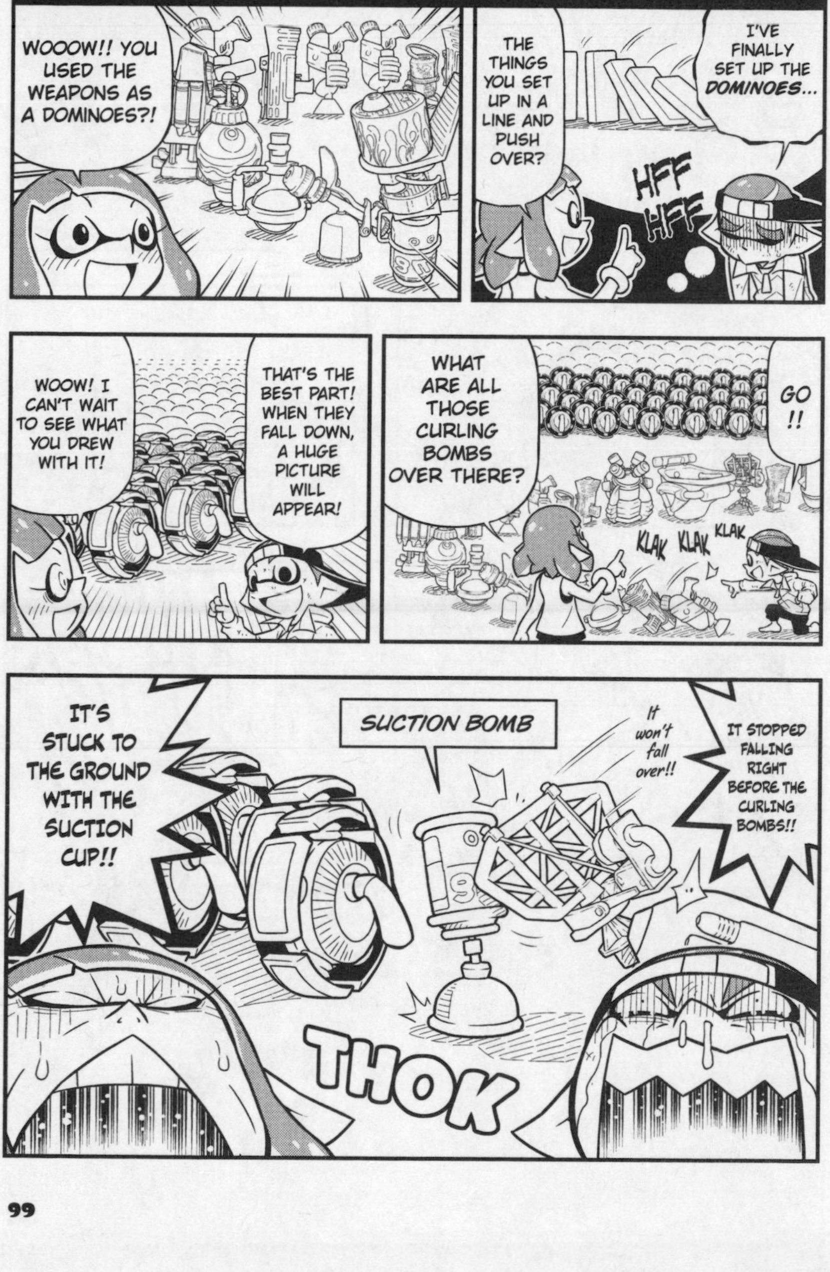
I'VE FINALLY SET UP THE DOMINOES...
HFF HFF
THE THINGS YOU SET UP IN A LINE AND PUSH OVER?
WOOOW!! YOU USED THE WEAPONS AS A DOMINOES?!
GO!!
WHAT ARE ALL THOSE CURLING BOMBS OVER THERE?
KLAK KLAK KLAK
THAT'S THE BEST PART! WHEN THEY FALL DOWN, A HUGE PICTURE WILL APPEAR!
WOOW! I CAN'T WAIT TO SEE WHAT YOU DREW WITH IT!
IT STOPPED FALLING RIGHT BEFORE THE CURLING BOMBS!!
It won't fall over!!
SUCTION BOMB
IT'S STUCK TO THE GROUND WITH THE SUCTION CUP!!
THOK

SPLATTER STACKED DARUMA

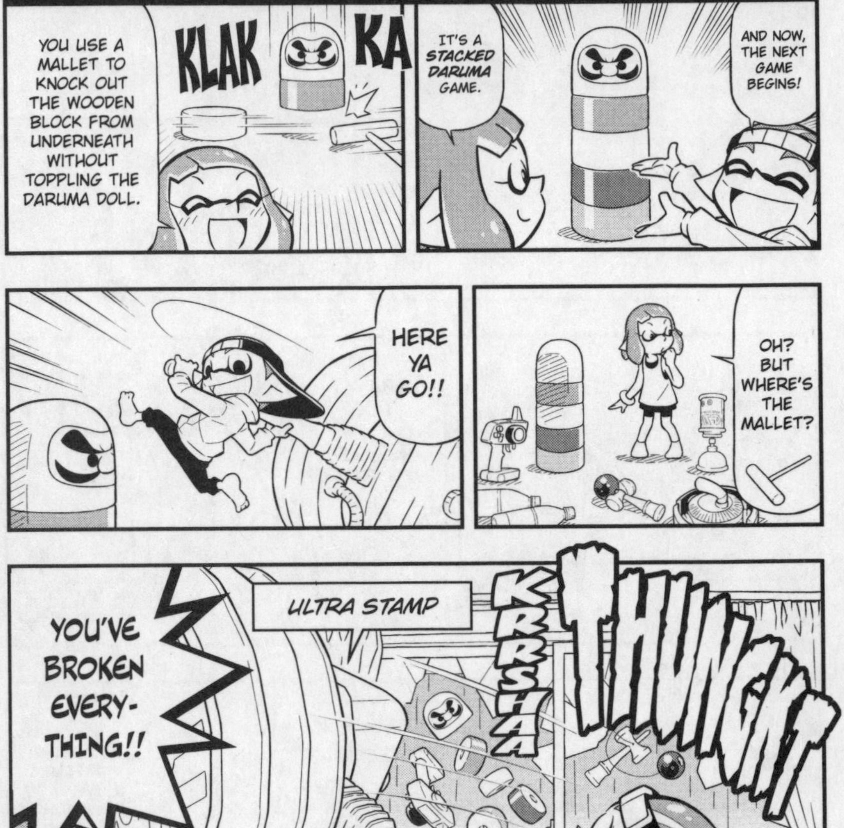

AND NOW, THE NEXT GAME BEGINS!
IT'S A *STACKED DARUMA* GAME.
KLAK KA
YOU USE A MALLET TO KNOCK OUT THE WOODEN BLOCK FROM UNDERNEATH WITHOUT TOPPLING THE DARUMA DOLL.
OH? BUT WHERE'S THE MALLET?
HERE YA GO!!
THUNGK!!
KRRSHAA
ULTRA STAMP
YOU'VE BROKEN EVERY-THING!!
...

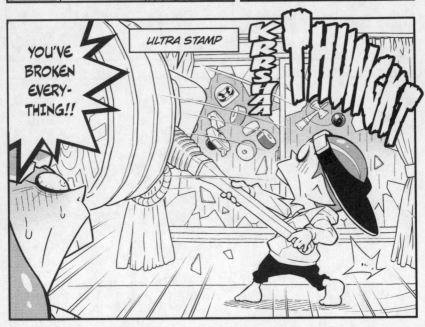

Splatoon SQUID KIDS COMEDY SHOW

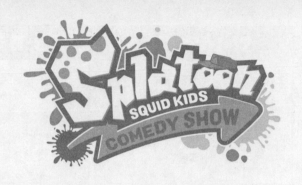

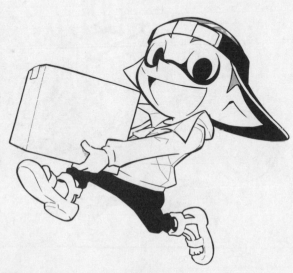

Splatoon SQUID KIDS COMEDY SHOW

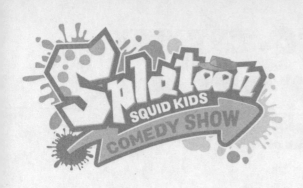

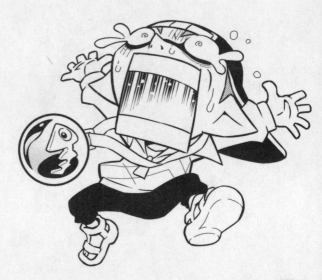

TIME TO GET THE GOLD IN TRACK-AND-FIELD!

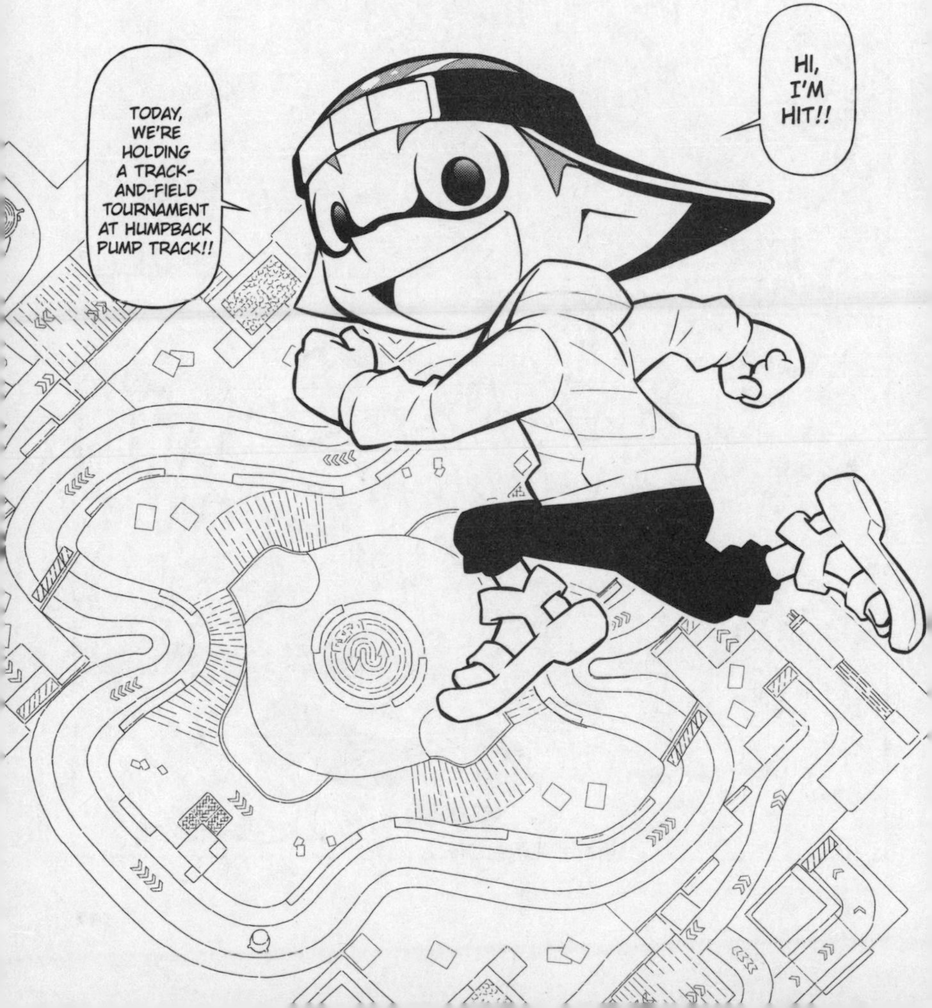
HI, I'M HIT!!
TODAY, WE'RE HOLDING A TRACK-AND-FIELD TOURNAMENT AT HUMPBACK PUMP TRACK!!

HUNDRED-METER DASH

FIRST GAME IS THE 100-METER DASH. GOOD LUCK EVERYONE!!
Watch me, Maika!
GET READY...
Ready
GO!
BWOOSH
SPLAM
KRA
SPLAM
YOU USED THE TENTA MISSILES AS A STARTING PISTOL?!
They're locked on!
SPLAM

HIGH JUMP

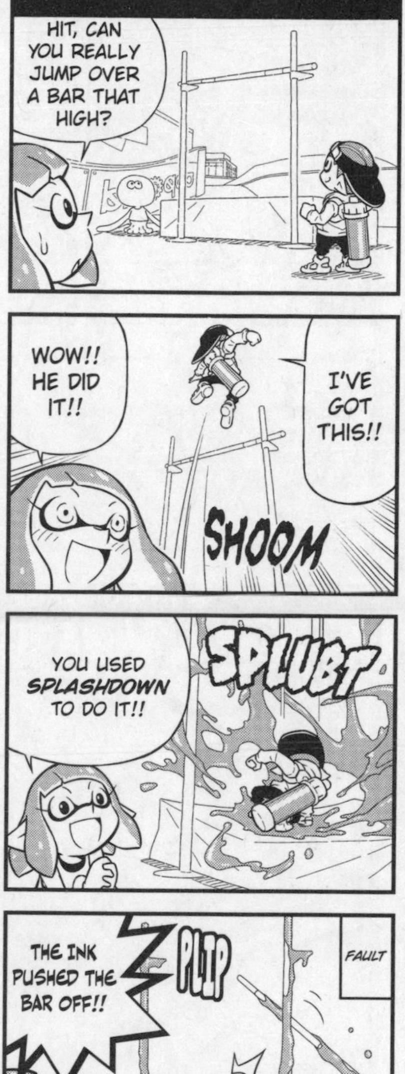
HIT, CAN YOU REALLY JUMP OVER A BAR THAT HIGH?
I'VE GOT THIS!!
WOW!! HE DID IT!!
SHOOM
SPLUBT
YOU USED *SPLASHDOWN* TO DO IT!!
FAULT
PLIP
THE INK PUSHED THE BAR OFF!!

HAMMER THROW

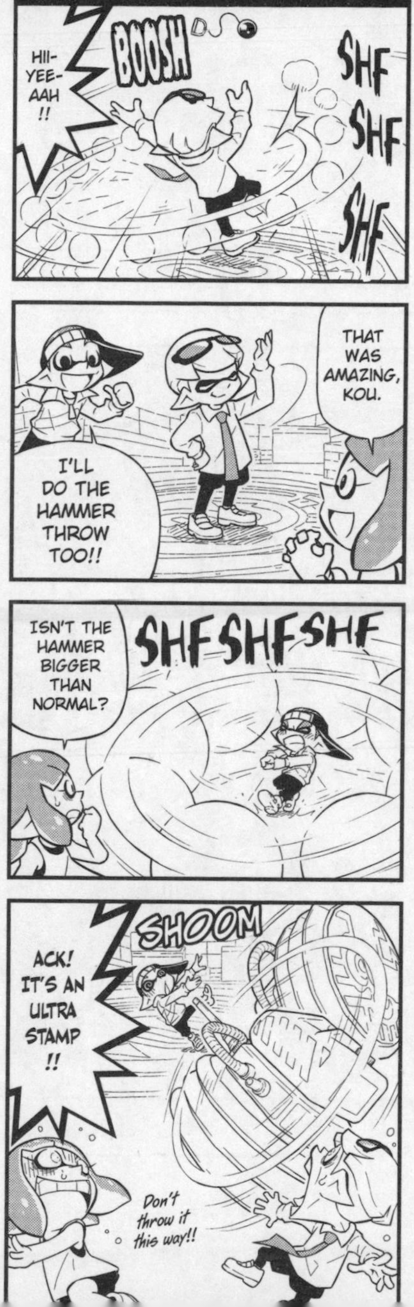
SHF
SHF
SHF
BOOSH
HII-YEE-AAH!!
THAT WAS AMAZING, KOU.
I'LL DO THE HAMMER THROW TOO!!
SHF SHF SHF
ISN'T THE HAMMER BIGGER THAN NORMAL?
SHOOM
ACK! IT'S AN ULTRA STAMP!!
Don't throw it this way!!

HURDLES

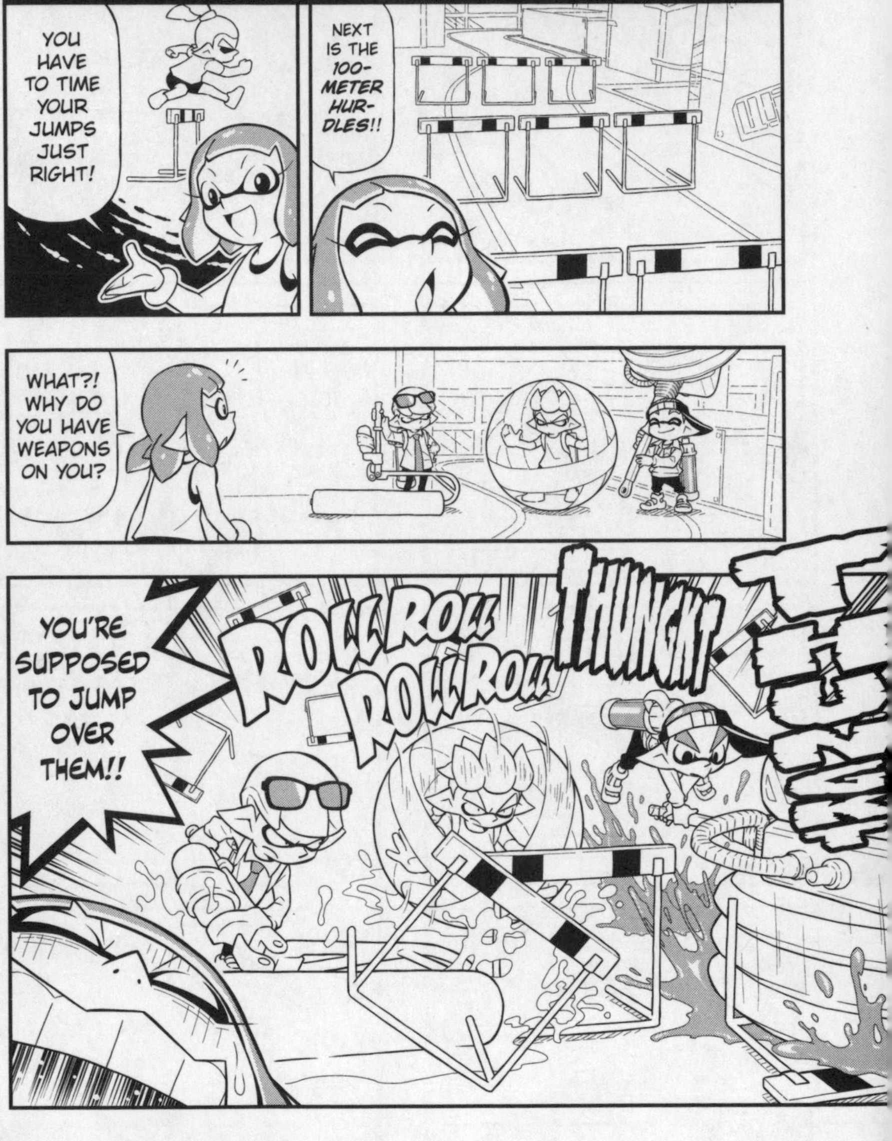
NEXT IS THE 100-METER HUR-DLES!!
YOU HAVE TO TIME YOUR JUMPS JUST RIGHT!
WHAT?! WHY DO YOU HAVE WEAPONS ON YOU?
THUNGK
ROLL ROLL
ROLL ROLL
YOU'RE SUPPOSED TO JUMP OVER THEM!!

LONG JUMP

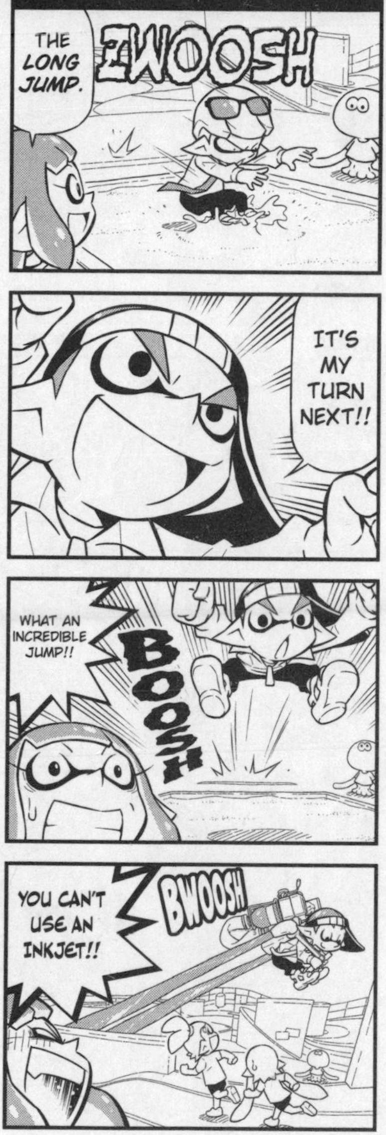
IWOOSH
THE LONG JUMP.
IT'S MY TURN NEXT!!
BOOSH
WHAT AN INCREDIBLE JUMP!!
BWOOSH
YOU CAN'T USE AN INKJET!!

RELAY RACE

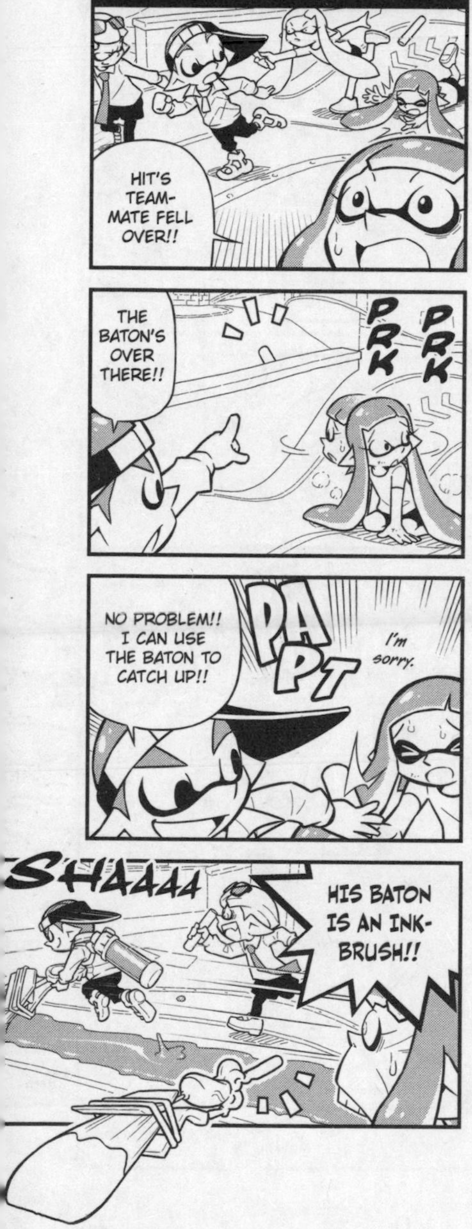
HIT'S TEAM-MATE FELL OVER!!
PRK PRK
THE BATON'S OVER THERE!!
PAPT
I'm sorry.
NO PROBLEM!! I CAN USE THE BATON TO CATCH UP!!
SHAAAA
HIS BATON IS AN INK-BRUSH!!

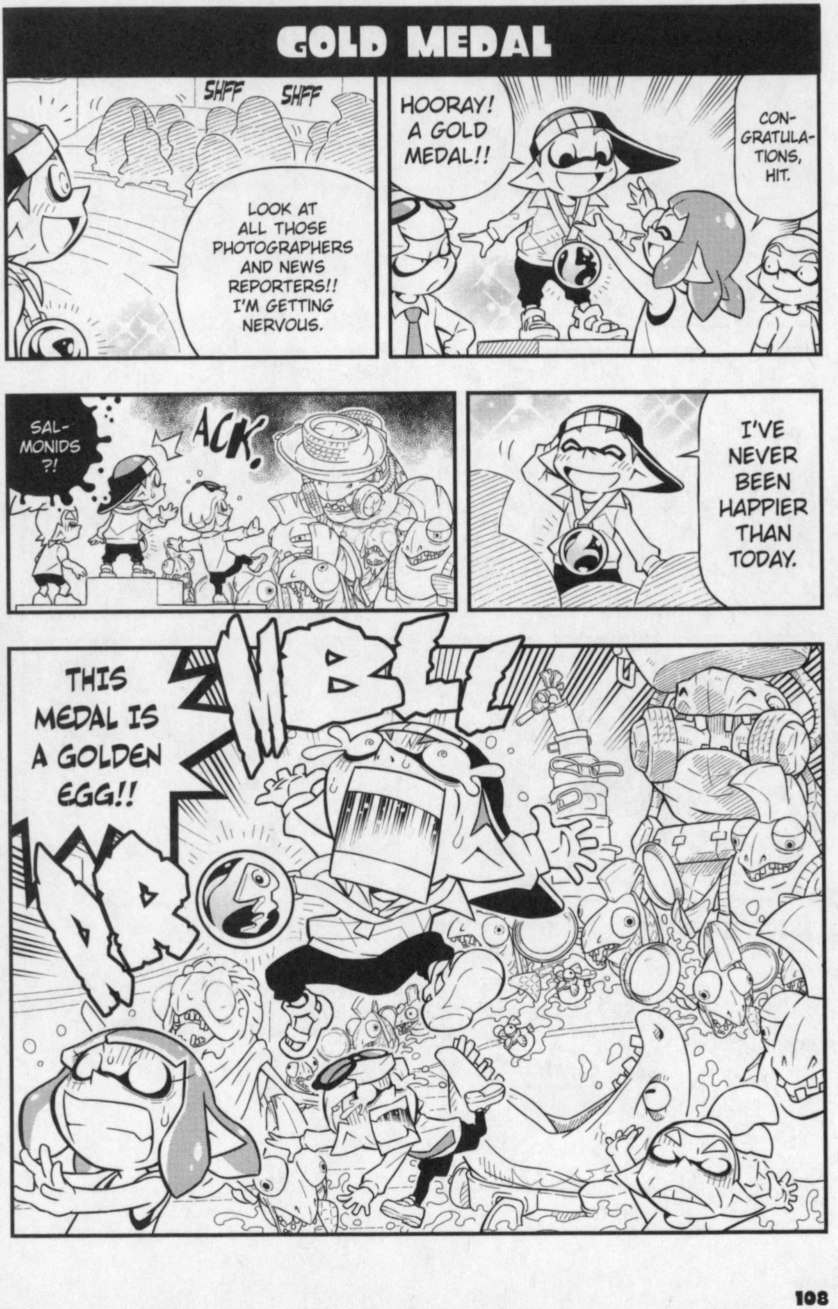
GOLD MEDAL
HOORAY! A GOLD MEDAL!!
CON-GRATULA-TIONS, HIT.
SHFF SHFF
LOOK AT ALL THOSE PHOTOGRAPHERS AND NEWS REPORTERS!! I'M GETTING NERVOUS.
I'VE NEVER BEEN HAPPIER THAN TODAY.
ACK
SAL-MONIDS ?!
BLL
THIS MEDAL IS A GOLDEN EGG!!
DR

Splatoon
SQUID KIDS COMEDY SHOW

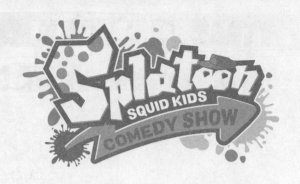

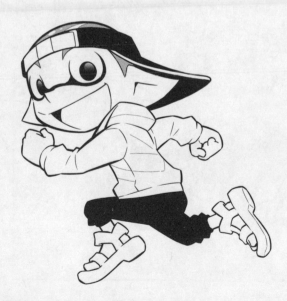

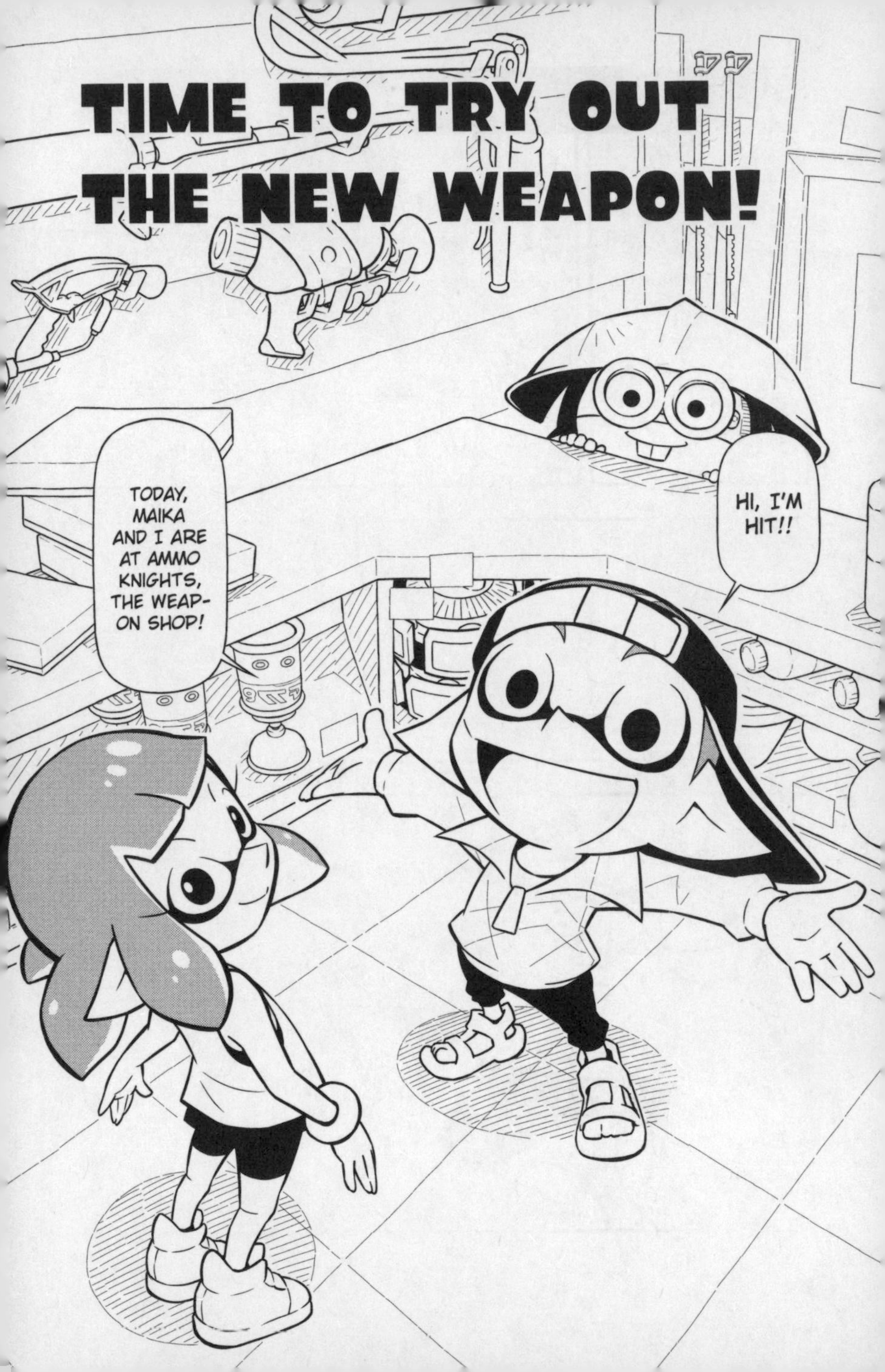
TIME TO TRY OUT THE NEW WEAPON!
HI, I'M HIT!!
TODAY, MAIKA AND I ARE AT AMMO KNIGHTS, THE WEAP-ON SHOP!

SHELDON

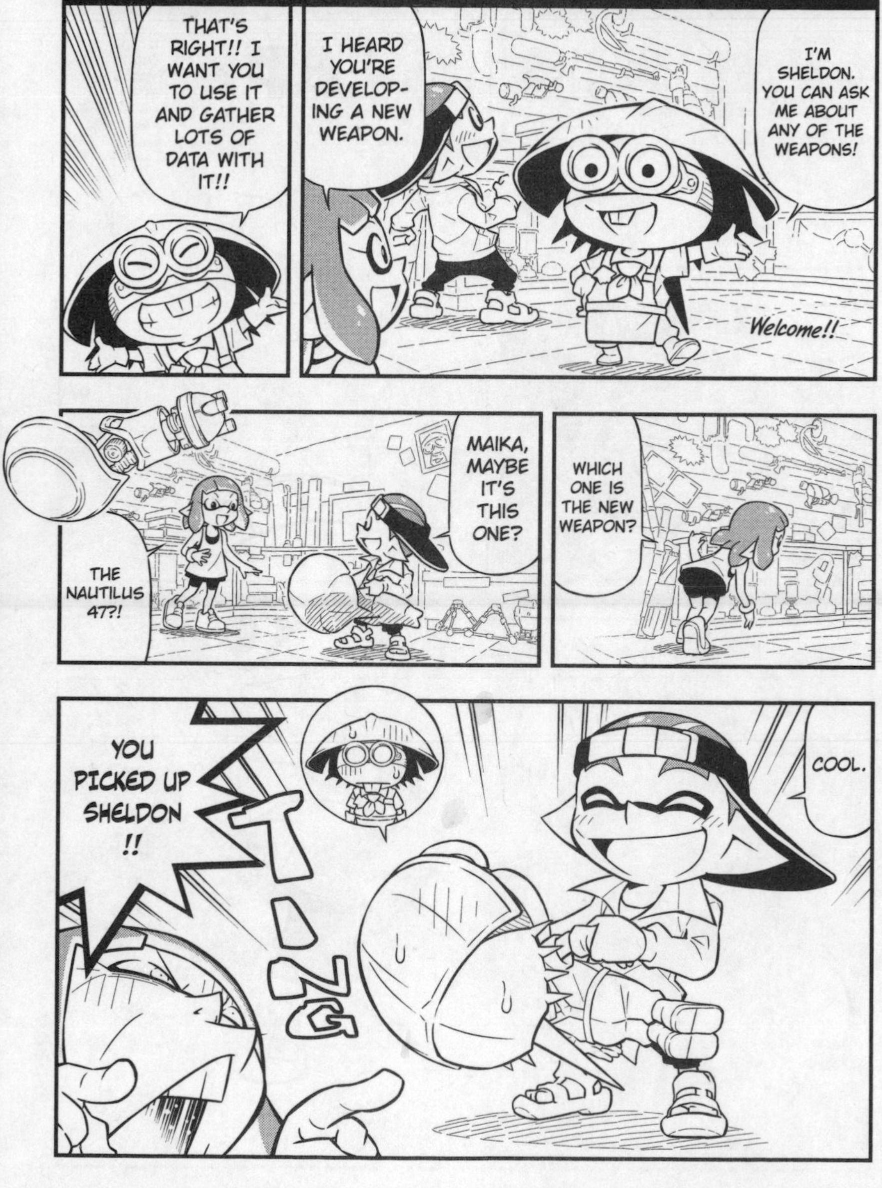
I'M SHELDON. YOU CAN ASK ME ABOUT ANY OF THE WEAPONS!
Welcome!!
I HEARD YOU'RE DEVELOP-ING A NEW WEAPON.
THAT'S RIGHT!! I WANT YOU TO USE IT AND GATHER LOTS OF DATA WITH IT!!
WHICH ONE IS THE NEW WEAPON?
MAIKA, MAYBE IT'S THIS ONE?
THE NAUTILUS 47?!
COOL.
YOU PICKED UP SHELDON !!

SMALL ENOUGH TO CARRY!!

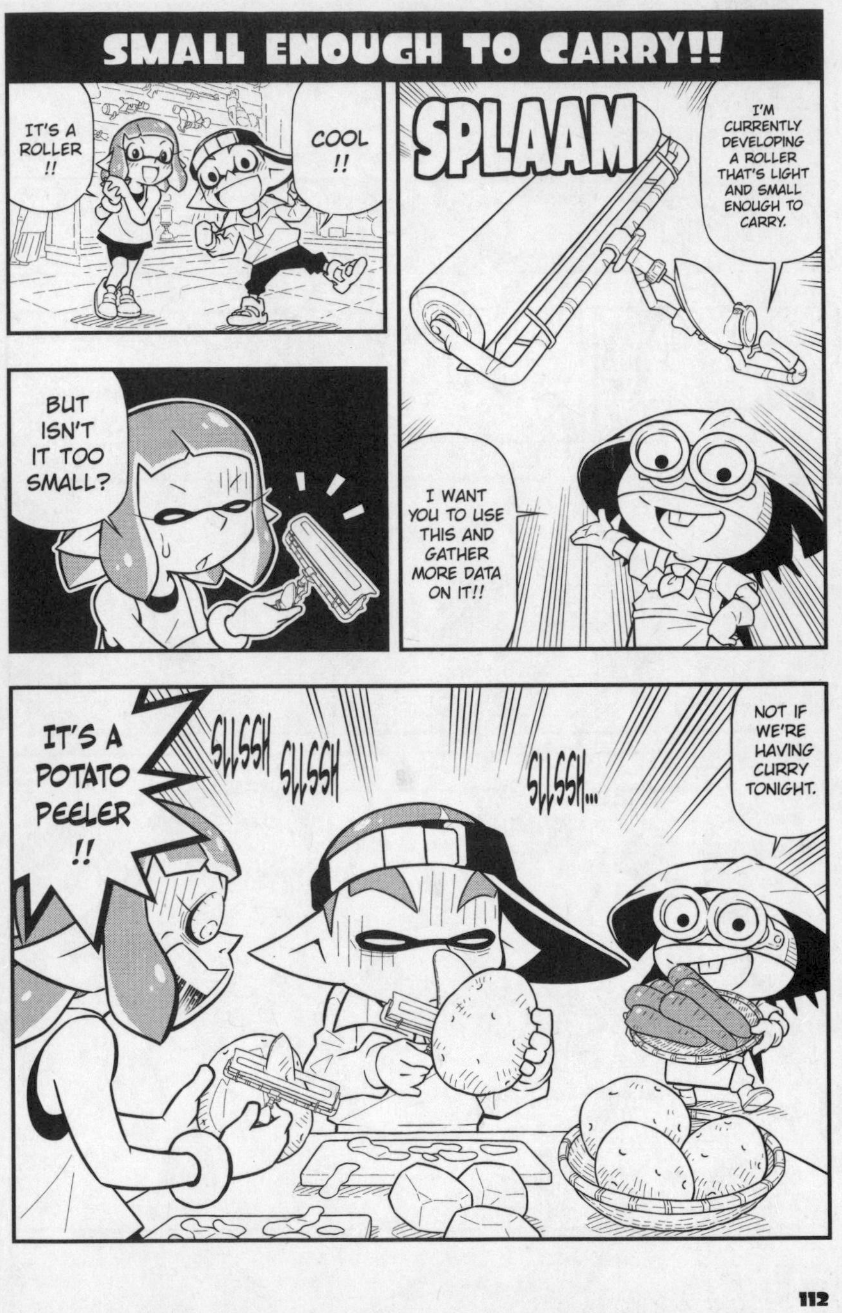
I'M CURRENTLY DEVELOPING A ROLLER THAT'S LIGHT AND SMALL ENOUGH TO CARRY.
SPLAAM
I WANT YOU TO USE THIS AND GATHER MORE DATA ON IT!!
COOL!!
IT'S A ROLLER!!
BUT ISN'T IT TOO SMALL?
NOT IF WE'RE HAVING CURRY TONIGHT.
SLLSSH...
SLLSSH
SLLSSH
IT'S A POTATO PEELER!!

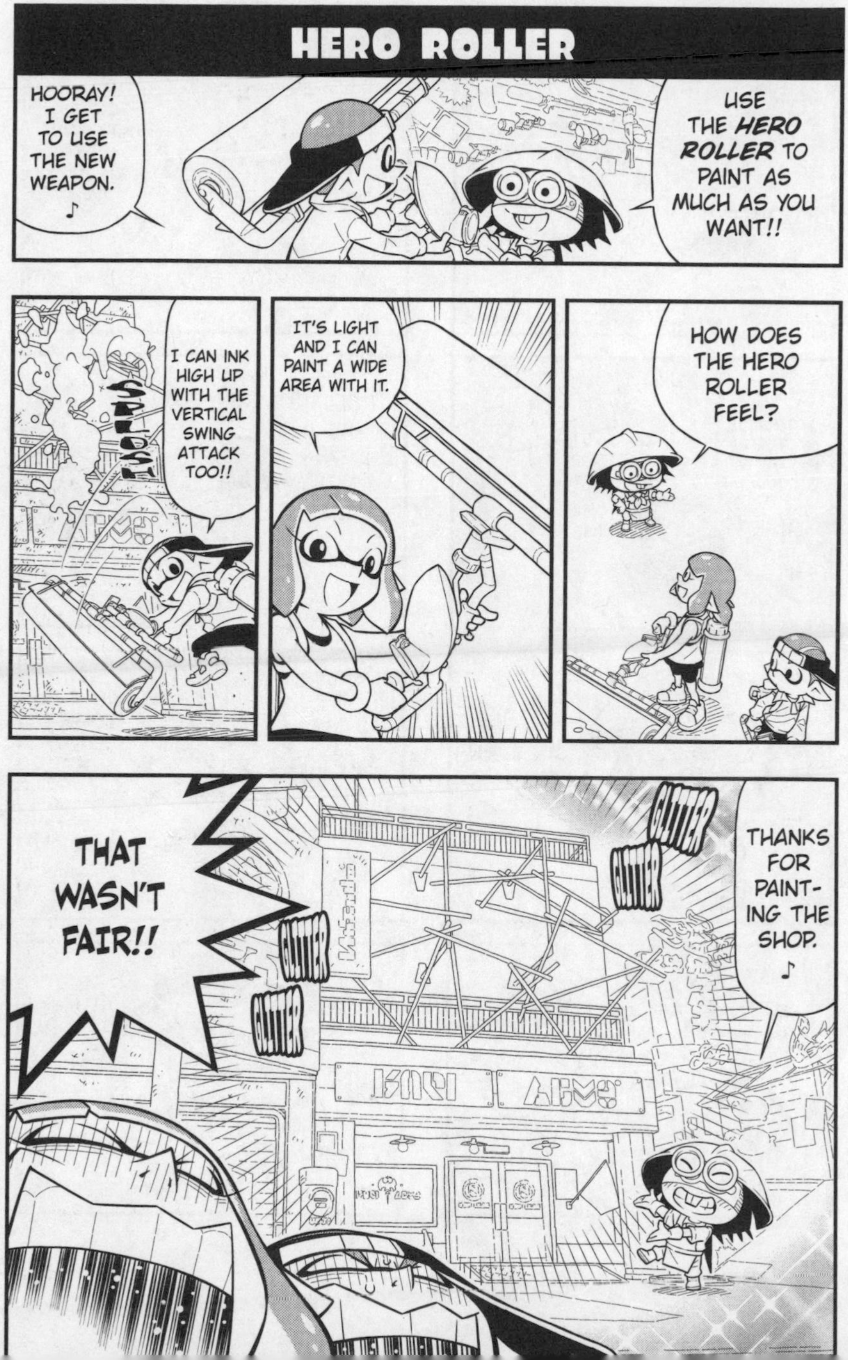
HERO ROLLER
USE THE *HERO ROLLER* TO PAINT AS MUCH AS YOU WANT!!
HOORAY! I GET TO USE THE NEW WEAPON. ♪
HOW DOES THE HERO ROLLER FEEL?
IT'S LIGHT AND I CAN PAINT A WIDE AREA WITH IT.
I CAN INK HIGH UP WITH THE VERTICAL SWING ATTACK TOO!!
SPLOOSH
THANKS FOR PAINT-ING THE SHOP. ♪
GLITTER
GLITTER
GLITTER
GLITTER
THAT WASN'T FAIR!!

FLOOR ROLLER

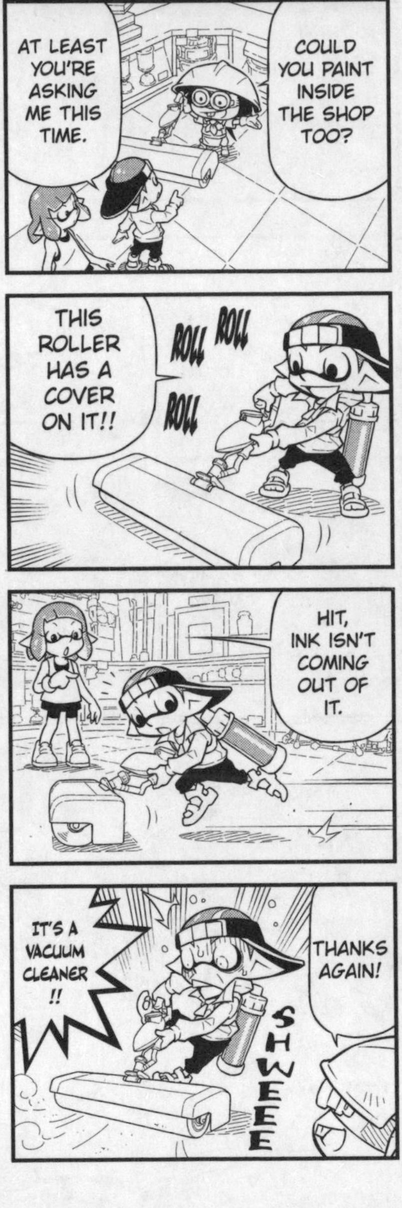
COULD YOU PAINT INSIDE THE SHOP TOO?
AT LEAST YOU'RE ASKING ME THIS TIME.
ROLL
ROLL
THIS ROLLER HAS A COVER ON IT!!
ROLL
HIT, INK ISN'T COMING OUT OF IT.
THANKS AGAIN!
SHWEEE
IT'S A VACUUM CLEANER !!

REMOVING WRINKLES

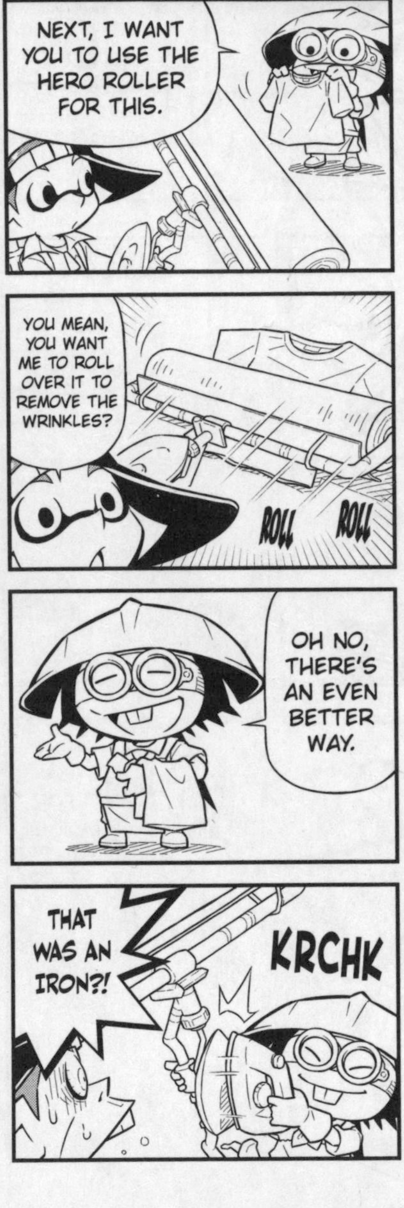
NEXT, I WANT YOU TO USE THE HERO ROLLER FOR THIS.
YOU MEAN, YOU WANT ME TO ROLL OVER IT TO REMOVE THE WRINKLES?
ROLL
ROLL
OH NO, THERE'S AN EVEN BETTER WAY.
KRCHK
THAT WAS AN IRON?!

WRAPPER

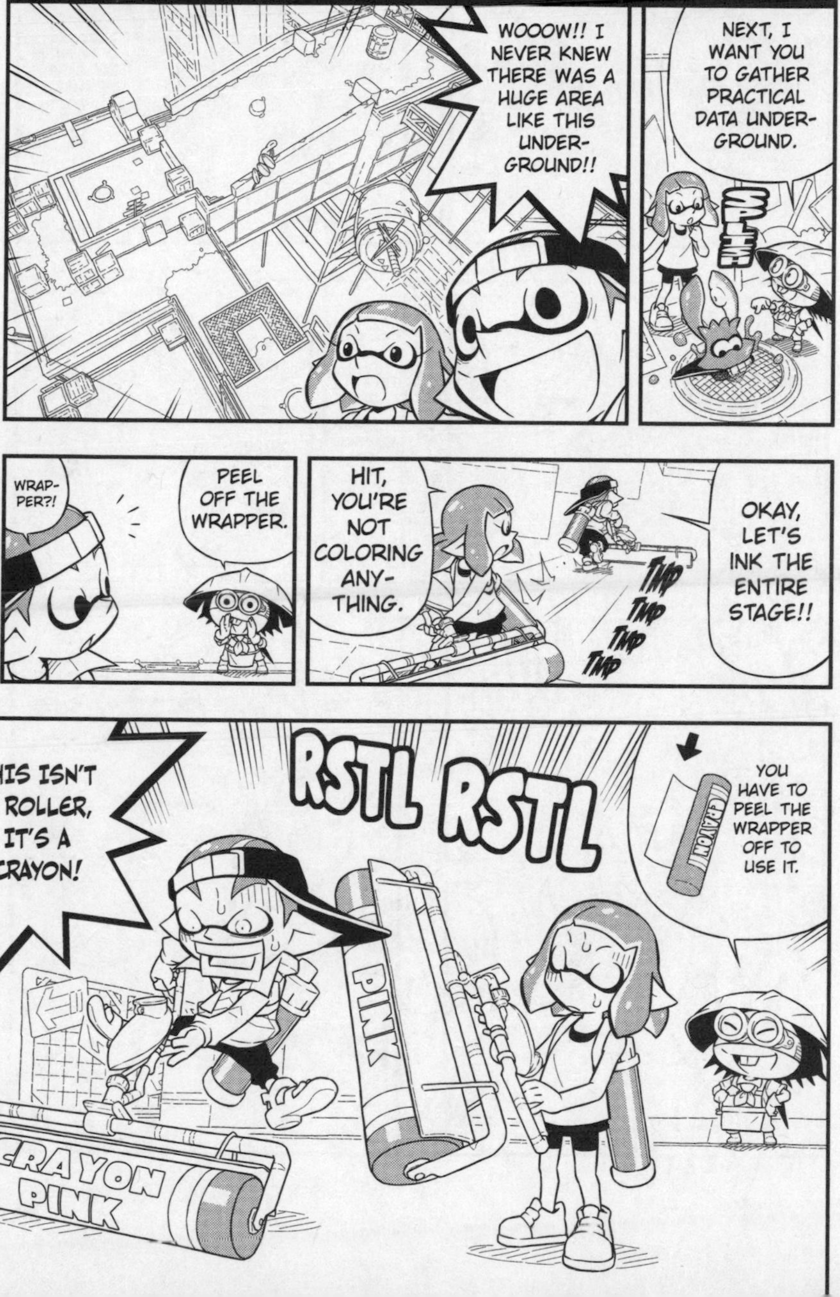
NEXT, I WANT YOU TO GATHER PRACTICAL DATA UNDER-GROUND.
SPLISH
WOOOW!! I NEVER KNEW THERE WAS A HUGE AREA LIKE THIS UNDER-GROUND!!
OKAY, LET'S INK THE ENTIRE STAGE!!
TMP TMP TMP TMP
HIT, YOU'RE NOT COLORING ANY-THING.
PEEL OFF THE WRAPPER.
WRAP-PER?!
YOU HAVE TO PEEL THE WRAPPER OFF TO USE IT.
CRAYON
RSTL RSTL
THIS ISN'T A ROLLER, IT'S A CRAYON!
PINK
CRAYON PINK

GATHERING PRACTICAL DATA

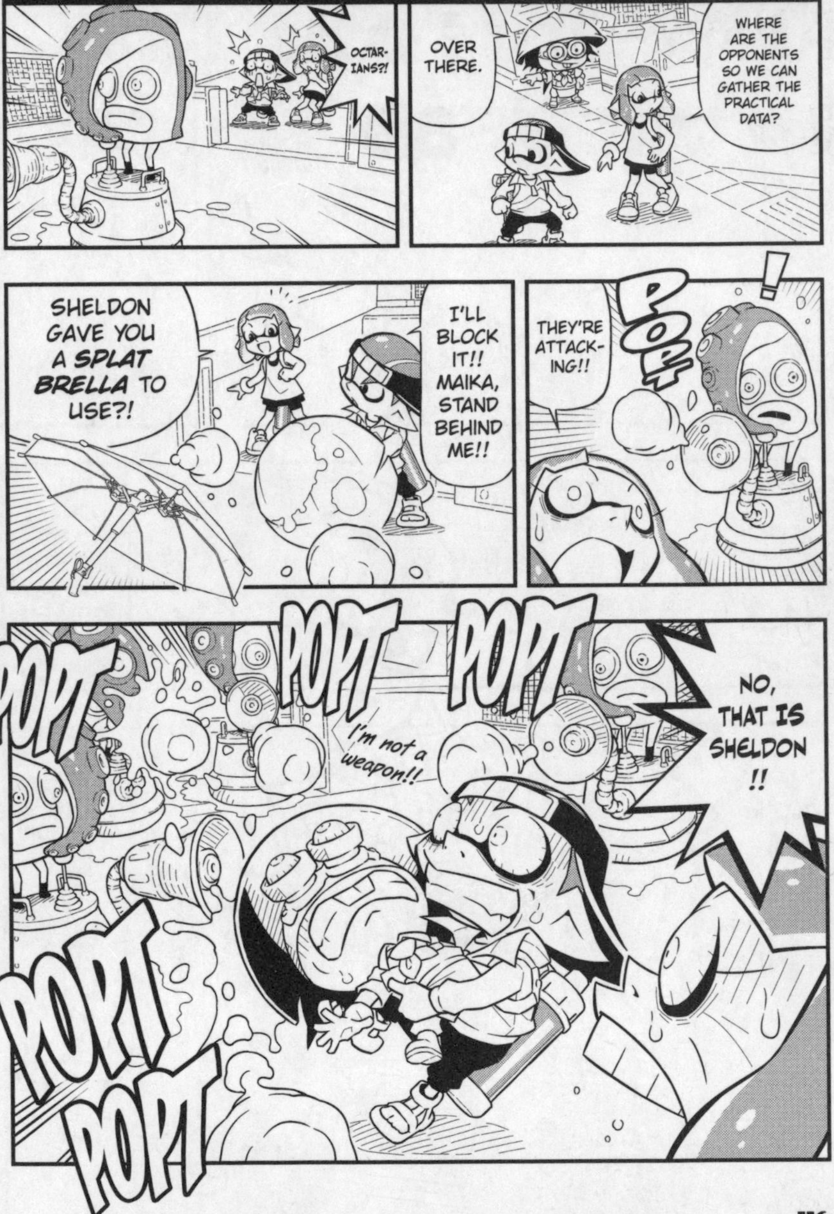

WHERE ARE THE OPPONENTS SO WE CAN GATHER THE PRACTICAL DATA?
OVER THERE.
OCTAR-IANS?!
!
POP
THEY'RE ATTACK-ING!!
I'LL BLOCK IT!! MAIKA, STAND BEHIND ME!!
SHELDON GAVE YOU A *SPLAT BRELLA* TO USE?!
NO, THAT IS SHELDON!!
POPT
POPT
POPT
I'm not a weapon!!
POPT
POPT
POPT

TIME TO WORK PART-TIME AND FIRE UP THE FOOD TRUCK!

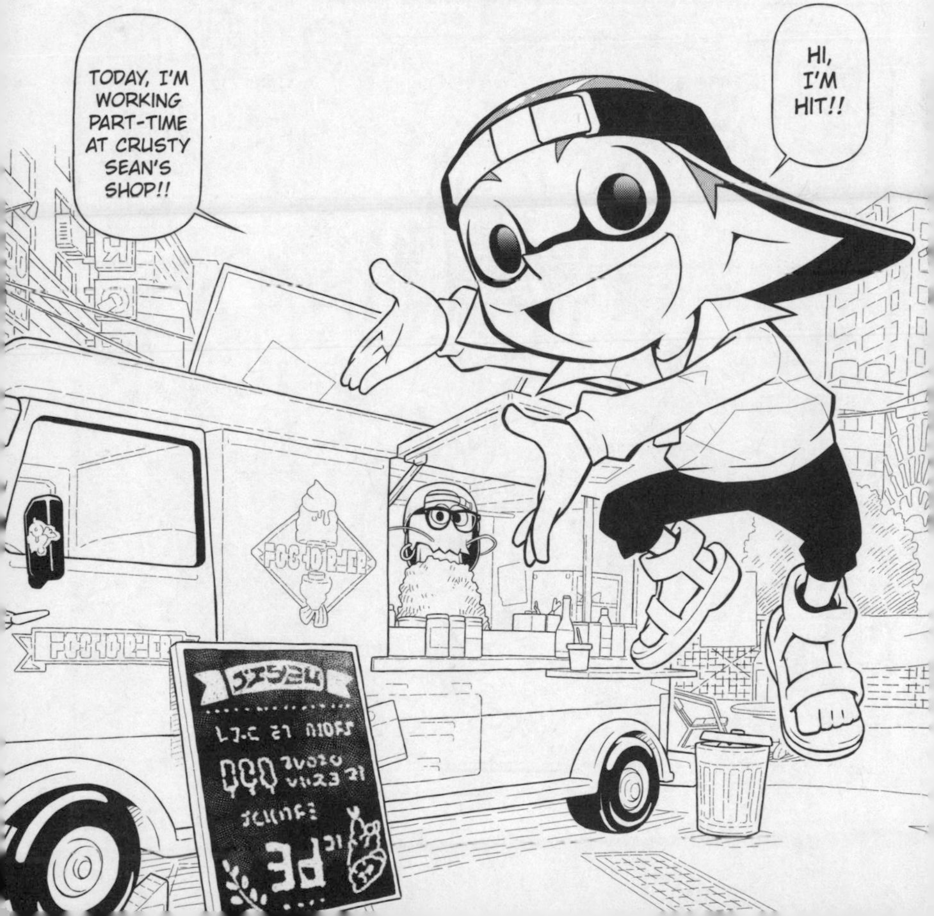
HI, I'M HIT!!
TODAY, I'M WORKING PART-TIME AT CRUSTY SEAN'S SHOP!!

CRUSTY SEAN'S EXCITING FRIED-FOOD TRUCK!

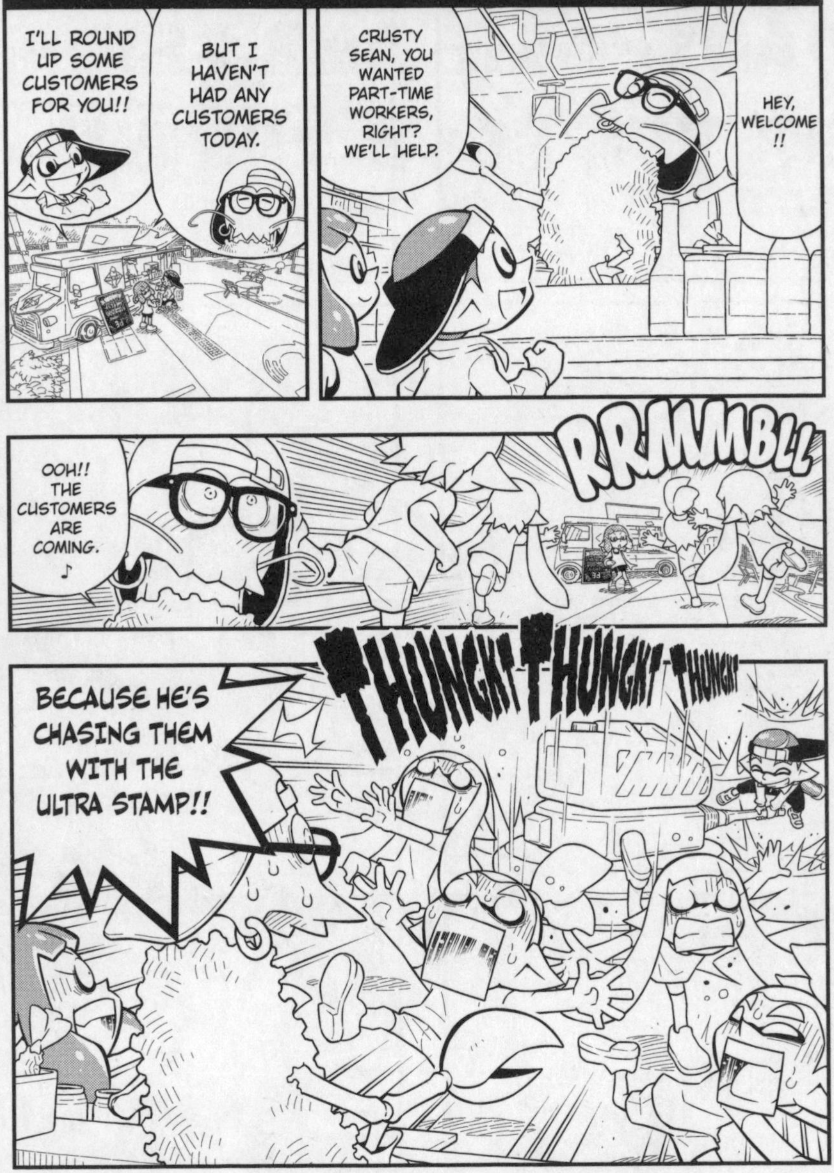
HEY, WELCOME !!
CRUSTY SEAN, YOU WANTED PART-TIME WORKERS, RIGHT? WE'LL HELP.
BUT I HAVEN'T HAD ANY CUSTOMERS TODAY.
I'LL ROUND UP SOME CUSTOMERS FOR YOU!!
RRMMBLL
OOH!! THE CUSTOMERS ARE COMING. ♪
THUNGK THUNGK THUNGK
BECAUSE HE'S CHASING THEM WITH THE ULTRA STAMP!!

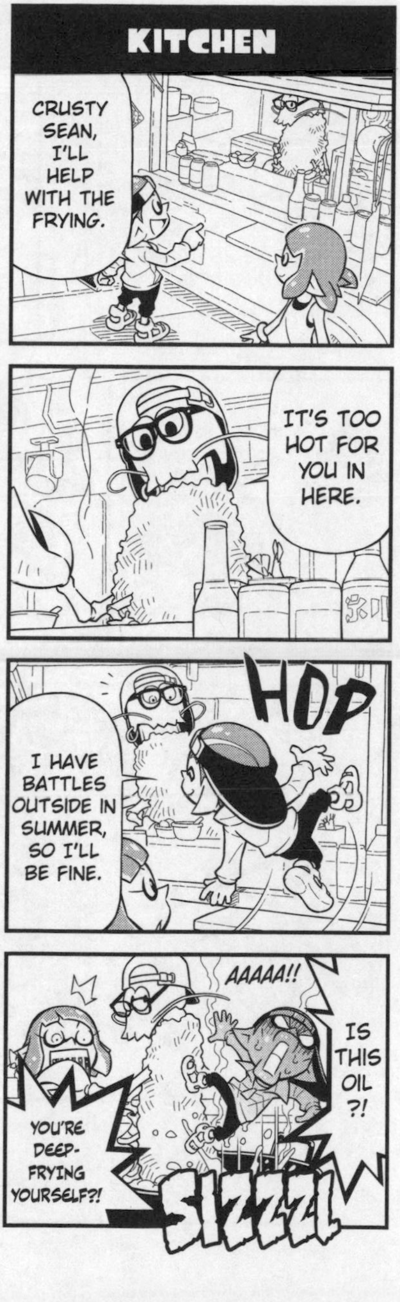
KITCHEN
CRUSTY SEAN, I'LL HELP WITH THE FRYING.
IT'S TOO HOT FOR YOU IN HERE.
HOP
I HAVE BATTLES OUTSIDE IN SUMMER, SO I'LL BE FINE.
AAAAA!!
IS THIS OIL ?!
YOU'RE DEEP-FRYING YOURSELF?!
SIZZZL

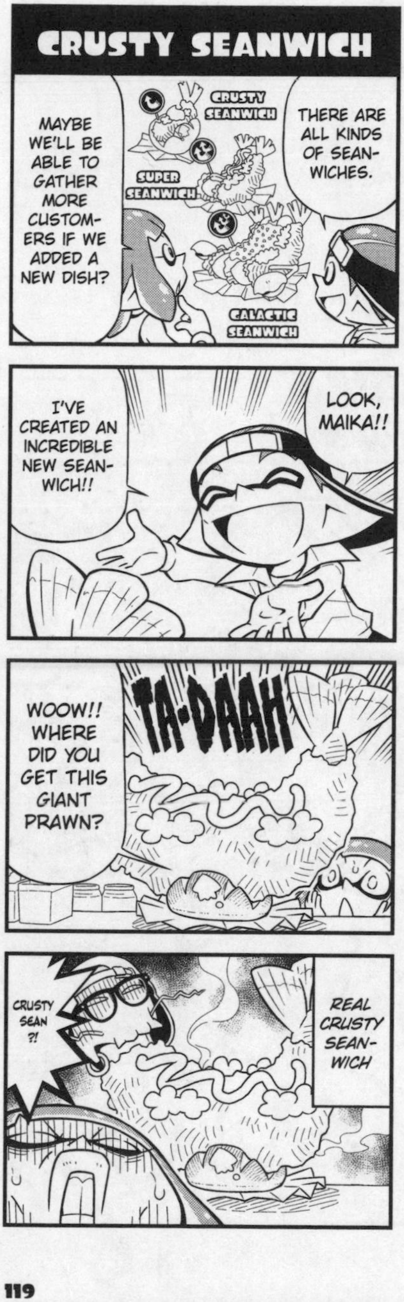
CRUSTY SEANWICH
THERE ARE ALL KINDS OF SEAN-WICHES.
CRUSTY SEANWICH
SUPER SEANWICH
GALACTIC SEANWICH
MAYBE WE'LL BE ABLE TO GATHER MORE CUSTOM-ERS IF WE ADDED A NEW DISH?
LOOK, MAIKA!!
I'VE CREATED AN INCREDIBLE NEW SEAN-WICH!!
TA-DAAH
WOOW!! WHERE DID YOU GET THIS GIANT PRAWN?
REAL CRUSTY SEAN-WICH
CRUSTY SEAN ?!

JUMBO FRIED PRAWN

HI, KOU.
MAIKA, YOU'RE WORKING PART-TIME AT CRUSTY SEAN'S SHOP?
WE DON'T HAVE ANY DONUTS, DO-NUT KOU.
IT'S KOU WITH THE THREE D'S, FOR DAPPER, DEBONAIR, AND DOLLARS!!
YOU WANT TO TRY THE NEW DISH?
FWUMP
THIS FRIED PRAWN IS HUGE!!
IS THAT CRUSTY SEAN AGAIN?!
Oh, he's here...
KRRRCH
IT'S A DEEP-FRIED RAINMAKER!!

POPULAR FOOD TRUCK

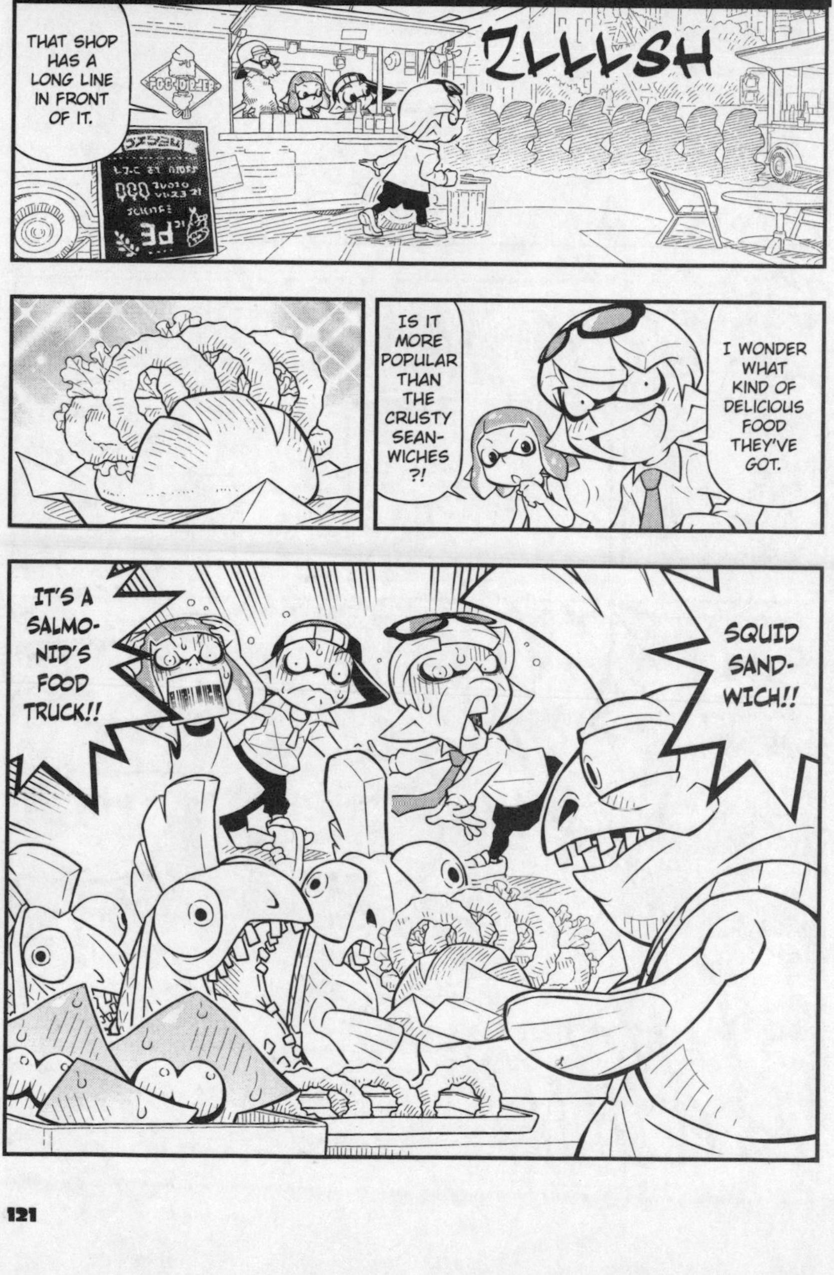
ZLLLSH
THAT SHOP HAS A LONG LINE IN FRONT OF IT.
I WONDER WHAT KIND OF DELICIOUS FOOD THEY'VE GOT.
IS IT MORE POPULAR THAN THE CRUSTY SEAN-WICHES ?!
SQUID SAND-WICH!!
IT'S A SALMO-NID'S FOOD TRUCK!!

POWER DRINKS

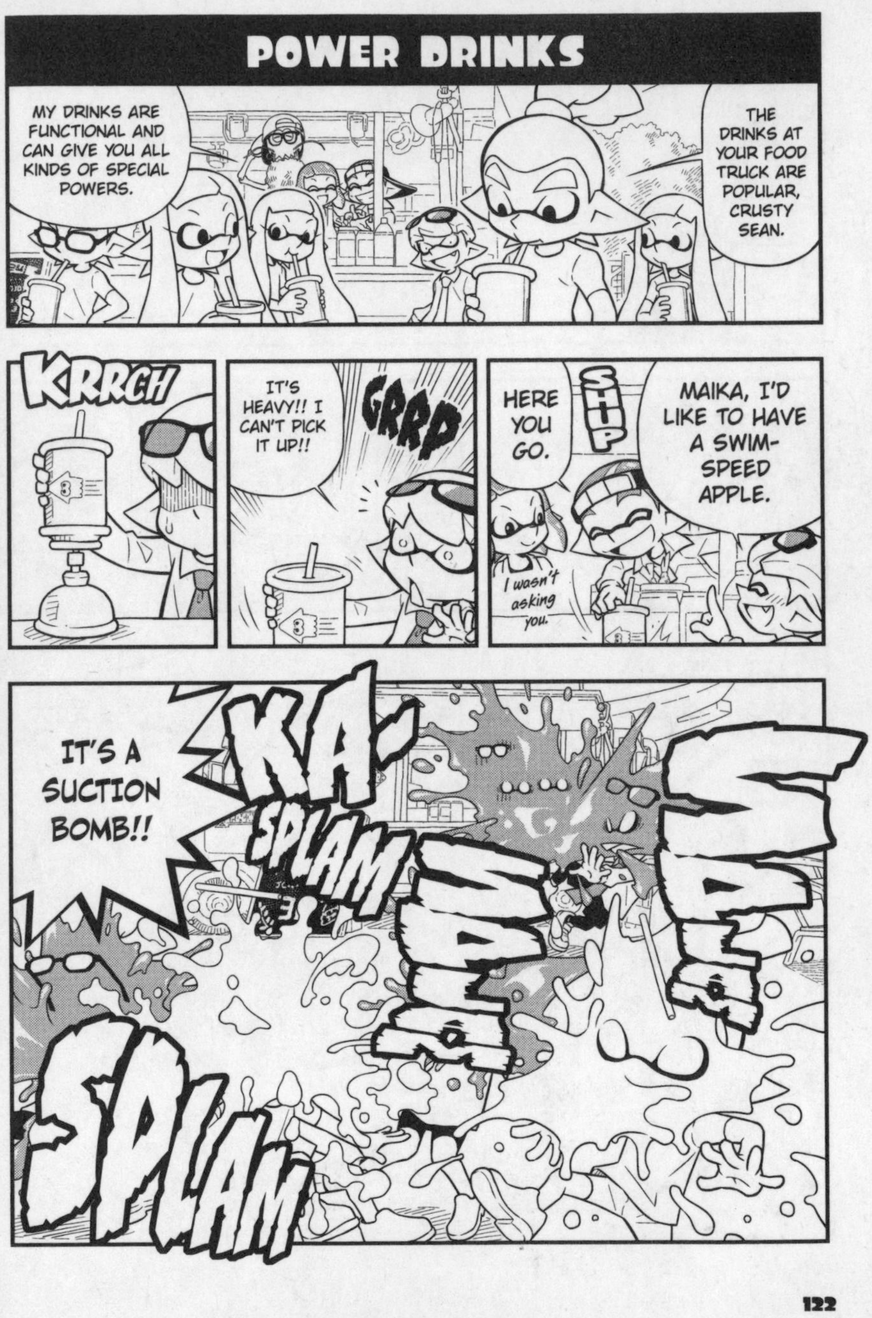
THE DRINKS AT YOUR FOOD TRUCK ARE POPULAR, CRUSTY SEAN.
MY DRINKS ARE FUNCTIONAL AND CAN GIVE YOU ALL KINDS OF SPECIAL POWERS.
MAIKA, I'D LIKE TO HAVE A SWIM-SPEED APPLE.
SHIP
HERE YOU GO.
I wasn't asking you.
GRRP
IT'S HEAVY!! I CAN'T PICK IT UP!!
KRRCH
SPLAM
SPLAM
KA-SPLAM
IT'S A SUCTION BOMB!!
SPLAM

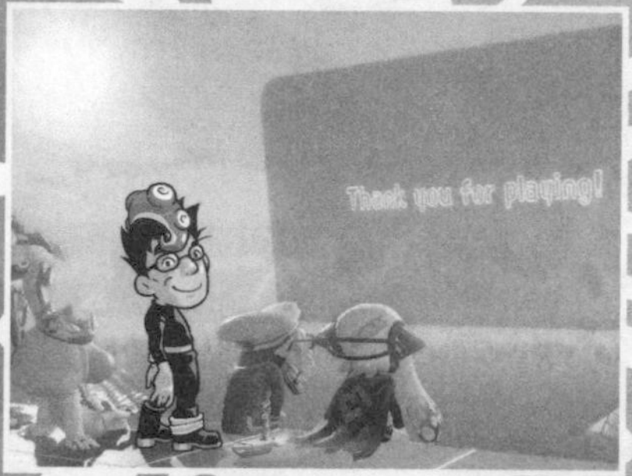
Thank you for playing!

HIDEKI GOTO

I've finally managed to beat the Hero Mode and *Octo Expansion* on *Splatoon 2*!!

Hideki Goto was born in Gifu Prefecture, Japan. He received an honorable mention in the 38th Shogakukan Newcomers' Comic Awards, Kids' Manga Division in 1996 for his one-shot *Zenryoku Dadada*. His first serialization was *Manga de Hakken Tamagotchi: Bakusho 4-koma Gekijo*, which began in *Monthly Coro Coro Comics* in 1997. *Splatoon: Squid Kids Comedy Show* began its serialization in *Bessatsu Coro Coro Comics* in 2017 and is Goto's first work to be published in English.

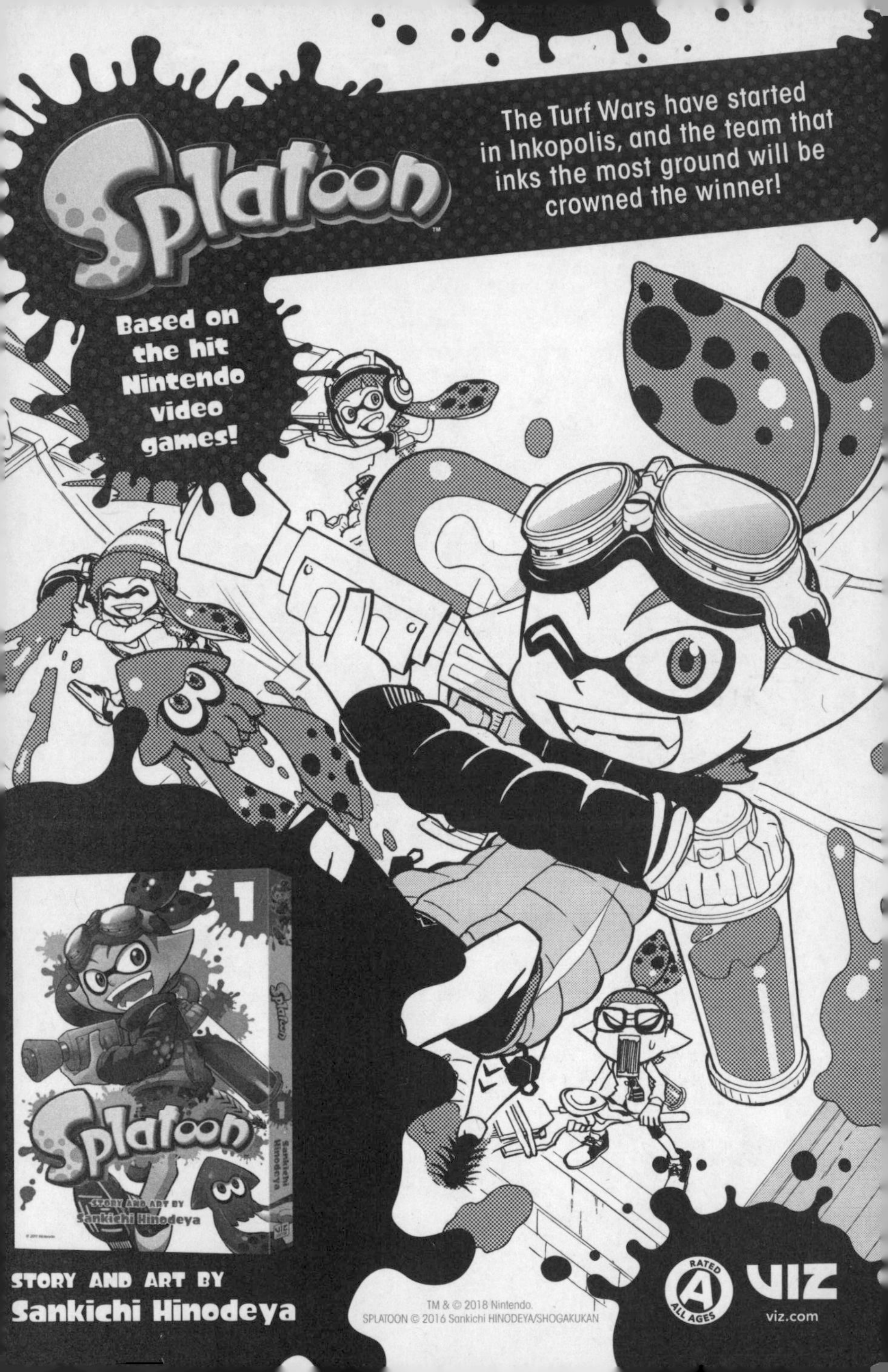
Splatoon™
The Turf Wars have started in Inkopolis, and the team that inks the most ground will be crowned the winner!
Based on the hit Nintendo video games!
1
Splatoon
STORY AND ART BY
Sankichi Hinodeya
STORY AND ART BY
Sankichi Hinodeya
TM & © 2018 Nintendo.
SPLATOON © 2016 Sankichi HINODEYA/SHOGAKUKAN
RATED A ALL AGES
VIZ
viz.com

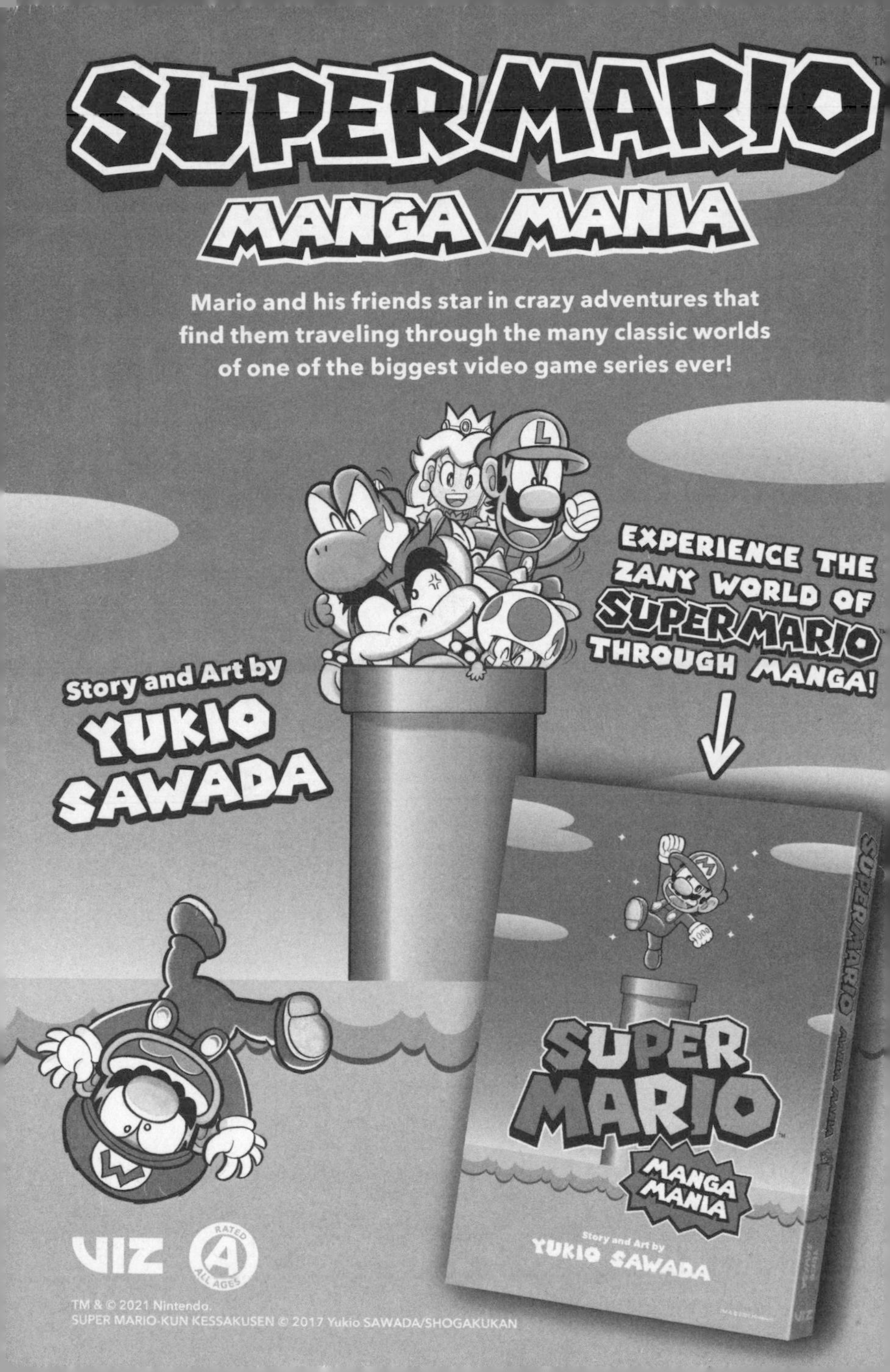
SUPER MARIO™
MANGA MANIA
Mario and his friends star in crazy adventures that find them traveling through the many classic worlds of one of the biggest video game series ever!
EXPERIENCE THE ZANY WORLD OF SUPER MARIO™ THROUGH MANGA!
Story and Art by
YUKIO SAWADA
SUPER MARIO™
MANGA MANIA
Story and Art by
YUKIO SAWADA
VIZ
RATED A ALL AGES
TM & © 2021 Nintendo.
SUPER MARIO-KUN KESSAKUSEN © 2017 Yukio SAWADA/SHOGAKUKAN

THE LEGEND OF ZELDA ™

LEGENDARY EDITION BOX SET

Story and Art by **Akira Himekawa**

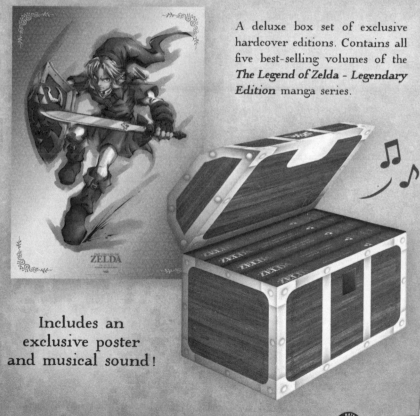

A deluxe box set of exclusive hardcover editions. Contains all five best-selling volumes of the *The Legend of Zelda - Legendary Edition* manga series.

Includes an exclusive poster and musical sound!

RATED A ALL AGES

VIZ

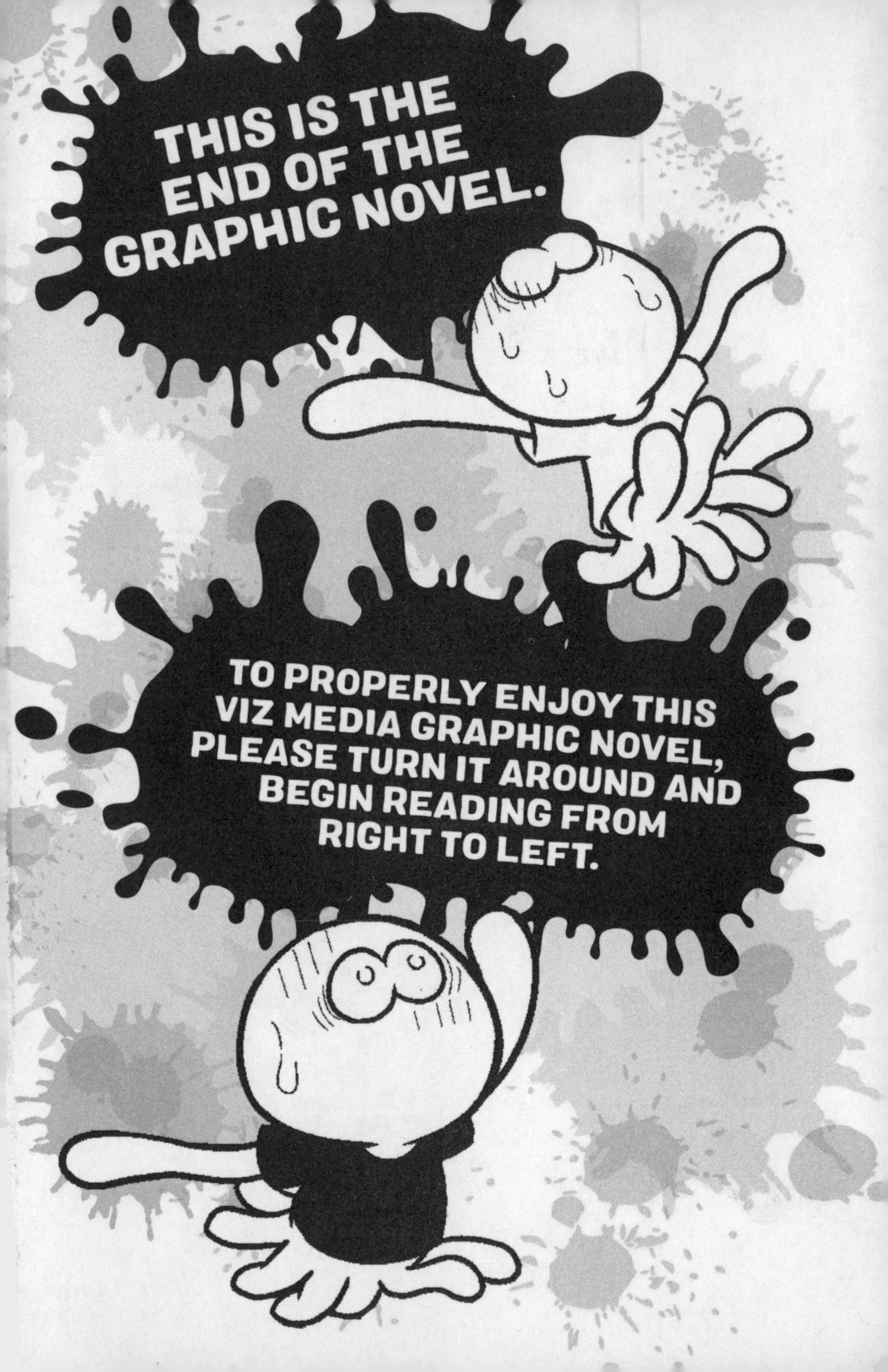
THIS IS THE END OF THE GRAPHIC NOVEL.
TO PROPERLY ENJOY THIS VIZ MEDIA GRAPHIC NOVEL, PLEASE TURN IT AROUND AND BEGIN READING FROM RIGHT TO LEFT.